INDIAN-WHITE RELATIONS

A Persistent Paradox

This Special Edition published by Howard University Press for the
National Archives Trust Fund Board
National Archives and Records Service
General Services Administration
Washington, D.C.

NATIONAL ARCHIVES TRUST FUND BOARD
        James B. Rhoads
        Archivist of the United States

        Gale W. McGee
        Chairman, Senate Post Office and
        Civil Service Committee

        David N. Henderson
        Chairman, House Post Office and
        Civil Service Committee

INDIAN-WHITE RELATIONS
A Persistent Paradox

EDITED BY Jane F. Smith
AND Robert M. Kvasnicka

HOWARD UNIVERSITY PRESS
WASHINGTON, D.C.
1981

Copyright © Howard University Press

All rights reserved

First paperback edition 1981

NOTICE: Contributions by the following persons are in the public domain and are not covered by the copyright to this volume: Louis R. Bruce, Robert M. Kvasnicka, James B. Rhoads, Carmelita S. Ryan, Jack Eckerd, Jane F. Smith, and Herman J. Viola.

Printed in the United States of America

Library of Congress Cataloging in Publication Data

National Archives Conference on Research in the History of Indian-White Relations, Washington, D. C., 1972.
Indian-White relations.

(National Archives conferences ; v. 10)
Includes index.
1. Indians of North America—Government relations—Congresses. 2. Indians of North America—Government relations—Sources—Congresses. 3. United States. National Archives and Records Service. I. Smith, Jane F., 1916– II. Kvasnicka, Robert M., 1935– III. United States. National Archives and Records Service. IV. Title. V. Series: United States. National Archives and Records Service. National Archives conferences ; v. 10.
E93.N24 1972   323.1'19'7073   75-22316
Hardcover ISBN 0-88258-055-8
Paperback ISBN 0-88258-094-9

FOREWORD

Since 1967 the National Archives and Records Service has held a series of conferences for the exchange of ideas and information between archivists and researchers. These conferences are designed both to inform scholars about the wealth of useful research materials available in the National Archives and Records Service and to provide an opportunity for researchers to suggest ways in which their use of these records could be facilitated.

The National Archives and Records Service, a part of the General Services Administration, administers the permanently valuable, noncurrent records of the federal government. These archival holdings date from the days of the Continental Congresses to the present.

Among the approximately one million cubic feet of records now constituting the National Archives of the United States are such significant documents as the Declaration of Independence, the Constitution, and the Bill of Rights. However, most of the archives, whether in the National Archives Building, the regional archives branches, or the presidential libraries, are less dramatic. They are preserved because of their continuing practical utility for the ordinary processes of government, for the establishment and protection of individual rights, and for their value in documenting our nation's history.

One goal of the National Archives staff is to explore and make more widely known these historical records. It is hoped that these conferences will be a positive act in that direction. The papers of each conference are published in the belief that this exchange of ideas and information should be preserved and made available in printed form.

Jack Eckerd
Administrator of General Services

NATIONAL ARCHIVES CONFERENCES / VOLUME 10

Papers and Proceedings of the National Archives Conference on Research in the History of Indian-White Relations

Sponsored by
THE NATIONAL ARCHIVES AND RECORDS SERVICE

June 15-16, 1972
The National Archives Building / Washington, D.C.

PREFACE

The National Archives Conference on Research in the History of Indian-White Relations, held on June 15-16, 1972, was the tenth in a series of semiannual conferences sponsored by the National Archives and Records Service to foster improved communication and a continuing dialogue between archivists and the scholarly community. These conferences are designed to focus attention on the rich research potential of materials in the National Archives and at the same time to provide federal archivists with guidance and counsel on how best to meet the research needs of scholars.

The specific purpose of the Conference on Research in the History of Indian-White Relations was to provide an opportunity for scholars, archivists, government officials, and other interested persons to engage in a stimulating and frank exchange of information and ideas about a subject that has been too long neglected by historians and lay people alike. It was hoped that by encouraging open discussion of the diverse points of view presented in the conference papers, as well as changing research trends and their implications, the participants would gain a better appreciation of their mutual interests and needs and that new perspectives might be opened that would contribute to increased understanding of Indian-white relations.

The theme of the conference was proposed by Jane F. Smith, director of the Civil Archives Division, who has had responsibility for most of the Indian-related records in the National Archives for many years and is deeply interested in all aspects of American Indian history. Robert M. Kvasnicka, a specialist in Indian records (now assistant chief, Natural Resources Branch), was asked to serve as conference codirector.

James B. Rhoads
Archivist of the United States

CONTENTS

FOREWORD   v
   JACK ECKERD

PREFACE   ix
   JAMES B. RHOADS

INTRODUCTION   xvii
   JANE F. SMITH/ROBERT M. KVASNICKA

DOING INDIAN HISTORY   1
   FRANCIS PAUL PRUCHA

I

MAJOR RESOURCES OF THE NATIONAL ARCHIVES AND RECORDS SERVICE FOR INDIAN HISTORICAL RESEARCH: HISTORY, USE, AND POTENTIAL OF THE RECORDS

Introduction   11
   ROBERT H. BAHMER

Indian-Related Records in the National Archives and Their Use: Observations over a Third of a Century   13
   OLIVER W. HOLMES

Special Study of the Appraisal of Indian Records   33
   CARMELITA S. RYAN

II

INDIAN ASSIMILATION: THE NINETEENTH CENTURY

Introduction *LORING B. PRIEST*	43
From Civilization to Removal: Early American Indian Policy *HERMAN J. VIOLA*	45
The Board of Indian Commissioners and Ethnocentric Reform, 1878–1893 *HENRY E. FRITZ*	57
Commentaries *ROBERT F. BERKHOFER, JR.* *LORING B. PRIEST*	79 87
Discussion Note	96

III

INDIAN COLLECTIONS OUTSIDE THE NATIONAL ARCHIVES AND RECORDS SERVICE

Introduction *THURMAN WILKINS*	99
Artifacts and Pictures as Documents in the History of Indian-White Relations *JOHN C. EWERS*	101
Major Indian Record Collections in Oklahoma *ANGIE DEBO*	112
The Archives of the Duke Projects in American Indian Oral History *C. GREGORY CRAMPTON*	119
Discussion Note	129

Contents

IV

THE ROLE OF THE MILITARY

Introduction ROBERT G. ATHEARN	131
The Frontier Army: John Ford or Arthur Penn? ROBERT M. UTLEY	133
Commentary RICHARD N. ELLIS	146
Discussion Note	152

V

RECENT RESEARCH ON INDIAN RESERVATION POLICY

Introduction DONALD J. BERTHRONG	155
The Reservation Policy: Too Little and Too Late WILLIAM T. HAGAN	157
John Collier and the Controversy over the Wheeler-Howard Bill KENNETH R. PHILP	171
Commentaries	
ROY W. MEYER	207
MARY E. YOUNG	212
W. DAVID BAIRD	215
Discussion Note	222

VI

SOME ASPECTS OF TWENTIETH-CENTURY FEDERAL INDIAN POLICY

Introduction 225
ALVIN M. JOSEPHY, JR.

John Collier and the Indian New Deal: An Assessment 227
LAWRENCE C. KELLY

The Bureau of Indian Affairs, 1972 242
LOUIS R. BRUCE

Commentary 251
D'ARCY McNICKLE

Discussion Note 258

BIOGRAPHICAL SKETCHES 260

APPENDIX: NATIONAL ARCHIVES RESOURCE PAPERS 267

INDEX 269

PICTURE CREDITS: Unless otherwise noted, the illustrations in this volume are of records in the National Archives and are identified by record group and file symbol.

LIST OF ILLUSTRATIONS

FIGURES

National Archives Identification Inventory sample page	14
Page from a volume of letters sent by the Office of Indian Affairs	18
Entries in a register of letters received by the Office of Indian Affairs	19
Thomas L. McKenney	46
Nez Percé teachers	64
Lace square made by an Oneida Indian girl	106
Sketch of C. M. Bell photographing an Indian delegation	109
Cherokee Female Seminary, Indian Territory	114
Sauk and Fox Day School, Indian Territory	116
Chief Washakie and a General Order announcing his death	139
John Collier	170
Crow Creek Agency	203
Nez Percé Agency	203
Sketches of the principal buildings at the Sisseton Agency	204
Interior of the office at the Rosebud Agency	205
Frame farmhouse with wickiup-type dwelling	206
Poster explaining the Indian Reorganization Act	236

MAPS

Plat of the Chilocco Indian School, 1919	63
Areas of Indian Cultures	124
Map of the Chiricahua Reserve, Arizona Territory	135
Map of the Mission Indian Reservations in Southern California	176
Executive Order of April 9, 1874, creating the Hot Springs Indian Reservation, New Mexico Territory, with map	201
Map of the Cheyenne River Agency, 1889	202

INTRODUCTION

The efficacy of conducting a conference that would focus attention on the rich resources among the National Archives of the United States for research in the history of the North American Indian was apparent from the initiation of the conference series. Because the vast quantity of materials in the National Archives documenting virtually all aspects of relations between the federal government and the Indian tribes that have come under its jurisdiction has been so heavily used by scholars and other researchers for various administrative, legal, and research purposes over a span of many decades, it was generally recognized that such a conference would engender unusual interest and response.

The specific topic on which it was decided to focus the conference—Indian-white relations—seemed singularly appropriate because of the current and long overdue concern about minorities and, in particular, the North American Indian. This recent burgeoning interest has been evidenced not only in expanded and new programs of the federal government, but in unprecedented scholarly research activity on all facets of Indian history. It has been reflected also in the publication of numerous books about Indian history and culture, many of them written by American Indians.

Perhaps the most significant, exciting, and hopeful signs of this interest, however, can be found in the programs and activities undertaken by Indians themselves. Thus, in 1964 the newly founded American Indian Historical Society, an all-Indian organization, established as its official organ the *Indian Historian,* a journal of history, information, and literature about the American Indian. The society has also sponsored two convocations of American Indian scholars, the first held at Princeton University in March 1970 and the second at Aspen, Colorado, in September 1971. Funded by the Ford Foundation through grants to the American Indian Historical Society, these interdisciplinary convocations have brought together Indian scholars, linguists, students, and tribal leaders to discuss problems confronting the scholars and to provide a forum for discussion by Indian voices of the vital practical questions affecting the Indian populace.

A continuation of this trend since the conference at the National Archives may be seen in the establishment in 1974 of the *American Indian Culture and Research Journal,* published quarterly by the American Indian Culture and Research Center, University of California, Los Angeles, and the *American Indian Quarterly: A Journal of Anthropology, History, and Literature,* relating "to the study and understanding of Indians in the United States, Canada, Mexico, and Central America."

The last decade has also witnessed the emergence of a new direction in American Indian study, particularly in the education of Amerindian youth. This has been reflected specifically in the establishment at many universities of new departments of American Indian studies, as well as in their sponsorship of symposia and conferences and the introduction of courses dealing with the Indian in American culture.

Another significant development is the recent establishment of several centers and institutes designed to collect and publicize information and materials on Indian contributions to the culture of the United States and their contemporary problems. Especially noteworthy are the new Center for the History of the American Indian at the Newberry Library and the Inter-American Indian Institute headquartered in Mexico City.

Concern about the North American Indian has also been evidenced by the federal government, both in expanded programs of the Bureau of Indian Affairs and other old-line organizations, and in the new approaches represented by such agencies as the former National Council on Indian Opportunity and the Office of Economic Opportunity.

Nowhere in the federal government or elsewhere, however, has the tremendous interest in Indian history been demonstrated more clearly in recent years than in the use of the Indian-related documentation that has been incorporated into the National Archives of the United States. Accordingly, it was decided that the conference would seek to highlight the rich potential of these holdings for the study of Indian-white relations. The conference title was carefully designed to indicate, as accurately as possible, the objectives and scope of the projected program. It was the intention of the conference directors to emphasize that the papers presented at the sessions would be concerned primarily with the "history" of Indian-white relations as revealed in "research" by the program participants among the records in the National Archives that chronicle much of the story of the relationship between the federal government and the American Indian tribes. It was not their purpose to present a thesis and, with the exception of remarks by the commissioner of Indian Affairs, the conference papers do not deal with the administration of current Indian policy. Nor was it their intention to discuss or attempt to solve the many

Introduction

difficult and controversial problems involved in this area but rather, through the historical background presented in the papers, to provide a framework that would help to place these matters in proper perspective.

Admittedly, many topics that were dealt with during the conference are still the subject of controversy and sometimes acrimonious discussion, not only between Indian and white historians but among white historians themselves. The program was consciously structured, therefore, to present many diverse points of view regarding the history of Indian-white relations, some of them quite different from the convictions of many conference participants. Although well aware of these differing convictions and differing points of view, the National Archives staff believes that it is the mark of an "open society" to candidly recognize such differences and to provide a forum for their discussion.

The program was planned to focus primarily on resources for Indian historical research in the National Archives and elsewhere, as well as certain facets of Indian-white relations including Indian assimilation in the nineteenth century, the reservation policy, and some aspects of twentieth-century Indian policy. During the two-day conference twelve formal papers were presented at six separate sessions, three of which were held concurrently. Several sessions also featured comments—critiques and elaboration of the formal papers—by well-known scholars. This volume consists of these papers, the additional commentaries, and summaries of the discussion that followed each session. Not included are the several National Archives resources papers that were prepared by staff members and distributed at the conference. These individual papers are no longer available, but they form the nucleus of the forthcoming guide to records in the National Archives relating to American Indians.

The program participants, virtually all of whom had made extensive use of the holdings of the National Archives, included an admixture of historians, English professors, and anthropologists but, unfortunately, few Indian scholars. Although the program planners were anxious to have maximum Indian participation, this was difficult to achieve as so few Indian scholars had ever visited the National Archives or were aware of the research potential of the Indian-related materials among its holdings. A major objective of the conference will have been attained if it helped to introduce the National Archives to young Indian historians and anthropologists and to establish the new lines of communication that are urgently needed by all scholars—Indian and white—working in this complex field.

As another means to this end the National Archives has actively participated in the American Indian Cultural Resources Training Program. Established in 1973 by Herman J. Viola, director of the National Anthropological Archives of the Smithsonian Institution, this program is designed to interest Indian Americans in becoming professional archivists and historians by acquainting them with records relating to their culture and history and the methodology necessary to use them.

The codirectors of this conference greatly appreciate the assistance and cooperation of the many persons who made its success possible. They are especially indebted to James B. Rhoads, former archivist of the United States, E. G. Campbell, assistant archivist for the National Archives, and Walter Robertson, Jr., executive director for the National Archives and Records Service. Without their generous support conference plans could not have been realized. The directors also are deeply grateful to all the program participants, particularly Francis Paul Prucha, S. J., William T. Hagan, and Lawrence C. Kelly who served as informal program advisors, and D'Arcy McNickle who, on short notice, graciously agreed to share with us some of his memories of John Collier. Also due a special note of gratitude are the members of the staff of the National Archives and its regional branches who prepared resource papers for the conference and Laura E. Kelsay whose paper on Indian-related cartographic records, originally distributed at the Conference on the National Archives and Research in Historical Geography, was reprinted for this conference. These acknowledgments would be incomplete without an expression of indebtedness to Virginia D. Keller who, in addition to her regular secretarial duties, handled nearly all the extra typing and clerical chores generated by the conference.

All conference participants agreed that one of the highlights was the reception held in the "Castle" at the Smithsonian Institution. Sincere thanks go to Meredith Johnson, special events officer, and all the other members of the staff of the Smithsonian Institution whose efforts contributed to making the event a memorable occasion.

For their assistance in preparing the conference papers for publication, the directors thank Carolyn Hunt, Rosa A. McDonald, and Deborah Clark. Deserving of special mention is Angela Wilkes of the Publications Division whose diligence, interest, and enthusiasm far exceeded her responsibilities of editing the manuscript and seeing the volume through the press.

JANE F. SMITH
ROBERT M. KVASNICKA
Conference Codirectors

INDIAN-WHITE RELATIONS
A Persistent Paradox

Doing Indian History

Francis Paul Prucha

The historian writing about Indian matters today is in a remarkably enviable position. After years of comparative neglect, Indian historical studies have come to the forefront. Experienced practitioners are in demand and in some circles are even treated by students and other lay people with new reverence and respect. Many historians, who turned to an investigation of Indian-white relations in the United States long before the subject was a popular one, may feel occasionally like minor prophets. Demand for one's services in this advisory capacity or that—while hardly on a par with the profitable consulting that our academic colleagues in the sciences enjoy—brings at least the heady feeling that comes from being wanted. And, though few fortunes have been made from scholarly books on Indian subjects, one cannot quite restrain the hope that his or her next work will ride the wave of consumer interest to the top of the bestseller list.

This rising interest in the history of Indian affairs, nevertheless, has ambivalent qualities. On the one hand, the new probing by scholars, both Indian and white, has sharpened our awareness of subjects to be investigated, has made it possible to delineate with greater exactness the scope of our discipline, and has already produced an impressive amount of work that has broadened our horizons and deepened our understanding of this subject. Yet, on the other hand, there is danger that the popularity will lead to haste and to disregard of accepted canons of historical research, if not, indeed, to a general slovenliness and, at times, alas, to downright dishonesty.

The good features of the present situation are sufficiently recognized and universally commended. I judge, therefore, that I may be excused from commenting on them further and that I may turn at once to a consideration of some of the problems that arise in doing Indian history.[1] My comments will be both explanative and hortatory—and on occasion, no doubt, also provocative.

There are, to begin with, problems of terminology. In large part, of course, it is all the fault of Christopher Columbus. His geographical inexactitude saddled his heirs with a name for the people he found in the Western Hemisphere that was inappropriate, to say the least. But the term "Indian" was not abandoned when more sophisticated geographical knowledge showed that it was a mistake, and it has been sanctioned by long usage. It seems unwise, if not impossible, to eradicate it and replace it in general usage with an artificially contrived term—such as "Amerind" or "Amerindian," which had a brief vogue—or with the more cumbersome "Native American," which is increasingly coming into use. Words are fundamentally arbitrary conventional signs to which certain meanings are attached. It is well to be reminded from time to time that some of them are not properly descriptive, but everyone knows what they mean. Intelligent discourse is not always advanced by substituting laborious circumlocutions or hyphenated nouns for simple words. I listened recently to a long disquisition on historical encounters between Native Americans and Euro-Americans, a discussion that would have moved along considerably better, and just as accurately and meaningfully, if the talk had been about Indians and whites.

But if we stick with "Indian" for our everyday discourse—and it is a point in favor of historians, I think, that they write in everyday language—what are we to do with the term "Indian history"?

Here we are on shifting ground. For too long United States history has been written exclusively by white historians. For many of them, "Indian" history has consisted of the story of events in which the Indians impinged in some way upon the course of white society. Indians, it has been noted to our shame, were often treated (along with mountains, deserts, rivers, and wild beasts) as part of the environment that had to be overcome. The commonly used textbook phrase, "the Indian barrier to white settlement" is indicative of this frame of mind, as is the repeated concern during the course of American history with the "Indian problem."

Now we are coming to see that "Indian history" might properly refer to changes within the Indian communities themselves, to Indian-Indian rather than Indian-white relations, and to the interaction of the red and white races from the Indian standpoint—in which no doubt there would be considerable concern about the "white problem."

Historians today, therefore, must be more careful than many of us have been in the past to differentiate between these different meanings of the term "Indian history"—between the history of the Indian experience in America and the history of Indian-white relations. That historians are still in a transitional and confused state is illustrated in a recent issue of a historical journal that was devoted entirely to the "American Indian."

Two articles dealt specifically with the writing of "Indian history"; the phrase was, in fact, used in their titles. One of the authors spoke about a "general history of the American Indian." He took a pretty dim view of the possibility of a "good," a "successful," or a "meaningful" general history (the adjectives are his), and his article became almost a litany of the different things that "Indian history" can mean, for his examples ranged all the way from books like the anthropological survey of Harold E. Driver to William T. Hagan's brief synopsis of government policy and Indian-white relations in the United States.[2]

The second author recognized the divergence in approach, and he made a clear decision. He declared categorically: "American Indian history must move from being primarily a record of white-Indian relations to become the story of Indians in the United States (or North America) over time." And he proposed a context in which his "new Indian history" might be developed.[3]

It is tempting to look upon the traditional history of Indian-white relations as passé, if not, indeed, morally unacceptable because of "racist" overtones, and to turn completely toward the new approach. Then scholars could draw upon traditional historical methodologies and social science theories and techniques alike, and anthropologists and historians could form a tight partnership. I personally think, however, that this would be a mistake—that the boat would list just as badly if we were all to rush from starboard to port.

It is an obvious fact which needs no belaboring that relations with the other group were of supreme importance both for the whites and for the Indians. To leave out these relations in the history of either group could easily lead to serious distortion. It therefore makes considerable sense for a member of the white society interested in its own history to investigate the ways in which contact with the Indians affected the course of events of the United States, just as it makes sense to study the impact of contact with foreign nations.

On the Indians' side, contact with whites was often a determining factor in their history. Great changes were wrought on Indian communities by contact with whites, and a history of strictly Indian-Indian relations would be partial to the point of inaccuracy.

So, while by no means denigrating the study of Indian history as the history of the Indian experience—a development that is long overdue—and by no means belittling cooperation between historians and anthropologists—a development that will certainly be valuable to both—I would like to assert my belief in the value of the historian's traditional tasks and in the value of the history of Indian-white relations. But I would, particularly, like to note some of the difficulties faced by practitioners of this historical inquiry.

Considering the significance and magnitude of the subject, there have been far too few historians who have devoted their careers to the study of Indian-white relations. Some periods and subjects in Indian policy have been almost entirely neglected by serious scholars. How many important works are there that deal with the period between the Dawes Act and the beginning of the reform movements of the 1920s? Yet that was the period of the working out of the allotment policy with its great and serious consequences. There is no satisfactory general history of government educational programs for the Indians. Too little attention has been paid so far to the administration as contrasted with the development of policies. And even the treaty system, so prominent in Indian relations, has not had adequate treatment. Largely untapped sources still exist that can help supply better answers to old questions, and new questions are continually being asked. All this is hard work—impatience is not a good virtue to promote the digging out of the necessary knowledge. It will require the work of many competent and dedicated persons.

The first requisite is accurate knowledge, which was the purpose of the conference on Indian-white relations. Historical events of the past are complex—they cannot be treated in one dimension, they cannot be pulled out of the context in which they occurred without grave danger of distortion, and they cannot be simplistically linked in a single chain of cause and effect. History, moreover, is a continuum. The beginnings and endings are often quite arbitrarily introduced by the historian for reasons of convenience, or fatigue. A history of a set period may be necessary, but if the knowledge of historians extends no farther forward or backward than their termini, some events may be considered as wonderfully unique phenomena when they are but examples of a continuing pattern. A history may properly treat a tightly limited area—a single Indian reservation, for example—but we know the fallacy of generalizing from a single example.

The facts dug out and the knowledge acquired and disseminated must be accurate and must be seen in proper perspective. But it is not an easy thing to maintain one's equilibrium when dealing with interracial relations. There is much to condemn in the treatment of the Indians by the United States government and its people. Injustice, callousness, and hatred, as well as ignorance, indifference, and neglect, have marked much of the whites' relations with the Indians. Many writers, some professional historians among them, have made these elements their stock in trade. Present-day activists and their sympathizers find it tempting to twist historical data to their own uses, an understandable reaction of minority groups seeking to redress an unjust balance and to gain overdue respect for rights that should have been indisputable.

But the historian's task is not activism or special pleading. History is a legitimate scholarly discipline, whose purpose is to reconstruct the past as accurately as the intelligence of the historian and the fullness of the historical sources permit. Its purpose is to supply enlightenment, understanding, and perspective and to provide sound information on which balanced judgments can be based. Its purpose is not to serve the special interests of any group or doctrine, nor to furnish ammunition for polemics and propaganda. It is a scientific study based on finely honed techniques. Its success depends upon long and careful training and on a critical evaluation of the remains of the past, seeking enlightenment for problems that plague the present.

Correction of existing historical writing comes from discovery of new sources, from application of new techniques, and from more sophisticated probing of the records with new questions. It does not come from unsubstantiated assertions about the past, nor by manipulating the evidence to suit one's preconceived positions. The goodness of a cause, moreover, is not a substitute for accurate and balanced information. Impassioned pleading for a cause and scholarly historical study both have their place, but they should not be confused as being the same thing.

Critical tools have long been at the historian's hand. Rules for the assessment of documents have been a staple of historical methods manuals and courses for more than a century, and I see no justification for throwing them out in doing Indian history. Their habitual use is what marks the "pro" from the amateur.

It is not enough, then, to write the history of the Modoc War with heavy and uncritical reliance on a story of the war told by a man who was the son of the interpreters in the conflict but who was only ten years old at the time and who never had a formal education. At least one might suspect that all the direct dialog of which the book is composed is not really verbatim.[4]

It will not do to accept uncritically everything that is put forth as the speech of a famous Indian. Indian orations recorded in the eighteenth century all came out sounding pretty much alike and usually sounding like the men and women who recorded them.[5] Chief Joseph's "surrender speech" apparently was not a speech at all but a report of his reply to the demand for surrender brought back by an intermediary.[6] Black Hawk's autobiography, while accepted as representing the chief's Indian viewpoint, was certainly not written by the Sac chieftain himself.[7] It is not necessarily a sign of authenticity when a man proclaims himself a Sioux chief, is 101 years old, and sells his memoirs to McGraw-Hill.[8]

And if one can be sure of the authenticity, the question of what weight to put on the contents of the speeches still remains. If we must interpret with great caution and critical eye the rhetoric of Andrew Jackson in his advocacy of Indian removal—as I have been repeatedly told we must— we must also cast a quizzical eye upon the rhetoric of the Indian leaders and the zealous missionaries who opposed him. If we must ask whether the statements of Andrew Jackson and Lewis Cass were self-serving, can we reasonably neglect to ask the same question in regard to the statements of John Ross or Jeremiah Evarts? Not every Indian who speaks is a chief representing his whole tribe, nor are all clergymen unbiased in regard to their own causes.

Statistics, so much discussed these days, can be used to promote causes as well as to portray accurately the past. I have been interested in accounts of the number of deaths on the tragic Cherokee "Trail of Tears," for the variety of figures is startling. Herbert Welsh, the crusading secretary of the Indian Rights Association, wrote in 1890: "The march through the wilderness caused the death of at least half the tribe."[9] Ralph Henry Gabriel declared in 1929, "A third of the people perished in the autumn and winter of 1838 when the Cherokee followed what they called the 'trail of tears.' . . ."[10] And a recent author, intent on showing the cruelty of Andrew Jackson toward the Indians, has repeated the figure of one-third.[11] Most historians speak of the death of one-fourth of the migrating Indians, although Edward Everett Dale in the *Dictionary of American History* notes with somewhat greater accuracy that "it is probable that nearly 10% of those who started died on this tragic journey."[12] What is disturbing is that few writers have made use of the records that do exist, which indicate the number of deaths in each of the emigrating parties.[13] That even 10 percent died is a damning commentary on the whole process of forced removal to the West, but sound historical judgment is hardly fostered by arbitrarily blowing up the figures beyond all measure of truth.

It is interesting to note, turning to a different and less controversial matter, that the Indian reformer of the 1870s and 1880s, Dr. Thomas A. Bland, mistakenly appears in a substantial scholarly account of post-Civil War Indian reform as Theodore A. Bland—a very small error, of the kind that creeps into every history book. But a subsequent study of the same period of Indian policy also calls him Theodore. The author of a third work on the same subject that appeared recently also thinks the doctor's name was Theodore. And on the tentative listing of non-Indians for whom brief biographies will appear in the new Smithsonian *Handbook of North American Indians* appears Theodore A. Bland. Anyone who comes along now with the correct name is likely to be ruled out of court.

These are examples—admittedly rather minor ones—of the tendency, even among professional scholars, to accept stereotypes, to copy uncritically from previous works when a reinvestigation of the sources is called for. The conference on Indian-white relations might serve as a rededication to the principles of scientific thoroughness and historical accuracy and critical use of sources that should mark such an important endeavor as doing Indian history.

The history of Indian-white relations presents, of course, the special problem of dealing with two diverse cultures. All historians need to understand the times and manners with which their histories deal, but added difficulties arise for the intercultural investigator. It is necessary to see the action on each side and to study the reaction on the other. This means, ideally, understanding two *others*, quite diverse in themselves. It is customary to insist that we grasp something of the worldview of the Indian cultures (because we instinctively know they are different from our own), and we try not to judge one culture by the norms of another. What is often forgotten is that we must also understand past white societies and not assume that the 1830s can be understood and judged entirely by the norms and values of the 1970s. The brilliance of hindsight must not blind a proper understanding of, say, the Jacksonian era's views of race, of religion, or of the future prospects and rate of Western expansion. One of the goals of writing about Indian-white relations in United States history must certainly be to explain that past to white Americans. Historians must learn to understand the intellectual equipment with which nineteenth-century Americans approached the terribly difficult problems that arose in intercultural contacts and conflicts.

If our goal is not to condemn or to praise but to understand, it is necessary to be more fully conscious of the historical context in which events in Indian-white relations took place. An appreciation of the Enlightenment minds of Jefferson and his contemporaries, for example, makes one question the easy analysis of Jefferson's Indian policy as, first of all, the desire to gain the Indians' land and only secondarily, a concern for Indian welfare, when these elements seemed to have been interwoven parts of one whole. Recent careful studies of the politics involved in the Cherokee cases decided by John Marshall's court, to take another example, make it impossible any longer to see a simple conflict between justice and morality on one side and expediency and illegality on the other, which so often has been the historian's judgment.[14]

Many times it is assumed and sometimes it is explicitly argued that a person cannot legitimately investigate the history of an ethnic group or cultural community without being a member of that group. I have the uncomfortable feeling that the argument is sometimes converted into a still more questionable form—that mere membership in the group itself supplies accurate information about all aspects of the group's past. Such ethnic or racial criteria of the validity of historical research are unacceptable because they are basically anti-intellectual. "It may well be," as a recent study on the discipline of history has pointed out, "that some things are knowable only to 'insiders'; but then there are other things that are especially perceptible to 'outsiders' precisely because they are outside. That is one of the ambiguities of historical research: the scholar tries to get as close to his subject as possible while maintaining enough distance of space and time to afford him a sense of context and significance."[15]

But I would like to hope that historians might advance beyond a concern for "insiders" and "outsiders," so that what might prevail in the study of Indian-white relations will not be charges and countercharges but a spirit of patience and cooperation, a willingness to aid one another in a common purpose. If that common purpose is to grasp the past with sympathetic understanding, let us be slow to judge and slow to condemn.

When judgment is necessary, however, we must take care to judge all parties alike. It is true that an understanding of a culture must be governed to a large extent by the culture itself, yet it is essential to avoid adopting a double standard of judging when dealing with two cultures and their interaction. It will hardly do to see all wrong on one side and nothing but sweetness and light on the other. Breast beating over the injustices done to the Indians may have a salutary effect on public policy—although there is little evidence that Helen Hunt Jackson's *A Century of Dishonor* had any direct effect upon the members of Congress to whom she eagerly sent copies or that the book significantly changed the effective Indian reform movements of the 1880s and 1890s. What effect Dee Brown's similar book, *Bury My Heart at Wounded Knee*, will have remains to be seen. The imbalance and distortions of such books, though serving an immediate purpose of stimulating public interest in a good cause, weaken their lasting importance, and the books themselves become part of the history of Indian rights movements, not histories that can stand the test of time.

A reviewer criticized a recent book on the history of Indian-white relations by saying, "Today, most treatises on the Indian are more or less biased, and this book is no exception. White invaders are portrayed as greedy, brutal, and faithless; Indians as uniformly ingenious and innocent. Anyone who has dealt as intimately with Indians as [the author] . . . knows that most were (and are) neither heroes nor villains but people trying (like the rest of us) to sustain their lives in a difficult environment." Those who are intent upon following professional norms would do well to heed the wise counsel with which this reviewer ends his criticism. "The historical record reveals . . . ," he notes, "that the Iroquois could be as brutal and merciless in their expansionist activities as any White frontier group; and it will not do so to absolve them of critical judgment by attributing the moral responsibility for their conduct to the temptations of White traders or missionaries. If moral judgment is to be rendered upon the latter, so should it upon the former. Or, if the Indians are to be absolved of responsibility on the grounds of being naive and illiterate victims of circumstance, by what right," he asks, "can we still impose judgment upon the traders, missionaries, and frontiersmen?"[16]

John C. Ewers has expressed a similar view. "I [do not] see the role of the historian of Indian-white relations," he said, "to be that of being kind to either party in this historic confrontation. But I do think he should study this very complex theme in both breadth and depth, consulting and weighing all the sources he can find, so that he can be fair to both sides."[17]

I will be accused of offering a counsel of perfection, but the goal of historians, no matter how we all fall short of it, can be no less. A historian's inability to eliminate biases altogether does not justify the abandonment of all efforts to minimize or to surmount them in the search for truth. Perhaps the goal cannot ever be attained, but we will assuredly not get closer to it if we fail to strive for it. "Some historians do in fact come closer to it than others," it has rightly been noted. "Some history is more objective and less biased, better documented and more cogently argued. Most of us would call that better history."[18]

We must seek the truth in the story we are telling, and in the history of Indian-white relations especially we must be alert to the pitfall of having too much sympathy either for our own preconceived ideas or for one side or the other of a controversy. To be a good judge, we must not care what the truth is we are seeking. We must be concerned only with finding it. Indeed, the more we care what it is, the less likely we are to find it. We must not let our personal interests or personal pique get in the way of our judgment. We must not be too much concerned about making points for one side of a controversy or another.

Let me close with the advice offered by a sixteenth-century religious leader to his followers. "Argue in such a way," he said, "that the truth may appear, and not that you may seem to have the upper hand." Let us proceed in such a spirit as we seek the truth about the history of Indian-white relations in the United States. Then we—and the world too—can acclaim the Indian history we are doing.

NOTES

1. The choice of my title, "Doing Indian History," was influenced by J. H. Hexter's article, "Doing History," *Commentary* 51 (June 1971): 53–62, in which he argues for excellence in traditional historical writing. I have been helped, too, by the following articles in addition to those cited specifically below: Jack D. Forbes, "The Indian in the West: A Challenge for Historians," *Arizona and the West* 1 (Autumn 1959): 206–15; Stanley Pargellis, "The Problem of American Indian History," *Ethnohistory* 4 (Spring 1957): 113–24; James C. Olson, "Some Reflections on Historical Method and Indian History," ibid., 5 (Winter 1958): 48–59; William T. Hagan, "On Writing the History of the American Indian," *Journal of Interdisciplinary History* 2 (Summer 1971): 149–54.
2. Wilcomb Washburn, "The Writing of American Indian History: A Status Report," *Pacific Historical Review* 40 (August 1971): 261–81.

3. Robert F. Berkhofer, Jr., "The Political Context of a New Indian History," ibid., pp. 357–83.
4. See Jeff C. Riddle, *The Indian History of the Modoc War and the Causes That Led to It* (n.p., 1914).
5. Alan E. Heimert, *Religion and the American Mind, from the Great Awakening to the Revolution* (Cambridge, Mass.: Harvard University Press, 1966), pp. 219–21.
6. Mark H. Brown, "The Joseph Myth," *Montana, the Magazine of Western History* 22 (Winter 1972): 2–17.
7. See the discussion of the autobiography in Donald Jackson, ed., *Ma-Ka-Tai-Me-She-Kia-Kiak, Black Hawk: An Autobiography* (Urbana: University of Illinois Press, 1955), pp. 31–38.
8. *The Memoirs of Chief Red Fox* (New York: McGraw-Hill, 1971). For an account of the charges leveled against the book, see *New York Times*, 10 March 1972.
9. Herbert Welsh, *The Indian Question, Past and Present* (Philadelphia, 1890), p. 7.
10. Ralph Henry Gabriel, *The Lure of the Frontier: A Story of Race Conflict* (New Haven: Yale University Press, 1929), p. 128.
11. Sidney Lens in "Book Forum," *Saturday Review*, 26 February 1972, p. 79.
12. *Dictionary of American History*, vol. 5, s. v. "Trail of Tears."
13. See Grant Foreman, *Indian Removal: The Emigration of the Five Civilized Tribes of Indians* (Norman: University of Oklahoma Press, 1932), pp. 310–12. Figures on removal, with the number of deaths, are given in U.S., Congress, House, *Report*, no. 288, 27th Cong., 3d sess., Serial 429, pp. 17–18.
14. See Joseph C. Burke, "The Cherokee Cases: A Study in Law, Politics, and Morality," *Stanford Law Review* 21 (February 1969): 500–531.
15. David S. Landes and Charles Tilly, eds., *History as Social Science* (Englewood Cliffs, N.J.: Prentice-Hall, 1971), pp. 16–17.
16. Murray L. Wax, review of *A History of the Indians of the United States*, by Angie Debo, in *Nebraska History* 52 (Fall 1971): 340.
17. John C. Ewers, "When Red and White Men Met," *Western Historical Quarterly* 2 (April 1971): 150.
18. Landes and Tilly, *History as Social Science*, p. 16.

I

Major Resources of the National Archives and Records Service for Indian Historical Research: History, Use, and Potential of the Records

INTRODUCTION
Robert H. Bahmer

Historical research implies that there are historical materials that will be used—documentary sources of one sort or another—and certainly the collections in the National Archives relating to Indian history and to Indian-white relationships are by far the largest and most complete in the nation. So the first two papers begin with some consideration of the materials that are in the Archives and available for research. The first paper, by Oliver W. Holmes, is on the present holdings of the National Archives relating to Indians, and the second, by Carmelita S. Ryan, relates to future holdings, since it deals with the appraisal of current records for ultimate deposit in the National Archives.

Indian-Related Records in the National Archives and Their Use: Observations over a Third of a Century

Oliver W. Holmes

Instead of producing some profound and arresting paragraphs with which I hoped to open this paper, my mind kept wandering to the spring months of 1938 when I spent many dirty but happy weeks in the basement of the old or North Interior Building in Washington (now known as the General Services Administration Building) preparing "identification inventories" of the old records of the Bureau of Indian Affairs that had been offered for transfer to our new National Archives Building, where great vault-like rooms containing thousands of shiny new steel shelves and containers stood empty waiting to receive them. It is still a shock to me to realize that more than one-third of a century has passed since those days.

It was in February 1938 that the first smaller shipments were made. Then we started on the main body of old files and letterbooks, including registers, indexes, and other control records, covering the years from 1800 down to 1921. Through April, May, and June of 1938, we moved in truckload after truckload—nearly one hundred in all—until by summer we had about seven thousand cubic feet of Indian Bureau records in the building, the contents of about one thousand four-drawer file cabinets or about two miles of shelving.

We made very detailed identification inventories in those first years, inventories which were signed in duplicate by authorized representatives of both the transferring agency and the National Archives. Naturally, we

```
                                              Accession No. 138
                                              January 11, 1938

                         THE NATIONAL ARCHIVES
                         Division of Accessions

                         Identification Inventory

Inventory No. 38-18, Part I            Preliminary Survey: P. M. Hamer,
                                       Parts of G-1 report Nos. 7,9,10,
Deputy Examiner: Oliver W. Holmes      17,18, and possibly others.

Archives of: Department of the Interior   Subdivision: Office of Indian
                                          Affairs, Mail and Files Division
Location of Depository: Ground Floor,
                       Old Interior Building, Sheet 1 of 8 sheets
                       18th and F Streets


                         - - - - - - - -


Description of Records

    A.  Records of the Indian Division, Secretary's Office, 1849-1907.

        1.  Original Letters Received, 1849-1907, folded and compressed in
            Woodruff files (pink charge slips in some of these files indi-
            cate papers now in use which will be sent to The National Archives
            as they are returned to the Mail and Files Division).  These
            letters are arranged in several serials, as follows:

            a.  From the War Department, 1849-1880, eleven file boxes
            b.  From the Treasury Department, 1850-1880, three file boxes
            c.  From the Executive, 1852-1880, three file boxes
            d.  From the State Department, 1857-1880, one file box
            e.  From the Attorney General, 1852-1880, three file boxes
            f.  From the Commissioner of the General Land Office, 1862-1880,
                two file boxes
            g.  From the Commissioner of Indian Affairs, 1869-1877, five file
                boxes
            h.  Miscellaneous, 1849-1889, twenty-three file boxes
            i.  From Board of Indian Commissioners, 1874-1880, one file box
            j.  General chronological file, 1849-1907, seven hundred and thirty
                file boxes
            k.  Special case files, all labelled, such as "Red Cloud trouble",
                "White River Massacre", "Committee on the Boundary between
                Indian Territory and Texas", "Report of Sioux Commissions",
                "Eastman Matter", etc., in ten file boxes.
            l.  Seven file boxes labelled "Old Miscellaneous Papers from
                Indian Office".
```

First page of an Identification Inventory describing some Indian Division records accessioned from the Office of the Secretary of the Interior. (Natural Resources Branch) wanted to know very exactly just what we were taking legal and professional responsibility for. Also, these inventories were supposed to provide information to aid the classifiers and catalogers in the National Archives Building who were expected to create an overall consolidated card catalog and other finding aids for administrators, scholars, and interested citizens of the future. One identification inventory that I prepared on this Indian Bureau assignment was over seventy single-spaced, typed pages in length. Others were thirty and forty pages. It was only later that lawyers advised against such detailed inventories lest the National Archives be held responsible for every little item described, which descriptions might not always be that accurate. Make them more general, they counseled. But in the late 1930s we, as staff members of the old Accessions Division, examined every volume and analyzed every file.

To one as interested in Indian affairs and the Indian story as I am—after a Minnesota and Montana background, not to mention a course in the history of the frontier from Solon J. Buck—it was a thrilling experience to learn how much had been saved. Some records had become disarranged and mixed up in the many moves to which the bureau had been subjected, yet dedicated employees had kept most of the records in far better shape than they were found to be in most older bureaus. Few busy twentieth-century agencies, perhaps only the State Department and the General Land Office, had more need than the Indian Bureau to consult their old records for administrative and legal purposes. Already, lawyers working on tribal claims had their assigned desks among these records in the bureau's basement file rooms. And the bureau had also welcomed certain historians during the 1920s and early 1930s.

Perhaps half of the use by historians had been by scholars from Oklahoma, where Mr. and Mrs. Grant Foreman led the way. Foreman was not trained as a professional historian but as a lawyer, in which capacity he had worked with the Commission to the Five Civilized Tribes, 1899–1903, and become interested in, and concerned about, the records of their tribal governments, which were about to end with the abolition of Indian Territory when Oklahoma became a state in 1907. Later, when Foreman became director of the Oklahoma Historical Society, he promoted the Hastings Act of 1934, under which the federal government made the society custodian of the records of these abolished tribal governments. It was surely natural that Oklahoma historians, more than those of other states, felt the need to explore the Washington side of their story. It was Foreman, I am sure, who sent many Oklahoma scholars to Washington in the days before we had a National Archives—such scholars as Edward Everett Dale, Muriel Wright, Angie Debo, Morris Wardell, Berlin Chapman, and others. Oklahoma, through its State Historical Society, its university, and the Oklahoma University Press, continued during the past generation to carry a torch, and I still feel Oklahoma has a sophistication about Indian history that other states need to consider.

But there were historians from other states who also knew these records before they were transferred to the National Archives. One, whose work has always fascinated me, was Annie Heloise Abel Henderson, who had the advantage of being on the bureau's staff as a historian for a number of years, beginning in 1910. I could say much more about her, but I think that should be done by someone in a special article after using her personal records, some of which now have been deposited in the National Archives. Another pioneer was Newton D. Mereness who made the so-called Mereness calendar for seven cooperating historical societies of the Midwest. His work alerted Upper Mississippi Valley historians to the richness of these records for their area and led directly to the project for publishing *The Territorial Papers* series. Edgar B. Wesley, Loring B. Priest, and Alban W. Hoopes also used these records and published influential books shortly before the records were moved to the National Archives. Unfortunately, the length of this paper prevents me from devoting more time to the experiences and the work of these pioneers, though it would be interesting to learn more about their adventures in those days.

Anyway, the basic records of the Bureau of Indian Affairs, from its establishment in 1824 (and some before 1824 that the secretary of the War Department had turned over to it) down to 1921, were brought into the National Archives Building in 1938. The New Deal was a great boon to the Archives in the days of its beginnings. The pressures for office space for the large emergency New Deal agencies could not be resisted. Dignified old agencies were jostled and squeezed out of their comfortable quarters by space control orders coming down from above. Secretary of the Interior Ickes was also named Public Works administrator, and the gigantic Public Works Administration, after the recession of 1937 (a further dip in the depression of the 1930s), had just been given additional billions to be spent in the shortest time possible in the hope of bolstering the sagging economy of the nation. The emergency agency was in a big hurry; nothing was to be permitted to stand in its way. When its young, haughty administrative officers decided they needed the long basement rooms occupied by the retired Indian Bureau files, there was no help for the bureau. There were no other available retreats, it appeared, where these files could rest in peace except at the National Archives. So, reluctantly, with sentimental laments, the Indian Bureau gave up part of its heritage—the records covering 120 years of the federal government's administration of Indian affairs.

Once the ice had been broken, smaller shipments came from time to time to fill the gaps—older records that had up to then still been retained in the operating divisions of the bureau. Additional records came when the Mail and Files Division found it had to trim further to fit into the space allocated to it in the new Interior Building. "I don't know what we would have done if the National Archives hadn't taken care of these old records," was now the typical comment of Indian Bureau personnel. The bureau had been reassured by the efficient service the National Archives was providing on these complex files in response to many calls each working day. The bureau even sent over some of their own specialists, such as Brent Morgan, to help with their more complex demands and to teach the staff at the Archives.

Under the impact of even greater space pressures engendered by World War II, the Indian Bureau was forced to move out of Washington entirely —to Chicago. Proof of the confidence that the bureau now had in the National Archives was the decision that the files from 1921 to 1933, up to the beginning of the Roosevelt administration (and in Indian Bureau history of the Collier regime), could be left with the Archives in Washington and serviced by mail. So more than two thousand additional feet were transferred in 1942. All in all, by the end of World War II there were over ten thousand cubic feet of records of the Indian Bureau proper in the National Archives. Later, in 1953, the central classified files for 1933–39 were transferred, representing several thousand feet more, relating mainly to the Collier period. The bureau had withheld the card indexes to these files from 1907 on, but in 1966 these too were transferred, so that the National Archives now has all the controlling finding aids created by the agency for these transferred files.

The one great misfortune is that the Archives has very little material for the period between 1789 and 1800, because the records of the centralized administration of Indian affairs were destroyed by a War Department fire in August 1800. We have only a few field office records of agencies and trading posts for these years (mostly for the Creeks and Cherokees) that were sent into Washington at a later date when these agencies and posts were abandoned. Therefore, scholars must search for materials for these early, important years of Old Northwest and Old Southwest Indian history in state and private collections, and they will find these records woefully scattered and incomplete. A special effort should, in fact, be made to collect, edit, and publish what can be found in all depositories for this very important period. But from 1800 to 1939, researchers will find the central records in the National Archives almost inexhaustible and in ever-increasing volume and detail.

While focusing on the very beginning of our life as an independent nation, I should mention the carefully kept records of the Continental and Confederation Congresses (Record Group 360) which are also in the National Archives Building. As the Revolution progressed, Indian affairs were handled centrally more and more, and after the Peace of 1783, it was

Post   To Col: 177.
Ante.   Greenwood Leflore,   Department of War.
        at Brown's Hotel.   Office Indian Affairs.
                                         March 10. 1834.
Sir,
        In a recent communication addressed to the Secretary of War, you particularized several instances in which G. W. Martin Esq, had committed errors in locating reservations under the Choctaw Treaty of Dancing Rabbit Creek. In consequence of your representation, Mr. Martin was instructed to report all the circumstances and facts touching those cases to the Department, that if mistakes or errors existed they might be corrected.
        It is the desire of the Department to execute with faithfulness all the provisions of that Treaty, and to render to all the Members of the Choctaw tribe complete justice. If errors other than those specified have occurred, and the Department shall be informed of them, there will be immediate measures taken to rectify them.
        You are therefore as one of their Chiefs solicited to communicate such cases to the Department, that it may apply without delay the proper remedy.
                                Very respectfully &c.,
                                Elbert Herring.

Post. 178. To General,   Department of War.
Ante. 172. William Clark,   Office Indian Affairs,
            Supt. Indian Affairs, &c.,   March 10. 1834.
Sir,
        Your letter of the 22d. ult?, enclosing one to yourself from Keo-Kuck & other Sac & Fox Chiefs, complaining of the intrusion of white men, by hunting on their lands, has been received.
        The course pursued by you in directing the agent to take measures for the expulsion of the intruders is approved, and it is hoped by this time the evil complained of is removed. — I am &c.,   Elbert Herring.

A representative page from one of the 192 volumes of letters sent by the Office of Indian Affairs during the period 1824–86. All general outgoing letters were copied into these volumes. During the years 1828–85 letters to high government officials were copied into a separate series of fifty-three volumes called Report Books. Both of these series are available as National Archives microfilm publications. (RG 75)

A typical page from one of the 144 registers of letters received by the Office of Indian Affairs during the period 1881–1907. These registers, combined with thirty-seven volumes of indexes, comprised the bureau's retrieval system for its incoming correspondence. Entry 69281 records the receipt of a letter reporting the death of Chief Joseph of the Nez Percé. (RG 75) increasingly recognized that the Confederation must assume greater control over Indian matters west of the Appalachian ranges. It was natural, therefore, that the new federal government in 1789 was given most of the responsibility for supervising Indian relations, although the original states retained responsibility for Indian tribes wholly within their boundaries. The records of the Continental and Confederation Congresses have just been carefully analyzed for the first time for Indian-related material by Howard H. Wehmann of the Special Projects Division at the Archives. His "Preliminary Guide" on Indian-white relations is now available, and researchers will find it both interesting and informative.

Since official records for the colonial period are not in the National Archives, we unfortunately miss the pleasure of having visits from scholars interested in Indian history for these important years. These scholars must go mainly to the earlier records of states that were once colonies and even back to Europe to consult British, French, Spanish, Dutch, and other records of Indian relations. Additionally, much that is relevant for the colonial period has come to rest not only in libraries and historical societies up and down the eastern coast but also in the important holdings of the Clements, Newberry, Huntington, and other libraries.

But to return our attention to records of our federal government, the transferred records of the Indian Bureau (designated as Record Group 75 in the National Archives control records) comprise 14,000 cubic feet of paper and represent the central core of documentary source materials for all research into the history of the American Indian insofar as the federal government has been concerned with that race. These materials are the proper starting place, for they will carry trail signs to relevant records in other record groups. The bureau records are well arranged and easy to work with. One may wish for more adequate indexes prior to 1881, but there is a series, numbering 126 volumes, of systematically maintained chronological registers of all incoming communications for the years 1824–81, which can be worked more rapidly for most purposes than the overly complicated indexes that are available after 1881. Overelaborate indexes can be a snare and a delusion, especially if a scholar begins depending on them. No worthwhile searcher will ever be satisfied with indexes for anything more than a starting point. Researchers will call for the papers themselves that relate to bureau field jurisdictions in the geographical areas that interest them or that cover their particular tribe or relate to a particular period and will go through them document by document. The Indian Bureau records lend themselves to that sort of research. There are some drawbacks, but in general working with them is exciting and satisfying.

Fitting hand and glove into these records of the Bureau of Indian Affairs, and of almost equal importance, are an additional thousand cubic feet of records of the Indian Division. This division existed from 1849 to 1907 in the Office of the Secretary of the Interior, handling Indian matters coming directly to the secretary's attention or referred to his office by the Indian Bureau. With these Indian Division records came also records of the Indian Territory Division, which had existed but a short time—from 1898 to 1907—when the Dawes Commission was active. During that time, however, it accumulated some five hundred cubic feet of valuable records relating to Indians inhabiting the old Indian Territory, now part of Oklahoma. But one must further mention records created by other divisions within the Office of the Secretary of the Interior, especially the records of the Appointments Division, where files relating to appointments and service of Indian superintendents and agents and cases relating to personnel investigations and disciplinary actions can be found. Certain files of the Patents and Miscellaneous Division of the secretary's office that relate to the administration of western territories after 1873, when that function was taken over by the Interior Department from the State Department, are also important because of heavy emphasis on Indian problems. Additionally, records of the Disbursing Office of the department should not be overlooked for there one can find well-indexed accounts of monies expended for all aspects of Indian administration. The custodians of these old records of the Interior Department learn to know the trails and read the signs that lead from one of these related groups to another, although, like the scouts of old, they sometimes run into difficulties when signs are old and difficult to decipher or have been tampered with.

Thus far, we have been referring to trails within the Records of the Bureau of Indian Affairs (Record Group 75) and the Office of the Secretary of the Interior (Record Group 48), but some of these trails lead into the records of other bureaus of the Department of the Interior. For instance, the same pressures that brought us the old Indian Office records also brought the old records of the General Land Office and Geological Survey of the Interior Department. In the Records of the General Land Office are to be found the story of the relentless pressures of the white population, the resulting Indian land cessions, the establishment of Indian reservations, the surveys of Indian lands, the management of Indian timber interests in the North Central states and Indian mineral and grazing rights in other areas, and, later, the breaking up and allotment of Indian reservations. There was within the General Land Office a separate division concerned with Indian lands whose activities dovetailed into those of the Land Division of the Indian Bureau. No research on Indian land matters, general or specific, is complete until both record groups have been searched. Records of the General Land Office relating to Indian affairs, if they could be segregated, would also amount to several thousand cubic feet.

Smaller in bulk but of genuine interest are the early records of the Geological Survey, especially those of the Great Western surveys that preceded the establishment of the Geological Survey, which are assigned to this record group because they were inherited by the Geological Survey. One must mention, especially, the records of the Powell surveys in Colorado and the Southwest, which contain almost as much material on the Indians of the region, past and present, as they do on its geology. From these surveys came the stimulus for the establishment in the Smithsonian Institution of the Bureau of Ethnology, with Powell as the first director. Further, one cannot overlook mention of the pictures of Indian life and Indian leaders preserved by the great cameramen of these expeditions— William H. Jackson, Timothy H. O'Sullivan, and John Hillers—many of whose finest plates are now in the National Archives. Materials of similar nature are to be found in diaries and other records of the surveys of western wagon roads and, to a still greater extent, in those of the Great Western railroad surveys. Of special importance are the records of the Northern Overland Survey of Gen. Isaac Stevens in 1853–54. Voluminous as are the printed reports of this expedition, there is much in detailed contemporary correspondence and other unpublished records that is fundamental for the Indian history of the Upper Missouri and Columbia River valleys. Into the records of these expeditions went a combination of the practical knowledge gained through years of experience of the mountain men of the West and the observations of the first trained scientific and artistic observers of Indian life. It is this blend that makes these records especially fascinating.

Records relating to Indians and Indian interests can also be found in the records of other bureaus of the Department of the Interior, notably among records of the Bureau of Reclamation relating to projects on Indian lands or adjacent to them where Indians and whites shared the water. Records of the Office of Territories contain much of importance for Alaskan natives. Records of the National Park Service relate to many areas associated with the Indians.

So far we have been describing only records relating to Indians that are found in records of the Department of the Interior and its constituent bureaus, where of course most, but not all, of them are, and searchers must always be aware of Indian-related records created by other government agencies, found in other records groups, that may be relevant to their studies. The signs and trails are frequent that lead from Indian Bureau records to those of the War Department for most of the nineteenth century, and all War Department records for this period are now in the National Archives. Responsibility for the administration of Indian Affairs was of course with the War Department until the Interior Department was established in 1849. The separately maintained records of the

Bureau of Indian Affairs, which had been established within the War Department in 1824, were taken along with the bureau into the new Interior Department, but letterbooks of the Secretary of War before 1849 could not be torn apart, nor could the files of incoming letters be searched document by document in order to remove letters that touched on Indian Affairs. These had to be left with all the other records of the Office of the Secretary of War and are still located in that record group. The clerks of the day were practical men and knew that it was impossible to separate a large, integrated body of records by subject when they were not created or organized by subject to begin with. The records of the Office of the Secretary of War for this earlier period, that is, before 1849, bear much the same relation to the Indian Bureau records proper as do those of the Indian Division in the Office of the Secretary of the Interior after 1849. But, in addition, the War Department records both before and after 1849 document an entirely different phase of Indian relations, that of military action against them. "Against them" is really not the proper expression, for often the War Department was called upon to protect Indians against the whites and sometimes against each other. The Army's primary mission was to enforce peace, although one tends to forget this in contemplating the record.

For peace or for war, military records of the War Department relating to Indian affairs are almost as voluminous as those of the Indian Office proper down to 1890, after which time one would have less occasion to consult them on this subject. The relations of the Indian Bureau and the War Department after 1849 were, perforce, close even if not always friendly. Travel on the record trails back and forth between these two great domains was difficult in those days of jealousy, one gathers, and may have augmented the rivalry between the two services and decreased the efficiency of both. Travel back and forth on these trails is still not easy today, even when the records are in the same building. The War Department and army records are incredibly complex to the uninitiated.

One reason for this complexity is that besides the records of the Office of the Secretary of War (Record Group 107) and the Records of the Headquarters of the Army (Record Group 108) created chiefly in Washington, there are also the records created by army commands in the field (Record Groups 98 and 393), seemingly always shifting in their territorial jurisdictions. These field records were, with minor exceptions, systematically retired to Washington when commands were abolished and military posts abandoned. Such retirement was also the rule in the Indian Bureau with records created in the regional Indian superintendencies, most of which were abolished in the 1870s and 1880s, but only in a few minor instances were the older records of Indian agencies under these superintendencies sent along to Washington. Most of the records of abolished agencies were destroyed or were rescued by collectors, historians, or other interested persons and eventually turned over to historical societies and libraries. Earlier records of agencies that continued in existence, especially in the trans-Mississippi West, have often been sent to the regional archives. But military records, in contrast, were conscientiously retired to headquarters in Washington. Here, then, in the army record groups, are the records of the army commands, posts, and detachments of the Indian frontier—complete down to muster rolls and morning reports—essential to all who write in any detail of military campaigns against the Indians or on the Indian history of a region.

To be considered logically with the War Department records are those of the old Pension Office, today part of the Records of the Veterans Administration (Record Group 15). In this record group are thousands of case folders replete with biographical facts concerning the old Indian fighters, from generals down to privates, that would help those writing on the Indian wars and frontier garrisons to identify the actors and give life to them as the writer fills in the narrative.

I recommend to researchers the "Guide to Records in the Military Archives Division Pertaining to Indian-White Relations." This guide cannot cover everything, but it covers a wide range of Indian-white relations, and I think the five archivists who prepared it deserve the special thanks of both Indians and whites, even though it deals with matters about which whites cannot always be happy.

Before continuing with the records of other old-line departments of the Executive Branch, we must mention the Records of the United States Senate (Record Group 46) and the House of Representatives (Record Group 233) and their influential committees on Indian Affairs. Their importance is surely obvious. Much of this material was printed in the long and amazingly rich series of congressional documents, but much was not printed and sometimes for significant reasons. There are still nuggets to be turned up in these voluminous papers, and it behooves the conscientious researcher to examine these important documents. Surely the records of the Congress; the Interior Department, with its Indian Bureau; and the War Department are the most important for the Indian story, but there are still others.

One thinks of the records of the State Department as useful only in studying our relations with foreign nations. But the Indian tribes were also once considered as foreign nations. In this department's records, therefore, are preserved the long series of ratified Indian treaties. Admittedly, since these have been printed, their value is perhaps chiefly sentimental or as exhibition pieces. But if there is any instance in which an original document holds a fascination that cannot be transferred to print, it is true in the case of these old Indian treaties. Treaties which were not ratified can be found, usually with accompanying documents of great value, among the records of the Senate, or, if they were never transmitted to the Senate for ratification, they are likely to still be among the records of the Indian Bureau with all the background records relating to the treaty negotiations. The State Department in its early years also handled a great variety of domestic business, including, as has been noted, the administration of the territories down to 1871. No one should overlook the fact that in its long series of "Domestic Letters" and in other sources, many documents can be found of importance relating to Indian history.

One would also expect to find important material relating to Indian matters in the Treasury Department. For example, the Office of the Treasurer of the United States has had custody of Indian tribal trust funds and their investment since 1870, when by law the responsibility was turned over to that official. Accounting for these trust funds produces records of no small importance. But the great mass of records accumulated over the years by the comptrollers and auditors of the Treasury Department, as they handled the settlement of all accounts from the early 1790s until the establishment of the General Accounting Office in 1921, were inherited by that new office and are now with the Records of the United States General Accounting Office (Record Group 217). Many of the accounts relating in some way to Indians and Indian affairs—and particularly those of the Second Auditor who handled War Department accounts—were sought out and taken over by the Indian Tribal Claims Branch, created in the General Accounting Office in 1925 to prepare the extensive financial reports called for by the Department of Justice in connection with settling tribal claims against the government. These records and personnel of the Indian Tribal Claims Branch were later moved into the National Archives Center in Suitland, Maryland, where the records are now part of the holdings of the General Archives Division.

There are thousands of cubic feet of these records, and, although used by accountants and lawyers in connection with tribal claims, they still very much represent unknown terrain to scholars. They are complicated and confusing and have never been described in any detail. In the early days of our government, when copies were not as easily made as now, many important original documents were sent to Treasury Department auditors, as evidence upon which payments were made, and have remained there. In disputed cases the evidence obtained may be extensive —orders and instructions, affidavits, reports, and at times even such documents as original diaries, submitted to prove compliance, may be found. Furthermore, the auditors appear sometimes to have taken over substantial parts of the records of early agencies, such as, for example, the Office of Indian Trade, to liquidate them and close out their accounts. We suspect, and hope, that some existing gaps may be accounted for in this way.

Now that the records are in better quarters and better arranged, scholars should be able to make wider use of them, and we plan to gain more adequate knowledge of them ourselves so that we can give more help to searchers than we have in the past.

Next, it must be mentioned that much is preserved in the records of the Department of Justice that relates to Indian rights and property and to claims—claims in behalf of Indians against the government, claims of whites against Indians, and claims of Indian tribes against each other. In connection with prosecuting or defending these claims, original testimony on historical events and happenings was presented in affidavits and other papers. The historian must sift through this evidence now as the officers of law did when the cases were tried, but the historian will usually do it for other purposes and against a wider background. Closely related to these records of the Department of Justice and again fitting into them hand and glove are the records of the courts and, especially in the case of Indian claims, of the United States Court of Claims. The user will be amazed at the volume of these records and will not find them to be trivial. The issues at stake were often important ones in the history of individual Indian tribes and sometimes in the history of the Indian population as a whole. Just as the War Department and army records, fortunately, have become less important since 1880, so the Justice Department and court records have become more important. The courtroom has been substituted for the battlefield in settling the issues that cannot be contained and handled within the Indian Bureau.

But before Indians as a tribe could bring a claims case before the Court of Claims in earlier years, they had first to obtain a special jurisdictional act from the Congress. As can be imagined, this was not easy unless the claim could be made to appear to have much validity to begin with. Over the years, almost all tribes had met with disappointment, some with many disappointments. These old problems festered and created new ones. And, after many years of effort, an Indian Claims Commission was created in 1946 which President Truman stated, in signing the act, would insure "the final settlement of all outstanding claims." Over the next twenty-five years, more than eight hundred fifty claims were filed, but these were consolidated into some six hundred ten docketed cases. As of March 1972, one hundred sixty-seven of these were reported disposed of by commission orders of dismissal and about two hundred four more were disposed of by awards certified to the Treasury Department aggregating well over $435 million. Records for many of these now closed cases have been transferred to and accessioned by the National Archives. The life of the Indian Claims Commission was extended another five years by Public Law 92-625, approved March 30, 1972, which provides also that the records of future settled cases will be transferred to the Archives. They will represent a very important body of material for the historian, who will be looking at them differently from the lawyers.

Theoretically, the government is completely impartial in these cases and is concerned only with seeing that justice is done. The laws provided that both government lawyers and lawyers representing the Indian claimants should be given equal access to all records in government custody, and this has been done, I feel, with respect to all accessioned records in the National Archives including those in the General Archives Division at Suitland, Maryland, and in the regional centers. One cannot guarantee that the lawyers have found everything that may be relevant, but they have brought together as evidence in these claims cases copies of all documents that they and various paid consultants and research experts could find on hundreds of very important issues of dispute between Indians and whites and sometimes between different Indian groups themselves. Added to official records from federal sources are copies of relevant documents that have been found in state archives, private manuscript collections, and other sources all over the country. Rarely do historians have so much collecting done for them.

There are other records in the National Archives that contain material of value for the student of the American Indian. Not all the smaller groups can be named in this paper. The one main body of government records relating to Indians that is not in the National Archives is made up of those created by the Bureau of American Ethnology. But they are well kept in the Smithsonian Institution just a few blocks away, along with important unofficial source materials that the bureau accumulated. The scholar has no difficulty obtaining access to these for he or she is dealing with a scholarly institution that has always been interested in promoting the study of the American Indian.

I must call to your attention several other unpublished guides that have been prepared on Indians in addition to the one on military records already mentioned. There is a "Guide to Records in the Civil Archives Division Pertaining to Indian-White Relations," prepared by Richard Crawford and Charles South, that goes into much more detail with respect to the records I have been describing and includes descriptions of other groups I have not discussed. And Edward Hill has prepared a guide to "Records in the General Archives Division Relating to the American Indian," which covers accessioned records located in the Suitland Center. Also available are special guides to audiovisual and cartographic records, which of course must be physically maintained separately from paper records, although they are supplements to them. Unfortunately, these guides are not brought together in one published book, but it is hoped that eventually they will be. The important thing is that after all these years records from many different sources have been brought together under the custody of an archival agency and in buildings dedicated to and equipped for research. One can now follow the trails back and forth between these record groups, not without still encountering obstructions, it must be confessed, but with fewer obstructions and more help than ever before.

We archivists of the late 1930s worked with the expectation that hordes of historians were waiting to descend upon the National Archives when the records were centralized and assembled there, but in this we were disappointed. We welcomed a few new historians from western states, such as Frank B. Reeves, Dale Morgan, and Mari Sandoz. But Washington was a long way from the West, and the word was slow in getting around. Then World War II intervened and younger historians were engaged elsewhere.

It is not that we were idle meanwhile, standing around looking for customers. The records were being used heavily, more heavily than we thought possible, for administrative purposes, especially after the bureau was removed to Chicago during the war. And many of the younger employees of the Archives were taken for military duty or departed for work in war agencies, and replacements were curtailed because of wartime economies in civilian agencies.

I have mentioned some of the other old records of the Interior Department that poured in upon us as increased space was sought in the department. All had to be arranged, boxed, and labeled. To organize and arrange these records on the shelves so that they could be found when needed was a major archival task. Once arranged, it was hoped that they could be described in "preliminary inventories," which would reflect the arrangement. Over the years, many persons worked on certain segments of such an inventory for the Bureau of Indian Affairs records, when they had time left over from reference service. Finally, Edward Hill, who had already produced a model inventory of the Reclamation Bureau records, took over and put all these contributions together in two paperback volumes issued in 1965. These, entitled *Records of the Bureau of Indian Affairs*, volumes 1 and 2, totaling 459 pages, are available to any scholar or library. Volume 1 describes the central bureau records created and maintained in Washington, including records inherited by the bureau from the Office of the Secretary of War and records of the Office of Indian Trade, which was abolished in 1822. Volume 2 describes such records of field offices, mainly superintendencies and agencies, as were sent to Washington when these offices were terminated and closed, plus records of the important Board of Indian Commissioners, 1869–1933. Hopefully, we will soon be able to bring these volumes up to date, by including records transferred since 1965, and issue them in a single well-printed volume. Meanwhile, I recommend this inventory as the single most important "finding aid" relating to the federal government and Indian affairs.

It was the Indian Bureau records that led the National Archives to embark on microfilm publication. Very early we discovered that there were certain files among the old records of the Indian Bureau that were of such general interest and historical value that we were asked repeatedly to make large quantities of microfilm copies of the same material in a file, either of the complete file or of selected documents. Even though care was exercised, it was soon realized that repeated microfilming was hard on the records. Bound volumes, such as letterbooks, had to be opened wide and made to lie flat as page after page was photographed through the entire book. When the process was completed, the volume had suffered considerably. Folded loose records tended to break at the folds when unfolded. Early in 1939 I wrote a memorandum suggesting the retention by the National Archives of a master negative whenever complete files were microfilmed in order to minimize deterioration of the records through repeated microfilming. Also, we could fill future orders with positive prints made from that negative at a much lower cost. Among the series I listed for which we had received repeated requests were the letterbooks, four in number, of Gov. Lewis Cass as superintendent of Indian Affairs of Michigan Territory, 1814–23. After discussion and planning, the complete records of the Michigan Superintendency of Indian Affairs, of which the Cass letterbooks were a part, were filmed on seventy-one rolls and became the first of the hundreds of microfilm publications of the National Archives. Records of the Oregon Superintendency, 1848–73, on twenty-nine rolls, was the second such publication. Now, most of the more important series prior to 1880 are on microfilm, and positive copies can be purchased by any institution or individual. These publications include the letterbooks containing copies of letters sent by the commissioner of Indian Affairs, 1824–81; the registers of letters received in the bureau, plus the letters themselves for the same period; the Indian census rolls from 1884 to 1940; and many special files. Unfortunately, the numerical filing system used for correspondence from 1881 to 1907 represents a file that does not lend itself well to microfilming, and we are still uncertain as to how to tackle that period. The files after 1907 are organized according to a usable subject classification scheme and will be more acceptable on microfilm when we can get to them.

There were complaints against microfilm at first and there still are, both justified and unjustified, but researchers now may have the satisfaction of getting copies of the records into their own workshop, where they can be consulted when time permits, in circumstances under the researcher's own control. The researcher can go back to them repeatedly whenever necessary and can make them available to others in a group for study, whereas the trip to Washington would provide researchers only with notes, which provide little satisfaction to the researcher and certainly none to anyone else. All complaints against microfilming seem rather petty compared to these advantages. By checking the catalog of microfilm publications against the inventory of the Bureau of Indian Affairs, one can determine just which of the series within this record group are now available on film and can understand to some degree the relations between them and the series that have not been microfilmed. Indeed, any new edition of the inventory for bureau records should make clear just what has become available on film up to the date issued.

Microfilm also is playing a key role in bringing together for the scholar the records of the central agencies in Washington concerned with Indian affairs and the records of the Indian Bureau's field offices that are being moved into the Archives's fifteen regional archives and record centers but mostly, of course, those in the West. The original records of all the field offices could hardly have been brought together unless all were to have been brought into Washington. This centralization was considered in the early days of the National Archives, but World War II and the atomic bomb convinced us that there was some danger in concentrating everything in Washington. Moreover, there were advantages in keeping regional records in the regions to which they were related. Establishing the regional centers and moving the older regional records into them was one of the great accomplishments of the National Archives, or the National Archives and Records Service as it became known in the 1950s. The records of Indian agencies, schools, and other field offices of the Indian Service had not been kept under as satisfactory conditions as those of the bureau in Washington. Many of the older records were destroyed or lost. Those remaining were frequently in a state of confusion when accessioned by the archives branches of the regional federal records centers. Nevertheless, these centers now have in custody a quantity of field office records of the Indian Service that, added together, would rival in footage the bureau records in Washington. Personnel of the archives branches in these centers have, for the first time, prepared summary descriptions of the Indian records in their custody, and researchers will find them of great interest.

But there is a danger in keeping the central office records and field office records in separate repositories a thousand miles or so distant from each other. Neither the central records nor the field records tell the full story. As I stated in an article on "Federal Field Records" in 1942:

> A knowledge of the policies, procedures, and programs of a central office is not enough. It must be supplemented by a knowledge both of the local conditions out of which such policies, procedures and programs grew and of the effectiveness of the enforcement and

execution of the same. The program found outlined in the records of a central office is one thing; the degree to which it is carried down through the hierarchy of field officials and made effective is another thing and the more important of the two. History has been written too much from the central records alone. It is equally dangerous to write history from the field records alone.

This is especially true, it seems to me, in the whole history of federal Indian administration. We need more grassroots studies of the operations of the allotment policy, the administration of tribal income, operations of Indian police and courts, education facilities and their use, the effectiveness of health programs, and Indian-white relationships on the edges of the reservations. These can only be made from the local records, yet the local records do not present the wider framework, furnish comparative data, or detail all the restrictions under which local administrators had to work. One might permit a master's thesis based on local records alone, but certainly a doctoral dissertation or any pretended scholarly monograph should only be written after both central and local records have been studied. It is microfilm publication that will save scholars from shuttling back and forth between Washington and the region and also permit them to compare and correlate the information in a way not hitherto possible. The Archives is now engaged in a program to put copies of all important central office microfilm publications in the regional archives so that the two bodies of records can be used together, as they should be.

I like to think I belong to an age of historiography that is concerned with the facts and the facts alone, leaving interpretations to others—to anyone interested, presumably for reasons of their own. One cannot expect a historian to understand all these individual and group interests, or even to know about them. And, if historians are concerned with the facts of the past—beyond their personal experience—they must be concerned with the documents remaining from the past. It is the business of historians to find and consult these documents and record their findings in interesting and objective narrative or present on film or in print the more important documents themselves so that others can take over from there and use the historians' findings with confidence.

Perhaps many historians feel this is going too far when it comes to Indian history because over 95 percent of all documentation originated with whites, and some may feel it becomes even more one-sided when we advocate more use of the records of federal agencies supervising Indian-white relations. I can only say that if historians want to know and understand what happened for good or for ill, they must use these records. In doing so, it may be surprising to learn that there were many in the Indian Service who were greatly concerned for the Indian—agents, physicians, and teachers—who gave much of their lives for what they felt was a good cause. I suspect, considering how they were appointed, that good Indian agents were in the minority, but I sometimes wish some of those who did their best could get credit—that we could perhaps have a book presenting the work of ten or twelve of the best of them. Anyway, the records of the best and the worst prior to our own generation are to be found mainly in these records.

The records in the Archives should not be expected to provide answers with respect to present policies and problems relating to the American Indian. They are not recent enough for that. We do not have the recent records, subsequent to World War II, that might chronicle, for instance, some of the pluses and minuses of the so-called termination policy. These may be coming in the next few years. But the records the Archives does have should help to put some of these problems in perspective. We must pay attention to background, for it is impossible to deal intelligently with Indian problems of today without background knowledge for the past fifty years, and more. The Indian Bureau should have had its own corps of historians over the years—as much or more than the State Department or the Defense Department—studying the history of all existing problems, for Indian policy and administration cannot ride on the surface of the present. Every important field jurisdiction of the bureau should likewise have its historian studying regional problems at the grassroots, and every tribe should have its official historian, and all should get together and compare notes. More and more of these historians should and can be Indians as more Indians receive the proper educational background.

Some of our academic historians may decry such official history, but more of it in our Indian Service would, I believe, be a very healthy thing. Academic historians can always sit on the sidelines and criticize. They may occasionally be able to supply some perspective. It should always be possible for bureau historians and other historians to get together and compare results. This would have been done previously if we had Indian Bureau historians, but we have only archivists interested in the bureau records and their greater use. We hope, in the future, to hold conferences in our regional archival centers, at least in those holding large quantities of Indian-related material, where we can give special attention to regional records and regional Indian history.

I am glad that more and more Indians are becoming interested in writing their own history, for I feel they will have a special contribution to make. They are welcome to come to the National Archives and the regional archives and to use these records as white historians have been—even more so. And I am sure they will be surprised at how much interesting material will be found about their own people even though most of the records to date, but not all, were created by those who happened to be on the white side of one of the greatest, if not always happiest, themes in American history.

Special Study of the Appraisal of Indian Records

Carmelita S. Ryan

The preceding paper is concerned with the different kinds of records in the National Archives—the various record groups and the many series within these records groups—in which information relating to the American Indian can be found. I will now discuss how those records came to the Archives, to give some idea of the kinds of records that can reasonably be expected to come to the Archives and to the regional archives in the future. This is not a detailed discussion of all the various series of records in the National Archives that contain information relating to American Indians but is confined to the records of the Bureau of Indian Affairs, whose records form the core of the holdings on Indian-white relationships.

Before going into the Indian Bureau records, I will mention briefly the archival concept of records appraisal and how that concept has been applied to the records of the federal government. Public records have two kinds of values: primary values, i.e., values to the creating agency itself, and secondary values, values to other agencies and to the general public. The officials of the creating agency judge the primary values of their records. Indeed, they are the only ones who know how long it is necessary to keep their records for their current needs, either in their offices or in some storage area. It is the secondary values of the public records, the values inherent in records long after they cease to be of current use to the creating agency, that interests archivists. One of the most important and difficult tasks archivists are called upon to perform is to determine by an analytical examination of a body of records whether they have sufficient secondary values to warrant preservation in an archival institution. This analytical examination is called records appraisal.

To aid practitioners in this demanding work, archivists and historians of several countries have devised a number of standards by which the secondary values of bodies of public records can be measured. At best, these appraisal standards can serve only as guidelines to those judging the secondary values of records. They can never be precise, nor can they be applied in the same way to each and every group of records. The standards must be used with good judgment and common sense—especially common sense. If you wish to know more about the standards used by the National Archives, I refer you to T. R. Schellenberg's *The Appraisal of Modern Public Records*, National Archives Bulletin No. 8, which discusses them in some detail.

Until the latter part of the nineteenth century, public officials of the federal government managed to survive without systematically appraising their records because the quantity of records they created remained, by today's standards, relatively small. Even had they felt the need to dispose of their useless papers, these officials had no effective statutory machinery to do so—there was no general disposal law until 1889. Prior to that time, an agency either had to throw out records illegally, allow them to accumulate (spilling over into less and less desirable storage space), or obtain from Congress a specific authorization, usually inserted in an appropriations bill, in order to permit them to destroy some of their records. With the passage of the 1889 law, agencies were provided with a method of disposing of records considered useless, but the act did not require a historical agency to appraise the records for possible research value. It simply stated that records that have no permanent value should be reported by heads of government departments to Congress, which reserved to itself the right of authorizing destruction. An executive order of 1912, however, modified this by directing that the departments submit their disposal lists to the Librarian of Congress to obtain his views on the historical values of the records so enumerated for destruction.

Although the 1889 act and the 1912 executive order provided a beginning, it was not until the passage of the National Archives Act of 1934, the Records Disposal Act of 1943, and the Federal Records Act of 1950, that an effective framework for the orderly and consistent appraisal of records was created. Under the 1950 act, federal agencies are required to take proper measures to preserve adequate documentation of their programs and operations, and the General Services Administration, through the National Archives and Records Service, is directed to establish standards for the selective retention of records of continuing value for research. In accordance with these and earlier provisions, three major types of retention and disposal standards have been developed over the past three decades.

The oldest program involves the use of records control schedules. These schedules, used widely by agencies of the federal government

Appraisal of Indian Records 35

since 1943, give various retention periods for all classes of records of a particular organizational unit and provide for their orderly retirement or disposal. They are mandatory authorizations for the periodic disposition of records and can be used repeatedly. The records of the Bureau of Indian Affairs are covered by three such records control schedules, which were issued in 1954.

The second program, inaugurated in 1946, provides for the use of general records schedules dealing with the disposition of certain types of records common to all major government organizations. The records covered by these schedules include those pertaining to civilian personnel, accounting, procurement, property, fiscal matters, and automatic data processing. This permissive, but not mandatory, program covers a large proportion of the total volume of records created by federal agencies. The Bureau of Indian Affairs applies general records schedules to their administrative or housekeeping records.

The third program, which began in 1961, involves the preparation of records retention plans designed to identify records of continuing value. The amount and complexity of federal records makes this identification quite difficult, and, as a consequence, it has often been neglected in the past. Now, however, records retention plans for each agency are being developed by the National Archives in cooperation with their own officials. Each agency is analyzed—its organization and activities studied—and its basic functions identified. Then the records created by the agency are examined. Finally, the appraiser determines which classes of records produced by the agency in carrying out its basic functions should be permanently retained. Although the principal purpose for preparing the plans has been to safeguard the permanently valuable records, an important by-product has been assistance to agencies in establishing realistic disposal periods for records found to lack enduring value. The Bureau of Indian Affairs has been covered by retention plans. Briefly, then, this is the history of the application of the appraisal concept to the records of the federal government.

The Bureau of Indian Affairs has been in existence since 1824, with connections in the Office of Indian Trade and the Office of the Secretary of War that take it back to the end of the eighteenth century. Although the BIA has been creating records at an ever-increasing rate for 150 years, the records did not pose a major storage problem until the end of the nineteenth century. Happily, the bulk of the records that were created by the bureau throughout the course of the nineteenth century have survived and are now part of the National Archives of the United States. Their survival is due, at least in part, to the lack of statutory authority to destroy records that were not needed by federal agencies in their current business.

With the passage of the Act of Congress of February 18, 1889, which authorized government agencies to schedule the destruction of their useless papers, the bureau began to weed out the records that they considered of no value. In effect, they began to appraise the worth of their records. The bureau prepared schedules of "papers which are not needed or useful in the transaction of the current business . . . and have not permanent value or historical interest" to be submitted to Congress "accompanied by a concise statement of the condition and character of such papers." The schedules were referred to a Joint Congressional Committee on the Disposition of Useless Papers. If the committee approved the recommendation, Congress authorized the Bureau of Indian Affairs to destroy the useless records.

The first such schedule submitted to the committee from the Bureau of Indian Affairs was presented three times—in 1900, in 1902, and, again, in 1904—before it was finally approved by Congress. This schedule contains several items that present-day researchers and archivists would find of considerable interest such as records relating to the issuance of traders' licenses during the 1870s and the reservation sanitary reports (actually a yearly survey of the medical condition of each reservation) for the years 1873 to 1880. It also contains many items that were unquestionably disposable, prime examples of which are one-half ton of drafts of letters sent and estimates of annuity goods required. The one item on the 1900 schedule that, in retrospect, appears startling, reads "accounts, correspondence, and letter books of superintendencies . . . abolished prior to 1880." Fortunately, this item was removed from the schedule, either by the congressional committee or by some bureau official before it was resubmitted to Congress in 1902. Saved from oblivion, these records were among the first offered to the National Archives by the BIA and today form the nucleus of the field office records of the bureau.

From the early 1900s the Bureau of Indian Affairs annually sent schedules of useless papers, as these lists of disposable items became known, to Congress until after the establishment of the National Archives in 1934, when the bureau began to send them to the Archives for approval. After they were examined and approved, the schedules were submitted to the Congressional Committee on the Disposal of Useless Papers, which later became the Joint Committee on the Disposition of Executive Papers. I might mention here that in 1970 the committee was abolished, and the National Archives now has the sole responsibility for determining whether a certain series of records merits disposition or should be permanently retained.

Most of the records proposed by the BIA for disposal since 1900 were undoubtedly disposable. Generally, the individual items present no problems. Sometimes archivists may have doubts about a single item or, in-

Appraisal of Indian Records

deed, no doubts at all—they may *know* that it is valuable. In that case the archivists simply refuse to agree to its disposition. They can modify the disposition of an item by extending its retention for a longer period so that its value can be verified by the passage of time, or they can ask that a sample of the records be saved. All of these procedures are cleared with the bureau, of course, but in the final analysis it is the decision of the archivist that determines whether the record is kept or destroyed.

In the late 1930s the BIA ceased submitting annual schedules of useless papers and instead listed items which it deemed worthless on a standard government form requesting that the records be disposed of. Since 1938 the National Archives has received thirty-seven disposal requests from the bureau. This number is fairly small compared with those received from other government agencies of comparable size and mission. Among these thirty-seven jobs are three comprehensive records control schedules, submitted in 1954, covering the records of the central office, the area offices, and the field offices of the Bureau of Indian Affairs. These three schedules contain provision for the retention as well as the disposition of almost all the records of the Bureau of Indian Affairs that were in existence when the schedules were prepared and for most of those created since that time. There are, of course, several series that are not covered under these plans, including records relating to the Job Corps or Head Start programs and the new Reservation Acceleration Programs. These, however, have been covered by the Retention Plans that have been prepared for the Bureau of Indian Affairs, which will be discussed at greater length later.

The dossiers documenting each of these thirty-seven external disposal jobs and the fifteen internal disposal jobs prepared by the National Archives on BIA records already in their custody contain extensive and exhaustive appraisal reports. In most appraisal reports each item has been carefully described, its relationship to other BIA and other federal government records noted, and its value to the government, the Indians, and to scholars set forth. Incidentally, all documentation on the appraisal of all records of the federal government on file in the National Archives Building is open for examination by interested persons. This includes all the various types of appraisal for disposal, for accessioning, and for retention planning.

Although since 1970 the National Archives has had sole responsibility for the disposition of all federal records, records relating to claims in which the federal government might be a party must also receive the approval of the General Accounting Office before the records can be legally destroyed. As a matter of course, the appraiser makes certain of GAO approval before any fiscal records are destroyed, and the written authorization of GAO is part of the job dossier. There are other agencies of the federal government that must also be consulted when the destruction of Indian records is contemplated, especially the Department of Justice and the Indian Claims Commission. These two agencies have special interests in Indian records and are consulted whenever records of interest to them are suggested for disposal. And there have been times when they have said no to a proposed disposal of BIA records. Whenever either agency has disapproved of the proposed disposal of certain Indian records, we have respected their wishes and retained the records in question. I may also say frankly that when the Indian claims cases are settled, some records will probably be resubmitted for disposal action.

Thus far this discussion has focused on appraisal of records lacking sufficient secondary values to warrant permanent preservation in the National Archives, but perhaps I should have started on a positive note, by discussing BIA records deemed permanently valuable since these are the records that will be kept and used by scholars. It would be impossible for the National Archives to accept for permanent retention all of the records created by the Bureau of Indian Affairs. The bureau, like every other agency of the federal government, creates too many records.

During fiscal year 1971, the amount of extant documentation of the BIA increased by 9,580 cubic feet, even though an additional 8,573 cubic feet of records were disposed of during the same twelve-month period. Currently, the bureau has on hand a total of 100,756 cubic feet of records stored or stashed away in their offices, file rooms, staging and holding areas, and in our federal records centers. None of these records have been accessioned by the National Archives, and, indeed, very few of them deserve permanent retention. In the past, using approximately the same appraisal standards that guide us today, we have selected for permanent preservation in this building only 10,650 cubic feet of BIA records for the period 1824–1939. After nearly forty years of studying the totality of the bureau's written documentation, from the presidency of James Monroe to that of Franklin Roosevelt, we have appraised as permanently valuable 10,650 cubic feet while in just one year of Richard Nixon's presidency the BIA has added 9,580 to its holdings!

The work of accessioning BIA records began even before the Archives building itself was finished and ready for occupancy. In the latter half of 1935, members of a team of special examiners assigned to the compilation of a list of the archives of the federal government in the District of Columbia surveyed and prepared reports on the records of the BIA. The reports, though brief in content, include a description of the various series of bureau records with both linear and cubic footage, note their exact location, and pinpoint any menaces to their safety and well-being. By 1936, their work had broadened to include preparation of inventories of records for identification purposes. These inventories contain recommendations for the transfer of the records to the National Archives. In addition, the special examiners appraised all records submitted for disposal as useless papers. Any series that they believed archival in nature was added to the growing lists of records that should be accessioned into the National Archives of the United States. In late 1937 and early 1938, the bureau agreed to let the National Archives accession their older records in order to make space for the records documenting the expanding activities of the Works Progress Administration, with whom they shared their office building. And so, in the spring of 1938, Oliver W. Holmes of the National Archives staff spent many hours in the bureau assembling the various series of Indian records that had been marked as archival in nature.

The BIA has made thirty-six offers of its records to the National Archives between 1938 and 1972. Each offer or transaction is covered by an accession dossier containing considerable information about the records in question, including rather complete appraisals of their worth and values. Each dossier also contains the accession inventory, signed by a representative of the National Archives and of the Bureau of Indian Affairs, which transfers legal custody of the records to the General Services Administration in the person of the archivist of the United States.

Not all of these accessioned records are in the National Archives Building. Over the past two decades the Archives has established a nationwide system of depositories that, besides the National Archives Building in Washington, now includes six presidential libraries, fourteen federal records centers, and eleven regional archives branches located in the federal records centers. The regional archives branches, established in 1968, preserve and make available for research those permanently valuable records of the federal government that were created and maintained by field offices and which document regional and local activities.

The latest NARS program for selecting the permanently valuable records of an agency is the preparation of a records retention plan. Working in close cooperation with the records staff of the agency involved, preparation of the plan begins with a careful analysis of the organization, functions, and activities of the agency. To this task appraisers usually bring a considerable store of information and knowledge which they have accumulated in their archival careers. With these weapons in their armory, they study statements concerning the agency, reports of congressional appropriation hearings, agency organizational and functional charts, and published reports and monographs concerning the agency's programs and accomplishments. The aim of all this study is the creation of a list of the major functions of the agency. Then the appraisers try to determine which classes of permanently valuable records are produced in carrying out each major function of the agency. In order to discover this they examine records control schedules, inventories, surveys of records, classification and filing manuals, and records management handbooks.

They also confer with records and program officials and examine representative portions of current and noncurrent records.

The first two functions designated under most retention plans and common to just about all federal agencies are, first, preparing and issuing policy, procedural, organizational, and reportorial documents and, second, providing executive direction for the agency's activities. In drawing up the BIA retention plan, we selected for permanent retention as documentation of the first function directives, organizational charts, annual work progress reports, speeches of high officials, and publications dealing with the overall program of the agency. Records selected relating to the second function included correspondence showing executive direction and top-level policy formulation and execution, reports of comprehensive audits and inspections, legal opinions and decisions concerning the bureau's operations, minutes of top-level staff meetings, and minutes and reports of advisory groups. Together these two groups of records will, we hope, document the policies of the agency and the decisions made on organizational and procedural matters. In brief, they will show what the mission of the agency is and how well it is being accomplished. The records are of historical value also, because they contain information useful for research in the administrative history of the agency, its area offices, agencies, and schools.

In addition to the two government-wide functions I have just discussed, the records retention plan for the BIA lists six distinct functions that produce records deserving permanent retention. The plan lists the bureau's educational program for both Indian children and adults as its third function. At present, the most important form of help provided the Indians is in the field of education, and education for Indian children and adults accounts for the largest share of the bureau's appropriation. The records designated for retention under this function, especially the individual Indian student case files and those relating to the Head Start programs, will be of considerable value to anthropologists, historians, and sociologists.

The bureau's role as trustee, assisting the Indians in making the most effective use of their lands and other resources, is the fourth function of the BIA retention plan. This role provides the legal basis for the bureau's existence, and it is this responsibility which has led to the development of other programs in the area of education and public service. Adequate documentation of this function is necessary to safeguard the property and other legal rights of individual Indians and of Indian organizations.

The fifth major function of the bureau is to assist the Indian people in developing programs leading towards complete Indian responsibility for the management of their own property and affairs. In pursuing this goal

Appraisal of Indian Records 41

the bureau has encouraged the creation and development of tribal governments, business councils, and other tribal organizations which tend to increase the active and direct participation of Indians in their own government, including the new reservation acceleration programs. The records thus created will be of great interest to historians and political scientists who wish to study the genesis and development of political organizations. The records will also prove useful to historians who want to compare the present Indian governments with the tribal leadership of earlier days.

The BIA provides public services for Indians living on reservations where such services would not otherwise be available to them. Because records created in the carrying out of this function, the sixth in the retention plan, not only contain information about individuals but document the nature and the effectiveness of the bureau's programs, these records were recommended for permanent retention.

The seventh function, assistance enabling the Indians to develop programs to attract industries to the reservation in order to broaden the tribal economic base, is one of the most promising of the bureau's newer programs.

Function number eight, the last in the BIA retention plan, is to provide the Indian people with viable options for either staying on the reservations or moving to nonreservation communities. Records relating to the Job Corps are being retained under this function. The great interest of these records to anthropologists and sociologists of the future seems obvious.

Records relating more exclusively to programs and administration of the bureau—those created at the headquarters level—will be retained in the Archives. The bulk of the records to be retained under the BIA retention plans, however, will contain information relating to individual Indians. They will be created in the area and field offices and will be eventually deposited in the archival branches of the federal records centers throughout the country. Some of these records have already been accessioned by the regional archives branches of the centers and are available for research now.

This discussion has concentrated primarily on the role of archivists in the records retention plans. Their work is supplemented by actions taken by the agency records officers, who complete a form listing the series of records specified by the archivist. The completed form shows the organizational unit within the agency that maintains the records in question and the titles by which the records are usually known. I am happy to say that the Bureau of Indian Affairs has completed its portion of the retention plans, and all the records that have been selected for permanent retention are specifically listed.

The records of the Bureau of Indian Affairs that are in the custody of the National Archives, both in Washington and in the archival branches in the federal records centers, and those that will be accessioned in the future under the provisions of the retention plans, should provide extensive and comprehensive information on the relationship of the Indian people with the federal and state governments and with the rest of the American people.

II

Indian Assimilation: The Nineteenth Century

INTRODUCTION
Loring B. Priest

My interest in American Indian history began with study under Frederick Merk at Harvard, which resulted finally with the publication in 1942 of *Uncle Sam's Stepchildren,* a study of the background of the Dawes Land-in-Severalty Act of 1887. This publication was well received at the time, but there was no indication that it would be considered a pioneer work in the use of archival resources or be included in the presidential library of 1963. Only the current revival of interest in Indian relations, I believe, accounts for its successful reprint and for my invitation to introduce this session since, following service in World War II, I have been primarily involved in administration at Lycoming College rather than in research. Occasional book reviews, however, have kept me in touch with developments in a field in which I expect to resume research upon retirement. [Dr. Priest retired from Lycoming College in May 1974. *Uncle Sam's Stepchildren* was reprinted in a paperback edition in 1975 by the University of Nebraska Press.]

The presentation by Herman Viola draws on his research and experience in his study of Thomas McKenney and the administration of the Bureau of Indian Affairs between 1824 and 1830, which is the subject of his thesis. Dr. Viola received his master's degree from Marquette University in 1964, under Father Prucha, and his doctorate from Indiana University in 1970.

The second paper is by Henry Fritz, a scholar whose interests in Indian research are closely related to mine. This is evidenced in his book on *The*

Movement for Indian Assimilation, 1860–1890, which was published by the University of Pennsylvania Press in 1963. Since receiving his doctorate from the University of Minnesota, he has combined interest in the effect of frontier expansion on nationalism and in the cattleman's frontier with his concern for postwar Indian policy. A variety of research work in the latter field illumines Dr. Fritz's paper on the Board of Indian Commissioners.

Joining me in presenting commentaries of these papers is Robert Berkhofer, a specialist in the American West and in synthesis and methodology in history. His interest in the subject of this afternoon's session is clearly illustrated by the title of his first book, *Salvation and the Savage: An Analysis of Protestant Missions and American Indian Response, 1787 to 1862.*

From Civilization to Removal: Early American Indian Policy

Herman J. Viola

Any fair appraisal of United States Indian policy in the period before the Civil War must take into consideration the genuine concern for the welfare and improvement of the Indians that existed among federal officials. Prominent among such men was Thomas L. McKenney, who was superintendent of the Office of Indian Trade (in fact the federal official most involved in all aspects of peaceful Indian relations) from 1816 to 1822 and then head of the newly created Bureau of Indian Affairs within the War Department from 1824 to 1830.[1]

It is easy enough to discuss Indian policy—beginning with Secretary of War Calhoun and extending through the administration of Andrew Jackson—as a heartless expulsion of the Indians from their ancestral homes in the East to new wilderness abodes west of the Mississippi. But what does such an interpretation do about such men as Thomas L. McKenney? I suggest that McKenney (with his views about the Indians and his proposals for their education and civilization) was too powerful a force in a crucial period of Indian relations to be ignored, that he supplied an important ingredient in Indian policy, and that his proposals were forerunners of policies that later became dominant. Let us look at the record.

A Quaker by birth and a humanitarian by choice, McKenney exemplified the strong reformist social climate of the early nineteenth century. He advocated the establishment of orphanages, Sunday schools, and Bible societies; he spoke out against the evils of dueling, whiskey, and slavery; he concerned himself with cruelty to animals. But he expended the bulk

Thomas L. McKenney *(National Anthropological Archives, Smithsonian Institution)*

of his humanitarian energies on behalf of American Indians. Once awakened to their need, he championed the cause of Indian reform, turning his office into a clearing house for humanitarian activities designed to help the Native Americans. He corresponded with church groups and philanthropists throughout the country; he encouraged the work of missionaries in their efforts to civilize and Christianize the Indians; and, above all, he tried to arouse a dormant America to the moral obligation it owed a suffering people.

How could their salvation be achieved? McKenney and his fellow humanitarians believed agriculture held the key. "Our object is not to keep these Indians hunters eternally," McKenney asserted. "We want to make citizens out of them," but first they must be "anchored in the soil, else they will be flying about whilst there is any room for them in the wilderness or an animal to be trapped."[2] As superintendent of Indian Trade, McKenney did his utmost to encourage the Indians to adopt agriculture. He urged his factors to set an example of self-sufficiency by cultivating garden plots. He shipped seeds, hoes, and plows to the factories. He required the factors to accept agricultural commodities from the Indians in exchange for trade goods: why not corn, wheat, and cotton, he reasoned, as well as furs? But even McKenney realized these unsystematic efforts were inadequate to affect the thousands of Indians scattered across the American frontier.

A proposal by the Reverend Cyrus Kingsbury of the American Board of Commissioners for Foreign Missions seemed to provide an ideal solution. In the spring of 1816, Kingsbury appealed for federal aid to establish a Cherokee school. The American Board wished to test the feasibility of instructing Indian children in farming, weaving, and carpentry. The War Department authorized the Cherokee agent to build a schoolhouse and quarters for a teacher and to purchase plows, hoes, spinning wheels, and whatever else the board needed for the project. If the experiment failed, all the property would revert to the government.

The new school, called Brainerd, opened in January 1817. Within a year there were fifty acres under cultivation and a mission house, schoolhouse, dining hall, kitchen, gristmill, sawmill, barn, stable, and five log dormitories. Moreover, forty-seven "promising Cherokee children" ranging from age six to eighteen and "from full blooded . . . to those apparently white" were receiving "a christian and civilized education."[3] Kingsbury used the Lancasterian system of instruction at Brainerd, a system using pupils as teachers devised by a Quaker schoolmaster to provide cheap education for England's poor.

McKenney was so taken with the idea, he urged Congress to establish a network of similar schools throughout the Indian country. The schools would cost only $1,000 each to build, he figured—$200 for rude but sturdy log cabins large enough to hold 100 children; lesson cards would cost $8, slates and pencils another $50, and a competent teacher could be hired for $700 or $800 annually.[4] When his letters to congressional leaders failed to arouse support, McKenney offered his services to those religious societies who seemed interested in establishing schools. "If I could aid in the promotion of a design so benevolent as that of reforming our Indians, of promoting amongst them, civilization and christianity, beyond the limits embraced by the [factory system] . . . , it would afford me great pleasure," he wrote to the corresponding secretary of the American Board. "There are no means within my controul, which, to promote such a work, I would not gladly put in immediate requisition."[5]

The value of having in government someone so friendly to their cause was not lost upon the religious groups. The Kentucky Baptist Society immediately made McKenney an honorary member of its board of directors, while the American Board appointed him a member of the two-man "Committee of correspondence and general agency near the seat of the National Government."[6] Suitably impressed by the plaudits, McKenney soon found the means he sought. President Monroe, in his first state of the union message on December 2, 1817, urged Congress to help the Indians on their way to civilized life. In response, the House appointed a select committee on Indian affairs, with Henry Southard of New Jersey as chairman.[7] Encouraged by such action, McKenney revived his proposal for a federally sponsored school system in the Indian country. In January 1818 he sent Southard a copy of his proposed school bill "in its renewed form," letters from two missionaries in the Indian country, and circulars he had received from the Kentucky Baptist Society. "I certainly think Congress has it completely in its power to erect out of the materials for Indian reform a monument more durable and towering than those of ordinary dimensions," he wrote, "a monument as indestructible as justice; interesting as humanity—and lasting as time. Who would not help to build it?" A week later, Southard introduced a bill proposing that profits from the factory system be used to support a network of Indian schools administered by the missionary societies.[8]

Immediately McKenney turned to his missionary friends. Specifically, he wanted the various benevolent associations to send petitions to their representatives in Congress beseeching them "to notice the subject." Despite McKenney's exertions, the bill did not fare well in the First Session of the Fifteenth Congress. An amendment eliminated participation by the missionary societies, and a limit of $10,000 was placed on the funds to be given the schools. Even with these changes the bill was defeated.[9]

McKenney viewed this as only a temporary setback and prepared for a new assault during the Second Session. His strategy consisted primarily of distributing a privately printed circular, which read in part: "I turn to the religious community and beg for help for our distressed and afflicted brothers—the heathen of our country. I turn to those whose motto is 'peace and good will toward men.' " The circular, dated July 1818, asked all Christians to petition their congressmen "to better the condition of our Indians." Suggest no means—a variety of plans would serve only to confuse the issue and "produce perplexity." The petitioners were only to urge adoption of the "grand object, . . . the security, preservation, and improvement of the Indians." The method by which it would be achieved would be "attended to at Washington."[10]

Petitions from all parts of the country flooded Congress. The First Baptist Church and congregation of Philadelphia, the Mississippi Baptist Association, the Blue River Baptist Association of Indiana, and Quakers from New York, New England, New Jersey, Delaware, Maryland, Pennsylvania, Ohio, Indiana, Illinois, and Virginia all asked Congress to help the Indians.[11]

McKenney's stratagem worked. In January 1819 Southard introduced a bill authorizing the president to select the tribes he thought prepared for the change to civilized life and to use whatever means necessary to civilize them. A month later the Senate introduced its own bill, which replaced the House version and became law on March 3. It provided $10,000 annually for the "civilization of the tribes adjoining the frontier settlements" and authorized the president "to employ capable persons of good moral character, to instruct them in the mode of agriculture suited to their situation; and for teaching their children in reading, writing, and arithmetic."[12]

With passage of the civilization bill, McKenney turned his attention to its proper implementation. He believed the small appropriation would do the most good when used in conjunction with existing schools. "And I further think," he wrote to Samuel Worcester, corresponding secretary of the American Board, "that its application should be where *Letters, The Christian Religion, & Agriculture*, are taught." But, he assured the clergyman, "I need not tell you how exactly your Brainerd establishment comes up to my way of thinking." A month later, McKenney again wrote to Worcester: "You may expect a share of the 10.000$—and your undertaking will justify, in my mind, a pretty large slice."[13]

Two printed War Department circulars announced the ground rules for distributing the money. The appropriation would be applied "in co-operation with the exertions of benevolent associations, or individuals, who may choose to devote their time or means to effect the object contemplated by Congress." The schools were expected to teach not only reading, writing, and arithmetic, but also the mechanical and domestic arts. Those groups interested in sharing in the appropriation were to write to the War

Department, listing the locations of their schools, funds available, number of teachers and children, the curriculum, and the amount of money desired. The government agreed to pay two-thirds of the expense of erecting the necessary buildings, but no money was to be given until construction had begun and one-fourth of the grant was to be reserved until the buildings were completed. In addition, the government would contribute annually to each school a sum proportionate to its enrollment. Not only were the administrators of the schools expected to be sober and upright people, one circular warned, but they had "as far as practicable, to impress on the minds of the Indians, the friendly and benevolent views of the government toward them, and the advantage to them in yielding to the policy of the government, and cooperating with it, in such measures as it may deem necessary for their civilization and happiness."[14]

When McKenney became head of the Indian Office in the spring of 1824, he quickly brought the school system under at least a rudimentary administrative control. By May he designed and sent to the school superintendents printed forms for their annual reports. The missionaries were to note "the prospects of the school, the dispositions of the Indians, whether more or less favourable to it, . . . any thing remarkable in the progress of any Indian child . . . the general health of the children, [and] their advances in the work of civilization with such remarks as may be deemed useful as to the climate, soil & productions of the surrounding country."[15]

Early returns indicated that the civilization fund had fulfilled its purpose beyond McKenney's most optimistic expectations. When the bill had been passed, there were only two Indian schools. Now there were thirty-two, all evidently patterned after Brainerd, teaching 916 Indian children. McKenney assured the secretary of war there was "good reason to believe that an entire reformation may be effected . . . in the course of the present generation." All that was needed, he concluded, was added support to the system and "the same zeal and Intelligence which have so far characterized those who superintend, and conduct it."[16]

McKenney believed that the right method of civilizing the Indians had finally been found. He was well aware that since the discovery of America there had been many attempts to civilize and convert the Indians, but the failures, he thought, had been the result of two basic mistakes. The early missionaries had learned the native languages and used them in instruction; the new system required the missionaries to teach the Indians English. The early missionaries began with instruction of the Indians in morality and virtue; the new system would teach the Indians first of all to work for a living.

McKenney considered the use of English the most important improvement. "I have always, myself, esteemed language to be the very centre of the power which is to reform and bless our Indians," he explained, "language I mean, not only of the right sort, itself, but *rightly applied*. It is this which, after all, is to effect the change in the character and destiny of these people. It is the lever by which they are to elevate themselves into intellectual and moral distinction." Although he had been impressed with the genius that George Guess displayed in his invention of the Cherokee alphabet, McKenney viewed the discovery as a mixed blessing, useful perhaps to the older generation of Indians who might not be willing or able to learn English. He prohibited teaching it to children. In fact, he admitted, "I care not how soon they forget altogether their own language —altho' this is not necessary—they may retain both. But I believe the less of it that is taught, or spoken, the better for the Indians. There [sic] whole character, inside and out; language, and morals, must be changed."[17]

McKenney also approved of the change in the subject matter. "Preaching of the Gospel is essential," he explained to Kingsbury, but "*teaching*, in the arts of life, and in the means appointed for man's more certain subsistence, ought not to be neglected." The Indian must first be taught to work. "It is in man's nature to be idle. Labor is painful. Education and habit alone, can reconcile him to it. It is upon this basis the present school system rests," he emphasized. "It is hoped it may never be departed from, for if it shall be, the work of reformation among the Indians is lost."[18]

With such good will and high intentions, with such enthusiasm and optimism, why did not McKenney's civilization program produce the hoped-for reformation of the tribes? Why was it that McKenney himself eventually came to question the validity of the entire program? These, too, are questions we must face. Several considerations appear to have influenced his thinking, not the least of which was a breakdown in personal communication. Antagonism often developed between the missionaries and the less idealistic Indian agents. The Creek agent thought the missionaries were wasting their time with "uninformed savages who neither understood their language nor believed in the truth of their doctrines" and told one "preaching was fudge." And, much to McKenney's chagrin, the missionaries were often in conflict with the Indians as well as the agents. "Some will be found among them, who are inefficient, bigotted, or overzealous," one Choctaw complained.[19]

Indeed, missionary zeal appears to have been a severe problem. The civilization act did not forbid preaching, and the missionaries' proselytizing was a source of friction. While the Indians may have been receptive to education for their children, so that they could deal effectively with the whites, they balked at religious instruction. The Creeks, for example, demanded assurances that no preaching would be done if they allowed a school to be built in their country. Despite the firm stance taken by tribal leaders, Lee Compere, the missionary to the Creeks, began giving religious instructions to those Indians who knew English and conducting worship services at his home. He preached not only to the Indians, but also to their Negro slaves. Compere ignored McKenney's repeated warnings and continued the practice. One Sunday in May 1828, a band of Creek warriors entered his house during services and ransacked the rooms "under the pretence of searching for the Black people." Those they found were taken into the yard where, Compere reported, "they beat them unmercifully." This incident ended Compere's effectiveness among the Creeks and he soon left.[20]

The Passamaquoddy Indians, many of whom were Catholic, were opposed to their schoolteacher's efforts to make Episcopalians of their children. Tribal leaders appealed to McKenney to remove the missionary. McKenney refused, but he allowed the tribe to divide its $300 grant from the civilization fund: $200 for maintenance of the school and $100 for the support of a Catholic priest. "It is no part of the policy of the United States Government to force upon the Indians the belief in, or observance of any of the religious creeds," McKenney assured the Passamaquoddy leaders. "If you prefer the Catholic Religion, there is not the slightest objection against your doing so."[21]

McKenney was further discouraged by the inadequacy of the school system. Seldom did a tribe have more than one school, which meant that only a few children had an opportunity to receive an education. These could exercise little influence on the rest of the tribe and once removed from the academic situation, the children quickly reverted to their former habits. The civilization fund quite successfully lured participants into the field of Indian education, but the $10,000 quickly proved insufficient to fill the demand. McKenney had presumed that once the system proved itself, Congress would enlarge the appropriation. But this it refused to do. As early as 1822, Congress considered repealing the civilization act because it regarded Indian reformation efforts an expensive waste of time. The act survived, but there was no hope of an increased appropriation. McKenney was outraged. "Numerous applications for assistance, and from the most respectable societies are now on file in this office," he complained to the secretary of war in the fall of 1826, "to which it has not been possible to return any other answer than that *the fund appropriated by the Congress is exhausted.*"[22]

While there had been a prospect of substantial federal support for the schools the religious societies had been more than willing to invest their own assets in the system. Through accounting errors, the societies shared $13,000 in 1824 and again in 1825, and they in turn invested about $170,000 during the two years. By the fall of 1825, there were almost 1200 children enrolled in thirty-eight schools. To compensate for the accounting errors, however, McKenney had to cut back the fund by $3,000 for each of the next two years, and expansion of the school system practically ceased. In 1826 the number of students was only thirty-five more than the year before, while the following year the number dipped slightly.[23] Although the full fund was restored in 1828, the school system never really prospered and had a negligible impact on the general Indian population.

Indeed, by the end of the decade, McKenney was ready to admit that the civilization program was a failure. The agonizing assessment had been forced upon him by a request from the Senate Committee on Indian Affairs for a report on the progress that had been made in the previous decade. McKenney turned to his field officials for the information, and reading their replies must have been painful. Gov. Lewis Cass claimed he was not aware that there had been any improvement in the condition of the Chippewa, Ottawa, and Potawatomi Indians. "On the contrary," he wrote, "from the progress of our settlements and the greater facilities afforded for the introduction of whiskey into their Country, I believe every year adds to the moral and physical evils which surround them." Equally depressing was the reply from John Dougherty, the Upper Missouri agent. "[I]t may be truly said," he wrote of the tribes in his area, "they have shown no improvement whatsoever, and as to 'education' there is not a single Indian man, woman, or child, to my knowledge, from the head of the Missouri to the mouth of the Kansas river, that knows one letter from another." Reporting to the Senate Committee, McKenney admitted that, except for those relatively few Indians who had attended school, no progress had been made. In fact, for the most part, the moral and physical condition of the Indians was growing worse each year.[24]

McKenney's disillusionment was caused in part by his experiences with James McDonald, a mixed blood Choctaw boy who had lived with him from 1818 to 1822. The boy was brought to Washington at the age of seventeen by Quakers who asked that he be given some gainful government employment. McKenney put him to work in the Office of Indian Trade and let him live at Weston, his magnificent estate on the heights of Georgetown. Since McKenney had a son of the same age, he raised the two like brothers. "I made no distinction between [them] . . . in dress or attentions," McKenney claimed. McDonald "had a horse at his service, when he chose to ride; took a seat with my family in the coach, rode with us to church, and visited where we did; and was never overlooked, in any of those social relations in which we indulged, whether in or out of Washington." Young McDonald demonstrated such remarkable ability that he was sent to Lebanon, Ohio, at government expense, where he studied law under Judge John McLean, later a Supreme Court Justice. After passing the Ohio bar in 1823, he returned to his home in Mississippi, where he opened a law office and became a justice of the peace. But McDonald never fulfilled his great promise, for despite his educational attainments he was rejected by the white world. Sensitive and introspective, he crumbled emotionally under the burden he carried, escaping through drink the demands made upon him by his humanitarian benefactors. When a white woman rejected his proposal of marriage, he committed suicide.[25]

This tragedy shocked McKenney into the realization that civilizing the Indians involved far more than simply teaching them English and making them into farmers. What was to become of those Indians who progressed enough to become assimilated into white society? Imitating a culture was one thing, being accepted by it was another. Obviously more time was needed—time for Indians to adapt to the complexities of a completely new way of life and time for Americans to bring themselves to accept the idea of a civilized Indian with equal rights and benefits. For this reason— to buy time—McKenney turned to the Indian removal program as the last hope for the Native Americans.

Although McKenney's plans for Indian civilization were not at once successful, we cannot ignore them. They indicate an early commitment of the federal government to the support of missionary and educational work among the tribes, a commitment that repeatedly reappeared in the course of Indian-white relations in the United States.

NOTES

1. Herman J. Viola, *Thomas L. McKenney, Architect of America's Early Indian Policy, 1816-1830* (Chicago: Swallow Press, 1974).
2. Thomas L. McKenney to Mathew Lyon, 18 May 1821, Letters Sent, vol. F, p. 197, Office of Indian Trade (hereafter cited as OIT), Records of the Bureau of Indian Affairs, Record Group 75, National Archives. (Hereafter records of the National Archives Building are cited as RG—, NA.)
3. Cyrus Kingsbury to William Crawford, 2 May 1816, and Crawford to Kingsbury, 14 May 1816, U.S., Congress, *American State Papers: Indian Affairs* (Washington, D.C.: Gales and Seaton, 1834), 2:477-78; Kingsbury to John C. Calhoun, 15 May 1818, enclosed with Return J. Meigs to Calhoun, 10 June 1818, Letters Received, Registered Series, Secretary of War, Records of the Office of the Secretary of War, RG 107, NA.
4. McKenney to Isaac Thomas, 14 and 23 December 1816, Letters Sent, vol. D, pp. 207-8, 214, OIT, RG 75, NA.
5. McKenney to E. Cornelius, 26 July 1817, Letters Sent, p. 373, ibid.
6. McKenney to Samuel Trott, 29 August 1817, Letters Sent, pp. 394-96, ibid.; Samuel Worcester to McKenney, 14 October 1817, Papers of the American Board of Commissioners for Foreign Missions (hereafter cited as ABCFM),

Houghton Library, Harvard University, Cambridge, Mass.; McKenney to Worcester, 30 October 1817, ibid.
7. U.S., Congress, House, *Journal*, 15th Cong., 1st sess., Serial 4, 3 December 1817, pp. 13-14, 20.
8. Ibid., 22 January 1818, p. 169; McKenney to Henry Southard, 15 January 1818, Letters Sent, vol. E, pp. 99-100, OIT, RG 75, NA; Original Bill 50, File HR15A-B1, Bills and Resolutions Originating in the House of Representatives, Records of the United States House of Representatives, 15th through 22d Congresses, RG 233, NA.
9. McKenney to Worcester, 14 February and 4 March 1818, ABCFM; U.S., Congress, House, *Journal*, 15th Cong., 1st sess., Serial 4, 3 April 1818, p. 417.
10. A copy of the circular, dated 4 July 1818, is enclosed with McKenney to Worcester, 29 July 1818, ABCFM.
11. File HR15A-G6.2, Petitions and Memorials Relating to Indian Affairs Received by the House of Representatives, RG 233, NA.
12. U.S., Congress, House, *Journal*, 15th Cong., 2d sess., Serial 16, 18 January 1819, p. 188; ibid., Serial 13, 19 February 1819, p. 288; U.S., *Statutes at Large*, 3:516-17.
13. McKenney to Worcester, 25 March and 3 May 1819, ABCFM.
14. McKenney to Calhoun, 14 August 1819, Letters Sent, vol. E, pp. 298-304, OIT, RG 75, NA; copies of both circulars, 3 September 1819 and 29 February 1820, respectively, are pasted inside the front cover of a volume entitled *Indian Office, Indian Civilization*, vol. A, RG 75, NA.
15. McKenney to Superintendents of Schools in the Indian Country, 22 May 1824, Letters Sent, 1:79-80, Office of Indian Affairs (hereafter cited as OIA), RG 75, NA.
16. McKenney to Calhoun, 24 November 1824, Letters Sent, p. 238, ibid.
17. McKenney to John Pickering, 18 April 1826, Letters Sent, 3:39, ibid.; McKenney to William Chamberlain, 25 July 1825, Letters Sent, 2:103, ibid.; McKenney to Kingsbury, 10 April 1826, Letters Sent, 3:20, ibid.
18. McKenney to Kingsbury, 10 April 1826, Letters Sent, 3:21-22, ibid.
19. John Crowell to Calhoun, 18 March 1824, Letters Received, OIA, Creek Agency, RG 75, NA; James L. McDonald to McKenney, 25 April 1826, Letters Received, OIA, Choctaw Agency, ibid.
20. Lee Compere to McKenney, 20 May 1828, Letters Received, OIA, Creek Agency, ibid.; McKenney to Southard, 4 June 1828, Letters Sent, 4:483, OIA, RG 75, NA; McKenney to Lucius Bolles, 22 July 1828, Letters Sent, 5:49, ibid.
21. McKenney to Leaders of the Passamaquoddy, 12 August 1828, Letters Sent, 5:82-83, ibid.; McKenney to John Eaton, 12 December 1829, Letters Sent, 6:184-85, ibid.
22. Francis Paul Prucha, *American Indian Policy in the Formative Years: The Indian Trade and Intercourse Acts, 1790-1834* (Cambridge, Mass.: Harvard University Press, 1962), p. 222; McKenney to James Barbour, 20 November 1826, Letters Sent, 3:30, OIA, RG 75, NA.
23. Data compiled from annual reports of the OIA, 1825-30: U.S., Congress, Senate, *Documents*, 19th Cong., 1st sess., no. 2, Serial 125, 30 November

1825, pp. 89-90; ibid., 2d sess., no. 1, Serial 144, 20 November 1826, pp. 507-8; ibid., 20th Cong., 1st sess., no. 1, Serial 163, 24 November 1827, pp. 144-45; ibid., 2d sess., no. 1, Serial 181, 1 November 1828, pp. 92-93; ibid., 21st Cong., 1st sess., no. 1, Serial 192, 17 November 1829, pp. 160-61; ibid., 2d sess., no. 1, Serial 203, 26 November 1830, pp. 160-72.
24. McKenney to Superintendents and Agents, 29 January 1830, Letters Sent, 6:247, OIA, RG 75, NA; Lewis Cass to McKenney, 11 February 1830, Letters Received, OIA, Michigan Superintendency, RG 75, NA; John Dougherty to McKenney, 20 January 1830, Letters Received, OIA, Upper Missouri Agency, RG 75, NA.
25. McKenney, *Memoirs, Official and Personal; with Sketches of Travels among the Northern and Southern Indians* (New York: Cady & Bros., 1846), 2:109-19. The quote appears on page 111.

The Board of Indian Commissioners and Ethnocentric Reform, 1878-1893

Henry E. Fritz

The role of the Board of Indian Commissioners as a reform agency seeking the assimilation of Indians has been imperfectly understood. In his book of 1942, Loring Benson Priest contended that by 1880 the board was entirely subordinate to the Interior Department and that it had lost public support by demonstrating "its inability to effect vital improvements," thus leaving the task of arousing reform sentiment to other organizations. The only previous challenge to this viewpoint is found in an unpublished master's thesis by Marshall Dwight Moody written at American University in 1951. Moody's thesis, titled "A History of the Board of Indian Commissioners and Its Relationship to the Administration of Indian Affairs, 1869-1900," pointed out that most of the board's major recommendations were eventually adopted, and that previous writers had stressed failures rather than accomplishments.[1]

In order to establish a basis for evaluating the importance of the board, it is essential that its powers and functions should be clearly discerned. Under the act of 1869, the ten philanthropists, who served without pay, were authorized to exercise joint control with the secretary of the interior in disbursing Indian appropriations, and they were to investigate and make recommendations regarding all issues that concerned Indian affairs. It does not follow that the board became impotent as a reform agency because it did not succeed in making the commissioner of Indian Affairs subordinate in reference to financial management and because Congress reduced the appropriations essential to the functions which the board was originally intended to perform.

During the 1880s, the board did labor with a minimum of financial support and with little appreciation from either Congress or the Interior Department. From 1883 until 1889, the annual appropriation for the board's work was only $3,000, forcing its members to exercise every possible economy. The salary of its secretary was reduced to $2,000 and the budget for rent and office expenses was set at $300, leaving only $700 for travel necessary to the investigation of affairs on the reservations. During these years, Chairman Clinton B. Fisk and Secretary E. Whittlesey pleaded in vain for a restoration of their funds. Fisk pointed out that the annual appropriation during the first years of the board's existence had been $25,000 but was cut down through certain influence "until it is impossible to continue the organization efficiently with the means placed at our control." He argued that the board's Purchasing Committee under the supervision of William H. Lyon, a leading merchant of New York, had likely saved the government an average of at least $100,000 annually in the making of contracts to supply the Indian agencies. In 1884, he pointed out the need to send two of the board members to visit the agencies in New Mexico, Arizona, Idaho, Washington, and Dakota, which he said was impossible because of a lack of means to defray the expense of travel.

These pleas were met with a refusal on the part of the commissioner of Indian Affairs to increase the estimate of appropriations and by considerable harassment concerning the manner in which the board expended its meager budget. The rental of a team of mules costing $40.00 for eight days while on an inspection tour in the Southwest was questioned, and the travel to Washington ($34.95) of a stenographer who donated her services was disallowed. Even hotel and board bills of the commissioners themselves in the amount of a single dollar had to be defended.[2]

It was under the Cleveland administration that the services of the board seemed to be in least demand by the Interior Department. In 1887 the commissioner of Indian Affairs even neglected to notify the board of the opening of bids for Indian supplies. Whether or not this neglect was "due to a mere oversight in the pressure of business," as Secretary Whittlesey surmised, the board felt obliged to pass a resolution that Commissioner J. D. C. Atkins be reminded of the law on this point. The government's attitude toward the board in the same year is further reflected in its objection to the use of an official envelope to cover a general mailing intended to publicize the Dawes Land-in-Severalty Act which had very recently become law. On that occasion, Whittlesey defended the right of the board to mail at government expense whatever in their judgment would "influence public opinion to help carry out the purposes of legislation."[3]

A change toward better relations with the Indian Office occurred in 1888 with the appointment of John H. Oberly, formerly superintendent of Indian schools, as commissioner. Oberly called a conference with the board to get advice on Indian matters and subsequently requested their services under authority of the Act of Congress of May 17, 1882, which among other things authorized the board members to visit and inspect Indian agencies. Oberly asked that one of their number investigate the personal character and business dealings of the traders at the Cheyenne and Arapaho Agency in the Indian Territory and also to inquire into the quality of the physician on the same reservation. That the Indian Office was anxious to have the service of a strong board was made apparent in 1890 when Commissioner Thomas J. Morgan made certain suggestions designed to strengthen its membership. He proposed the nomination of Andrew S. Draper, superintendent of public instruction for the state of New York, to fill the vacancy of the chairman caused by the death of Clinton B. Fisk. He also expressed the opinion that Francis Wayland, dean of the Yale Law School, and John D. Long, former governor and congressman from Massachusetts, might bring to the board "additional weight of character and influence."[4] These suggestions should be considered in relation to the fact that reform in the areas of education and law for Indians had been dealt with inadequately during the 1880s. Therefore, Morgan hoped for a reorganization of the board as a reform agency at the next Mohonk conference.

The key to an understanding of the primary role and importance of the Board of Indian Commissioners during the fifteen years from 1878 to 1893 is the abandonment of the appointment of Indian agents by religious denominations and a gradual return to political patronage during the administrations of Hayes, Garfield, and Arthur. Because the board had been responsible for the "peace policy" of the Grant administration, its members protested the departure from it and worked closely with the Protestant missionary societies in an attempt to prevent both political and military appointments to the Indian service.[5]

As long as the peace policy prevailed, the annual January meetings of the board at Washington with representatives of the missionary societies were primarily concerned with coordinating the efforts of the Protestant churches on the reservations to prepare Indians for assimilation. Then, between 1878 and 1882, the Interior Department gradually withdrew the prerogative of appointing agents from the missionary associations. As a matter of principle Secretary Carl Schurz was opposed to an official relationship between the government and the churches, but he was further motivated by reports that some of the denominational agents were unfit to hold the office. Thus in 1878 Commissioner Hayt decided to replace several of them with military officers until the mission boards concerned could name stronger candidates. At the same time, the practice was begun of having the Indian Office investigate and approve church nominees before their names were submitted to the president and to the Senate for confirmation. Shortly thereafter, the missionary associations were being asked to sanction the appointment of persons recommended by the chief executive of whom they had no knowledge whatsoever.[6]

It was under these circumstances that tensions developed vis-à-vis the Protestant mission boards and the Board of Indian Commissioners on the one side and the Interior Department and Congress on the other. Early in 1881, the Board of Foreign Missions of the Reformed Church resolved to inform the Indian Bureau that it would no longer cooperate with the government in the nomination of agents, and a break in relations on the part of other Protestant societies also became imminent.[7] In April James M. Reid of the Methodist Board of Missions requested that Secretary of the Interior Kirkwood define the relations of his society to the government and made the following comment:

> Until the late administration of the Department of the Interior, all proceeded satisfactorily. If an agent was unsatisfactory to the government or to us we nominated another. . . . For the last two years we have had the responsibility of these agencies but have, in *fact,* had no nomination. There are on file letters . . . in which our own Agents tell us plainly that they do not owe their places or any duties to us. It is clearly unwise for us to occupy this relation. We beg you to consider whether in the appointment of Indian Agencies [sic], the invitation must not continue to be with the religious societies, if the "peace policy" is to continue. . . . Allow us most respectfully to present our objections to the methods of the two years just passed. Vacancies have been created, and again filled without any information being given us. Nominations have been pressed upon us in various ways and forms from political sources, backed indirectly by the department, so situating us as almost to compel us to a given nomination. When nominations have been sent in, they have been detained in the department for months, and the candidate subjected to pressure from traders and others striving to make conditions of confirmation with him. An agent nominated for one post has been sent, without our knowledge, to another, to which there were grave objections to his being appointed. Agents of high character have been summarily dismissed, without our knowledge . . . on uninvestigated charges, from which they were at length vindicated after delays and costs more than equal to all remuneration received as

agent. . . . Our sole object in all this difficult work, is to fill as well as possible these important agencies, and we believe this can only be done by an adherence to the "peace policy" as understood and worked in the beginning. . . . But the responsibilities and dignity of this society will not admit of their making any nomination that may be dictated to them.[8]

In their report for 1882, the Board of Indian Commissioners acknowledged that the Indian agencies were no longer assigned to the several religious denominations.[9] The peace policy was ended.

Secretary Carl Schurz did not set out to antagonize the Protestant mission societies or the Board of Indian Commissioners when he initiated the departure from the peace policy in 1878, and certainly he did not favor a return to political appointments. Schurz was sincere in his advocacy of a merit system, but, as Commissioner Hayt explained, "he immediately found himself embarrassed by the pressure for political appointment, and in consequence of that he went back (temporarily) to the plan pursued under Gen. Grant's administration."[10] By the end of his term of office, the merit system was defeated by party politics, and Schurz found it difficult to maintain good relations with the board and the missionary associations. In January 1880 he received their joint delegation and "explained at length the perplexities and embarrassments under which he labored at the same time expressing his sense of obligation to the Religious societies for their aid in his administration." He also employed a committee of the board to investigate charges leading to the dismissal of Commissioner Hayt and, in recognition of this service, requested the appointment of a similar committee to make "further inquiries . . . into the conduct of Indian Affairs and the business methods and management of the Indian Bureau. . . ." The board reciprocated by appointing the committee, and it also acknowledged imperfections in the peace policy owing to "mistakes made by the societies in nominating suitable men for agents. . . ."[11] As late as January 1883, relations with the Interior Department appear to have been reasonably cordial for, during an interview that again included the mission society delegates, Secretary Henry M. Teller and Commissioner Hiram Price acknowledged that the services rendered by the board were valuable, and they "expressed the hope that the churches . . . would continue their mission and educational work for the Indians."[12]

During this same period, a growing concern among humanitarians over the fate of the Native Americans caused the members of the board and the delegates of the Protestant associations, who convened regularly with them, to become lobbyists for reform measures conducive to Indian assimilation. Since 1869, the board had recommended in each of its annual reports a policy of individual allotments of land in severalty within the reservations, and by 1876 the Interior Department was persuaded that this should be done. The remaining problem was to draft suitable legislation and to bring pressure to bear in Congress toward its enactment.[13]

The lobbying movement in Congress for a general land-in-severalty law was initiated with an attempt in 1878 to procure Indian homestead titles to land allotted within reservations under the provisions of treaties dating from 1854. For the most part these treaties involved small tribes in Oregon and Washington Territory, but the allotment and patenting provisions were modeled after the sixth article of the treaty with the Omahas of Nebraska.[14]

When the delegates of the religious societies met with the board at Washington in January 1878, they prepared a statement expressing deep interest in three proposed means of assimilation. These were the extension of law over all Indians, "legal provision for the common school education of Indian children," and the adoption of "regulations to secure to Indians the possession of land in fee and in severalty, in all practicable cases, by titles properly guarded." They asserted that these three reform measures were "essential to the civilization of the Indians," and they called "for the action of Congress without longer delay." Further, they expressed "grave doubts as to the wisdom of removing Indian tribes to the Indian Territory or to larger Reservations, in cases in which the Indians are in good measure prepared to abandon their tribal relationship, and to enter on civilized life." In the opinion of these Protestant reformers, such Indians should at least have the option of remaining where they were and of becoming citizens.[15]

On the following day, the board and the missionary delegates conferred with President Hayes who "expressed full sympathy with all the measures recommended," and suggested that a proper bill should be prepared covering the points given. Instead of attempting to provide for all three proposed assimilation measures in a single bill, the board determined to focus primarily on land in severalty and to establish a policy of patents in fee simple by emphasizing the obligations of the government in its unfulfilled allotment treaties. Thus they requested the solicitor of the Interior Department to draft a bill "to give civilized Indians rights of homesteads upon their reservations," and they formed a legislative committee to lobby for it in the Senate and House committees on Indian affairs. Several interviews with these committees were held during 1878 and the secretary of the interior was consulted regarding amendments.[16]

After lengthy deliberations, the board's bill was withdrawn with the explanation that it would expose Indians within the reservations to all of the dangers of taking a homestead including the trial before registration and would require them to pay a fourteen-dollar fee. Feeling an obligation

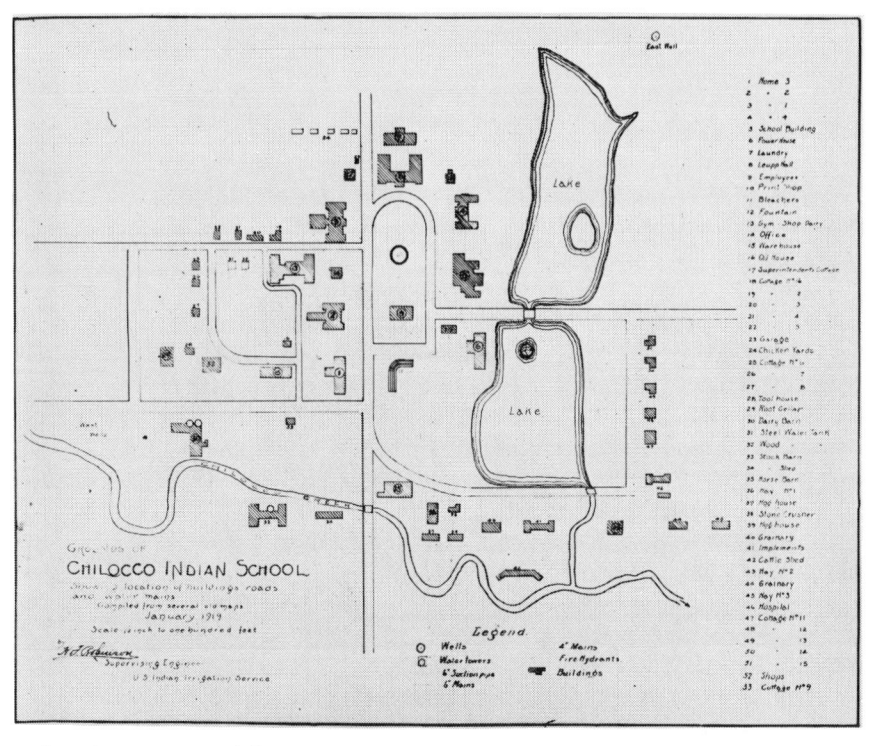

Education was one of the primary means of assimilation. Above is a diagram of the grounds of the Chilocco Indian Industrial School, Oklahoma, showing the location of the school buildings in 1919. The school opened on January 15, 1884, in what was then Indian Territory, with a student body of approximately one hundred seventy pupils drawn from the Kiowa, Comanche, and Wichita and the Cheyenne and Arapaho agencies. Over ninety years later it is still in existence although the school's superintendent in his annual report for 1885 expressed doubts about its prospects due to its "unfavorable" location: the school "is almost entirely isolated from all society, thus depriving the pupils of the benefits of direct contact with civilized life, which has been found to be so beneficial in the schools situated in the States." Moreover, its proximity to "one of the principal thoroughfares leading from the Indian agencies to the State of Kansas" prompted disruptive visits by hundreds of Indians. (RG 75, Central Map File, 9687)

Assimilation personified. Agent John B. Monteith with Archie B. Lawyer, Mark Williams, and James Reuben, three fullblood Nez Percé Indians appointed in 1878 by the Office of Indian Affairs as teachers for Chief Joseph's Band of Nez Percé in Indian Territory. Earlier, Reuben, a teacher at the Nez Percé Agency in Idaho for $20 per month, was detailed to Fort Vancouver, Oregon, where he served as an interpreter for $65 per month. Upon his return to the agency he went on strike for higher wages. For teaching in Indian Territory, Reuben and each of his colleagues received annual salaries of $700. (RG 75, No. 75-IP-1-44)

to provide an alternative, Commissioner Hayt drafted a new bill at the beginning of 1879 and went before the annual meeting of the board with representatives of the mission societies to discuss it. Nine days later he presented this proposed legislation to Secretary Schurz who in turn transmitted it to the Indian committees of Congress. This bill provided a basic model for the Allison and Scales bills of 1879 and for the Coke and Dawes bills at later stages in the legislative process. These bills were named after the chairmen of the Indian committees who took the responsibility for introducing them.[17]

The urgency of Indian assimilation was directly related to the political pressures brought to bear in Washington as the white population of the West clamored for the opening of reservation lands and, in some cases, for the removal of Indians to other locations. Missionaries got the idea that the rights of the Indians to their lands could best be secured by putting them on the same legal footing as their white neighbors. Furthermore, the concept of individual allotments of land in severalty with patents in fee simple was in perfect conformity with the purposes for which missionaries labored on the reservations during the years of the peace policy, namely, the conversion of Indians to the Protestant ethic. Because the Board of Indian Commissioners occupied a strategic position at the seat of government, the missionaries and their respective associations turned it into a lobbying agency.

Already in 1877 Alfred L. Riggs, missionary of the American Board of Commissioners for Foreign Missions to the Santee Sioux, was working with Board Secretary E. Whittlesey on a homestead bill for that tribe. It included a provision against alienation of any nonhomesteaded tribal land for ten years and required the consent of a majority of adult members, with supervision of the secretary of the interior, to dispose of tribal land after a decade had passed. The bill also proposed that when "any such Indian shall have perfected his homestead title, and can read and write his own or the English language, he may become a citizen of the United States on taking an oath to support the Constitution of the United States." Riggs was moved to take this action because of the demand by the Nebraska legislature that the Santees be removed to another location.

Isaiah Lightner, the Quaker agent for the Santees, shared Riggs's concern and was responsible for preparing the tribe's petition of 1877, asking that certificates of individual allotments, given under the provisions of the treaty of 1868, be reinforced with homestead titles.[18] Agent Lightner also circulated petitions among the white population near the reservation and from the response became convinced that "by far the larger portion of the citizens of Knox county were quite willing for the Santees to have a home there." As evidence of this, he submitted the petition of 1878 with a large number of signatures to the Board of Indian Commissioners in care of

Rush Roberts. Eight months later N. G. Clark, the secretary of the ABCFM, forwarded a draft of Riggs's bill to Henry L. Dawes and, simultaneously, asked Board Secretary Whittlesey to aid the senator "in any efforts that may be made in the right direction."[19] In February 1880, some time after Dawes had introduced the Riggs bill, agent Lightner also appealed to the secretary of the board to undertake the responsibility for lobbying it through. He did so in these words:

> Rev. A. L. Riggs and I consulted about this subject this morning. He will write to Senator Saunders to prepare his mind for any thing thee may offer in presenting these papers (more petitions) to him. . . . My views are that one of the Bills which are now before Congress should be pushed . . . and keep driving on until the object is accomplished. . . . I now ask thee as a friend of the Indian work to aid in bringing Senate Bill 333 or any other one that covers the ground to the end for which it was intended. We have some enemies here who are doing all they can to remove the Santees and I want all friends to work for us at this time.[20]

S. R. Riggs among the Sissetons in Dakota Territory was experiencing similar difficulties with the surrounding white population and was responsible for a broadening of the provisions of the original Santee bill to include the Sissetons and the Peorias who were located near Fort Sully.[21]

Confidence in the Board of Indian Commissioners, as an agency that might successfully promote legislation meant to assimilate Indians, continued to grow. In 1881 a committee on the Indian question appointed by the National Congregational Council addressed resolutions to Secretary of the Interior Samuel Kirkwood. After endorsing the idea of homesteads on reservations, providing that they could not be alienated in any way for twenty-five years, they expressed a desire "to act in cooperation with the Board of Indian Commissioners, . . . the Department of the Interior, and [the] Committees of Congress" to secure land in severalty and the same legal protection for Indians as that enjoyed by other citizens.[22]

During the meeting with the board at Washington in January 1882, the delegates of the Protestant denominations endorsed a resolution presented by the Presbyterian Indian Committee which stated "that all of the friends of the Indian are under great obligations to the Board of Indian Commissioners, that their integrity and painstaking fidelity in the discharge of delicate duties have demonstrated the value of this Board, and that we earnestly recommend that it be continued and cordially supported by the Government." This document makes clear that the question of the board's survival reached a breaking point in conjunction with the ending of the peace policy.[23]

That the board was linked to the policy of denominational selection of Indian agents in a period when the Indian service was being returned to the system of political patronage probably goes far to explain the diminishing appropriations in support of its work. Given these circumstances, Congress would hardly have welcomed an independent board amply funded to keep the agencies under scrutiny. Yet the board itself survived and became both a lobby and a forum, supported and attended by representatives of all of the important Indian reform associations that emerged in the early 1880s.

The board adopted the practice of using the annual gatherings of Protestant delegates as an occasion to visit the White House, the Interior Department, and the Indian committees of Congress in support of legislation for assimilation by means of individual land allotment, education, and the protection of law. In 1883 Albert Smiley, a member of the board, invited the Protestant delegates and others interested in the Indian question to a three-day conference at Lake Mohonk in New York. From this time forward, there were at least two general meetings of Indian rights advocates per year.

By that time it had become clear that a united effort of the Indian rights associations would be necessary if the Coke bill, or something similar to it, was ever to become law. Despite the bombardment of the Indian committees of Congress with petition forms circulated by the Women's National Indian Association and others, the measure failed in the House of Representatives, though it did pass the Senate in 1882 and 1883.[24]

The meeting of the board in Washington with the secretaries of the missionary societies in January 1884 was an unusual affair. On that occasion ex-Justice of the United States Supreme Court William Strong, who greatly influenced the Mohonk conferences, led the joint delegation to see President Arthur and Secretary of the Interior Teller. In the evening a public meeting was held at the Congregational Church, with Senator Dawes as the presiding officer and main speaker. Other speeches were given by Commissioner of Indian Affairs Hiram Price, Rep. Byron Cutcheon of Michigan, and Capt. Richard Pratt of the Carlisle Indian School. Entertainment was provided by the Carlisle band.[25]

During the regular meeting at the Riggs's house, which included representatives of the Boston and Washington Indian rights associations, a resolution was adopted approving the "chief features of the general 'Land in severalty Bill' framed by the Senate last Session [and] especially as amended & introduced by Mr. Throckmorton in the House this Session." They urged that "some such bill for allotting lands in severalty and extending the laws of the states & Territories over the Indians" be adopted with all feasible safeguards in reference to the Indians' interest "in surplus lands when opened up for settlement by whites." Among other important resolutions was one providing that a committee of the conference be appointed to draft a bill for the creation of a Division of Education within the Indian Bureau. They proposed that such a division be headed by an eminent educator for the purpose of developing a school system for all Indians except the Five Civilized Tribes. This latter resolution forecast the main emphasis of the board after the Dawes bill became law.[26]

When the second Mohonk conference convened the following September, the program committee included the officers of the Indian Rights Association of Philadelphia together with General Whittlesey and Samuel C. Armstrong of Hampton Institute. Clinton Fisk and Herbert Welsh were chosen chairman and secretary, respectively. This conference directed Chairman Fisk to appoint a committee of twenty-five to lobby in the House for Senate bills 48 and 1755 (the Sioux Bill) during the next session of Congress.[27] That Fisk served in a double capacity as chairman of both the board and the Mohonk conference illustrates the nature of relations with the new Indian reform groups. The confidence of the national organizations in the board as an agency to coordinate lobbying activity was again made apparent in 1885 when the Women's National Indian Association, with representatives of eight Protestant churches on its executive board, asked Chairman Fisk to sign and present their anniversary resolutions to President Cleveland and to both houses of Congress. These resolutions called for education, lands in severalty, citizenship, and the fulfillment of "all existing treaty stipulations."[28]

In appointing the Committee of Twenty-five following the Mohonk conference of 1884, Fisk had successfully courted the Women's National Indian Association into a working relationship with the board, thus completing the coalition of reform groups that advocated Indian assimilation. Among the members chosen was Amelia S. Quinton, secretary of the WNIA, who participated in the January, September, and November meetings of the board in 1885. That Fisk knew how to create an effective lobbyist coalition is evident as well from other persons named to the committee. Besides members of the board and of the Indian Rights Association, these included Sara T. Kinney, president of the Connecticut Indian Association and wife of the editor of the Hartford *Courant;* Lyman Abbott, editor of the *Christian Union;* Erastus Brooks, a distinguished journalist and philanthropist retired from the New York *Express;* and Alice C. Fletcher, who could speak about individual land allotment from first-hand experience among the Omahas and simultaneously bring the prestige of an ethnologist to the support of the committee's recommendations.[29]

The appointment of Alice Fletcher to the Committee of Twenty-five is especially significant in reference to the fact that, during 1885, the board returned to the strategy of using unfulfilled treaties to press for a general land-in-severalty law with patents in fee simple. In 1881 Fletcher, who adopted the methods of Alfred Riggs concerning the Santees, had prepared a petition which, despite the initial opposition of Senator Dawes, resulted in the Omaha Land-in-Severalty Act of 1882.[30] Thus in 1885 the Omahas were used by the Committee of Twenty-five to illustrate the potential of individual land ownership among other tribes. Fletcher prepared a table of "unfulfilled treaty obligations for the allotment of lands in severalty" which was presented to President Cleveland when the committee met with him in November.[31]

The pressure upon the administration in reference to treaty obligations became evident in January 1886 when the secretary of the interior ordered the issuance of patents to the Puyallups of Washington Territory near Tacoma. Their treaty of 1854 gave the president authority to survey and assign allotments "to individuals and families on the same terms as . . . provided in the sixth article of the treaty with the Omahas." Since 1879 the Interior Department had put off the implementation of this provision in hope that a general land-in-severalty law would give such Indians protection against future alienation of their lands. The sixth article of the Omaha Treaty allowed state legislatures to remove the restrictions against both leasing and forfeiture. In the opinion of the board, however, it was better for the Puyallups to have their allotments secured with land certificates, which were temporarily protected against alienation by treaty provisions, than to risk losing them to the Northern Pacific Railroad.[32]

Since 1878 the Department of the Interior had tried to find a compromise between the interests of white people who wanted Indian lands and the interests of the Indians who wanted a secure title to their remaining patrimony. Therefore, the Indian Office responded to the demands of these opposing forces by drafting two kinds of proposed legislation. The first kind consisted of bills to consolidate tribes by removing the smaller tribes to larger reservations and bills to reduce the acreage of the largest reserves outside of the Indian Territory.[33] The other kind of legislation provided for the division of reservations in severalty, with patents protected against alienation, and for the sale of surplus lands with tribal consent. In 1882 Commissioner Hiram Price drafted a composite measure titled, "A Bill to Provide for the Improvement of the Condition of Uncivilized Indians, the Reduction of Their Reservation to Proper Limits, the Making of the Same Permanent, and the Allotment Thereof . . . in Severalty." Known as the Kirkwood Bill, this measure would have created a "commission on Indian civilization" to determine the proper size of reservations, according to the pursuits to which the land was adaptable, and to define the reservation boundaries. A patent in fee simple was to be vested in the tribe with the provision that land held in common could not be conveyed to any other party except the United States and with further provision that tribal members could take individual allotments with patents inalienable for twenty-five years.[34]

By this time, Dawes had become chairman of the Senate Indian Committee, and he turned to the Board of Indian Commissioners for advice. Secretary Whittlesey responded that he much preferred the Coke bill but would amend it with features of H.R. 3180, "notably Sec. 6 which provides for Indian Citizenship." As far as a "commission on Indian civilization" was concerned, Whittlesey suggested that the board was prepared to assume that responsibility and could save the government the expense of appointing special agents to supervise allotments, as provided in the Scales and Coke bills of 1879 and 1881.[35]

By 1885 debate centered mainly on four questions: first, whether the application of the terms of a general allotment law to a particular reservation should require tribal consent; second, whether patents in fee should be issued to tribes in common; third, whether the sale of surplus land should be mandatory; and the fourth involved the requirements for making Indians citizens of the United States.

The Coke bill, as passed by the Senate in 1884, was a liberal measure in that it recognized tribal autonomy and the Indian tradition of holding land in common. It also provided for several options: A two-thirds majority vote of adult males was required before an entire reservation could be allotted in severalty, but lack of tribal consent could not prevent individual members from selecting allotments with patents inalienable for twenty-five years. The president was authorized to have patents issued to tribes in common, with the provision that individual patents would take precedence over those given to tribes. Tribal patents were intended to make reservations secure against white encroachment for at least a quarter of a century, and toward that end they were to be recorded in both the General Land Office and the Bureau of Indian Affairs with the same inalienability provision that applied to individual patents. Where land was mainly valuable for grazing, it could be assigned to a number of Indians who desired to hold it in common. After the process of allotting lands on a given reservation was completed, the secretary of the Interior Department was permitted to negotiate with the tribe for any portion of the remainder and the money could either be paid to the tribe or invested for its benefit. Neither the Coke bill of 1884 nor any general allotment bill preceding it contained a clause regarding Indian citizenship.[36]

Reaction to this proposed legislation at the Mohonk conference was divided. It was warmly endorsed by the officers of the Indian Rights Association and by several members of the board as a step in the right direction. But it encountered the strong opposition of Alice C. Fletcher,

Board of Indian Commissioners and Ethnocentric Reform 71

Capt. Richard H. Pratt, Lyman Abbott, and the Reverend H. Kendall, secretary of the Presbyterian Board of Home Missions.

Fletcher spoke the sentiments of this group when she said that under no circumstances should land be patented to a tribe and observed that it would be impossible "to get two-thirds of a tribe to vote in favor of allotting lands in severalty." Her main concern was that reinforcement of tribalism would make assimilation more difficult, if not impossible. Consequently, the Mohonk conference passed a resolution "strongly opposing any recognition by the Government of the tribal relation."[37]

The board had always favored the ending of the reservation system by means of lands in severalty, and wanted it done speedily. In 1885 Chairman Fisk warmly endorsed the view that the reservations of the Northwest should be allotted in severalty and the remaining lands thrown open to settlement "within a few years."[38] By this time, the board had been converted to the proposition of compulsory assimilation and brushed aside the argument that the tribal relation and the holding of land in common were the natural condition of Indians. Their ethnocentric attitude was fully evident in the reply: "So are superstition and sin."

The board was prompted to take this position in response to Secretary of Interior Lamar who, during an interview in November with the Committee of Twenty-five, stated emphatically that patents should be issued to entire tribes and the tribal arrangement upheld during a gradual transition from a primitive to a civilized state among the Indians. In his view it was premature to think of a quick end to the reservation system and of tribalism because that was "the normal condition of the existence of this race." Lamar wanted to reduce the size of reservations in proportion to the needs of their inhabitants and then rigidly enforce the exclusion of whites at the borders. After title had been vested in the tribe and the reservation subdivided in the form of individual allotments, it was the secretary's opinion that, "there ought to be a very considerable portion of the reservation still left undivided and undistributed." No reservation lands should be surrendered without the consent of the tribe. In nearly every respect it would seem that Lamar's views were in conformity with the provisions of the revised Coke bill of 1884.[39]

The board exerted every possible influence to combat Lamar's opinion. Later in November, Secretary Whittlesey sent letters to all Indian agents asking for a report on the number of allotments and patents already given on their respective reservations, as well as the number of Indians desirous of and prepared to receive them. The replies indicated that while many had received allotments, few patents had been issued and that many Indians wanted both allotments and patents, if only as a means of securing their lands against white encroachment. Whittlesey selected some of the more favorable responses for publication in his annual report (February 15, 1886) in support of a statement that, *"not less than 75,000 are asking for individual allotments and patents, and nearly all of these are, in the opinion of their agents, far enough advanced to receive and care for separate homesteads."*[40]

In the meantime, Senator Dawes had undertaken to make changes in the Coke bill to conform with the resolutions of the Mohonk conferences and with the persuasive arguments of the Committee of Twenty-five, headed by Board Chairman Fisk. Both were greatly influenced by Alice C. Fletcher, the ethnologist, whose experience in allotting land among the Omahas gave her views much respect. Dawes told the Mohonk conference in 1885 that the recent changes made by the Senate Indian Committee were meant "to put the Indian in severalty on a farm, . . . to sell all the rest of his reservation, . . . [and] to give him all the rights and privileges of any white man in the courts." In this same speech Dawes proposed to perfect the Coke bill by adding to it a provision that, "all those who take these allotments are hereby declared to be citizens of the United States."[41]

Both Dawes and the advocates of Indian rights had become interested in the question of Indian citizenship in November 1884, after the Supreme Court decision in the case of *Elk* v. *Wilkins*. Dawes first introduced a separate bill for the purpose of making citizens of all Indians who lived apart from their respective tribes and who adopted the habits of civilized life. This bill was particularly intended to encourage graduates of the industrial schools to assimilate with the white community, but it applied to any Indian who might choose to renounce his tribal relationship.[42] In their report for 1884, the board went further and proposed that every Indian within the territorial limits of the United States should be declared a citizen by congressional act—a recommendation that went side by side with demands for assimilation through education, law, and land in severalty. It was under these circumstances that Dawes was moved to incorporate a citizenship clause in the general allotment bill.[43]

During 1886 the board continued its drive for compulsory Indian assimilation. That the Indian was to be given no choice in the matter was made clear in a widely circulated pamphlet prepared by Merrill E. Gates, a board member and the president of Rutgers. Titled "Land and Law as Agents in Educating Indians," it laid down the thesis that the best way to kill an Indian was to make him a white man. The greatest obstacle, said Gates, was the tribe. Therefore, "we must as rapidly as possible break up the tribal organization and give them law, with the family and land in severalty as its central idea. We must not only give them law, we must force law upon them. We must not only offer them education, we must force education upon them."[44] These words capture the spirit in which the board carried on its effort to assimilate Indians from 1885 forward, and the results are seen in both the Dawes Act and in the compulsory Indian education acts of 1892 and 1893.

The efforts of the board to insure that Indians were educated in preparation for citizenship requires separate treatment. However, the evidence presented here would seem to support several conclusions. First, the board's inability to function independently of the Interior Department in reference to the inspection of agencies and the disbursement of Indian appropriations does not mean that it had ceased to be important. Second, the refusal of the Cleveland administration to request an increase of funds in support of the board's activities may be partially explained by differences with the Interior Department over proposed policies regarding Indian assimilation. Third, the argument that the board was rendered impotent as a reform agency by lack of funding is unsound and misses the main point. The board was not funded to arouse public sentiment in behalf of reform legislation. That task belonged to the Indian rights organizations who in turn relied upon the board to coordinate their lobbying efforts. Fourth, the board's claim to credit for the passage of the Dawes Land-in-Severalty Act was more than a vain exaggeration.[45] And, finally, the features of the Dawes Act that made possible a rapid dispersal of reservation lands owed at least as much to the ethnocentric motivation of the board and its Protestant constituency as to the influence of western landgrabbers.

NOTES

1. Loring B. Priest, *Uncle Sam's Stepchildren: The Reformation of United States Indian Policy, 1865–1887* (New Brunswick: Rutgers University Press, 1942), chap. 4.
2. Fisk to Congressman E. John Ellis, member of the House Appropriations Committee, 2 February 1884; Fisk at Seabright, N.J., to W. F. Vilas, secretary of the interior, 23 January 1889; E. Whittlesey to J. D. C. Atkins, commissioner of Indian Affairs, 21 April and 22 September 1885 and 6 February 1886; Whittlesey to Second Auditor, 9 March 1888, Board of Indian Commissioners (hereafter BIC) Letterbook, Records of the Bureau of Indian Afffairs, Record Group 75, National Archives Building. (Hereafter records in the National Archives are cited as RG—, NA.) Minutes of BIC, New York, 27 May 1884, RG 75, NA. It seems likely that Chairman Fisk's estimate of the savings in making contracts for Indian supplies through the services of the board was too high. The acting commissioner of Indian Affairs said in 1880 that the government had saved $50,000 in each of the two previous years by maintaining the Indian Department Warehouse in New York City. See copy of E. J. Brooks to Sen. William B. Allison, 2 March 1880, File HR46A-F16.4 (Various

Subjects), 46th Cong., House Committee on Indian Affairs, Records of the United States House of Representatives, RG 233, NA. The board held its annual spring meeting in New York for the purpose of assisting the Indian Office in making contracts.
3. Whittlesey to Commissioner of Indian Affairs, 8 January 1887, and Whittlesey to unknown addressee, 6 April 1887, BIC Letterbook, RG 75, NA. Internal evidence indicates that the second letter went to an official in the federal government.
4. Whittlesey to W. H. Waldby, 25 October 1888, BIC Letterbook, RG 75, NA; Oberly to Whittlesey, 9 February 1889, BIC, Letters Received, RG 75, NA; Secretary of the Interior Vilas to Commissioner Oberly, 15 December 1888, Office of Indian Affairs (hereafter indicated by OIA), Letters Received, 30811–1888, RG 75, NA; Morgan to Secretary of the Interior, 19 August 1890, OIA Letterbook, RG 75, NA.
5. BIC Minutes, 9 January 1880, Minutebook, RG 75, NA; *Thirteenth Annual Report of the Board of Indian Commissioners, 1881* (Washington, D.C.: Government Printing Office, 1882), p. 6; Henry E. Fritz, *The Movement for Indian Assimilation, 1860–1890* (Philadelphia: University of Pennsylvania Press, 1963), p. 76.
6. Commissioner J. Q. Smith to the Reverend R. C. Rogers, 8 August 1876; Commissioner E. A. Hayt to the Reverend J. M. Reid, 18 March and 31 October 1878; Hayt to the Reverend H. Dyer, New York, 16 May 1878, OIA letterbooks, RG 75, NA. Joseph T. Bender, acting chief clerk of the Indian Office, to L. C. Main, 23 February 1881, Letters Sent by the Chief Clerk and Assistant Commissioner, Letterbook, RG 75, NA.
7. The Reverend John M. Ferris, New York City, to Commissioner R. E. Trowbridge, 5 January 1881, OIA, Letters Received, 259–1881, RG 75, NA.
8. J. M. Reid, correspondence secretary of the Methodist Mission Board in New York, to S. J. Kirkwood, secretary of the interior, 18 March 1881, OIA, Letters Received, 6319–1881, RG 75, NA.
9. U.S., Congress, House, *Fourteenth Annual Report of the Board of Indian Commissioners, 1882*, Executive Document No. 77, 47th Cong., 2d sess., Serial 2110, p. 61.
10. Hayt to the Reverend S. S. Lawson, 3 June 1878, OIA Letterbook, RG 75, NA.
11. BIC Minutes, 9 January and 4 February 1880 (the latter includes a copy of Schurz to BIC, 2 February 1880), Minutebook, RG 75, NA.
12. BIC Minutes, 16 January 1883, Minutebook, RG 75, NA.
13. *Annual Report of the Commissioner of Indian Affairs, 1876* (Washington, D.C.: Government Printing Office, 1876), p. 9; *Annual Report of the Commissioner of Indian Affairs, 1887* (Washington, D.C.: Government Printing Office, 1877), p. 1.
14. *Tenth Annual Report of the Board of Indian Commissioners, 1878* (Washington, D.C.: Government Printing Office, 1879), pp. 7–8; C. Schurz to William Stickney, secretary of the Board of Indian Commissioners, 13 or 18(?) August 1879, BIC, Letters Received, RG 75, NA.
15. "An Address of the Convention of Friends of the Indians, Assembled in

Washington January 10, 1878, in Conference with the Board of Indian Commissioners," File 45A-E8 (Miscellaneous), Committee on Indian Affairs, Senate Records, 45th Cong., RG 46, NA.

16. BIC Minutes, 11 January, 11–12 April, 18–19 June, and 13–14 November 1878, Minutebook, RG 75, NA; A. C. Barstow, chairman of BIC, to W. B. Allison, chairman of Senate Indian Committee, 2 March 1878, Committee on Indian Affairs, Senate Records, 45th Cong., RG 46, NA; *Tenth Annual Report*, BIC, p. 8.

17. Hayt to Secretary of Interior, 24 June 1879, enclosed "draft of a bill authorizing the Department to allot lands in severalty on all Indian reservations, and to issue patents there for the restrictions as to the power of alienation . . . ," Records of the Office of the Secretary of the Interior, Indian Division, Letters Received, RG 48, NA. In sending one of the copies to Sen. William B. Allison, Schurz said, "The views of the Indian Office, and the proposed legislation presented, have the full approval of this Department; and the subject of the bill is earnestly recommended to the early and favorable action of Congress." Schurz to Allison, 27 January 1879, File 45A-E8 (Miscellaneous), Committee on Indian Affairs, Senate Records, 45th Cong., RG 46, NA; *Tenth Annual Report*, BIC, app., pp. 129–30, 132.

18. Lightner, Santee Agency, to Hayt, commissioner of Indian Affairs, 20 April 1878, with endorsements by Episcopal Bishop William A. Hare and Alfred L. Riggs (copy), BIC, Letters Received, RG 75, NA.

19. Riggs, Santee Agency, Nebraska, to Gen. E. Whittlesey, secretary of the Board of Indian Commissioners, 4 December 1877, enclosing a draft of "A Bill to allow certain Indians to enter homesteads from lands occupied by them"; Riggs to Whittlesey, 8 June 1878; N. G. Clark, Missionary Rooms, Congressional House, Boston, to Whittlesey, 19 March 1879; Lightner, Santee Agency, to Whittlesey, 7 February 1880, BIC, Letters Received, RG 75, NA. For other evidence that Riggs's bill likely influenced the board to seek the fulfillment of individual allotment provisions in treaties by means of homestead titles, see Solomon Draper, attorney at Niobrara, Nebr., to Riggs, 6 December 1877, BIC, Letters Received, RG 75, NA. Riggs sent Draper's letter to Whittlesey. It included this paragraph: "In regard to suggestions in case another bill is presented to Congress, I think that all that is necessary is that the amendment to the homestead law for the benefit of the Indians, be made to apply to lands held and occupied by them as reservations as it now does to lands outside of reservations." Also convincing is E. Whittlesey to Hon. W. B. Allison, 13 December 1877:

> Since I placed in your hands the bill relating to the Santee Sioux, I have received a letter from Rev. A. L. Riggs . . . in which he advises that the clause "Free from any fee or charge" be omitted. He says, "The Indians would rather pay their entry fees. It assures them that they stand on a common platform with white settlers. Then the land is worth more to them if they do something for it. And again they will have much more favor at the land offices if their entries bring fees." Mr. Riggs is also very anxious to include in the bill the

Sisseton and Peoria (near Fort Sully) Indians. They are as much in need of such legislation as the Santee Sioux; and so are several other tribes; but my judgment is that a specific act applicable to one reservation alone is more likely to succeed.

File 45A-E8 (Miscellaneous), Committee on Indian Affairs, Senate Records, 45th Cong., RG 46, NA. The movement to reinforce land certificates, given individual allottees under the Santee Treaty of 1868, with homestead titles was begun in the spring of 1877.

20. Lightner to Whittlesey, 7 February 1880, BIC, Letters Received, RG 75, NA. Also, see copy of Lightner, Santee Agency, to Hayt, commissioner of Indian Affairs, 20 April 1878, with endorsements by William H. Hare and Alfred L. Riggs, BIC, Letters Received, RG 75, NA.
21. S. R. Riggs, Beloit, Wisc., to Whittlesey, 8 December 1877, BIC, Letters Received, RG 75, NA; and Charles Crissey, Browns Valley, Minn., to Secretary of the Interior, 12 April 1884, enclosing a petition of Minnesota and Dakota citizens wanting Sisseton and Wahpeton reserves opened to settlement, OIA, Letters Received, 7463-1884, Dakota Petitions, RG 75, NA.
22. George H. Atkinson, Moline, Ill., to S. Kirkwood, 23 April 1881, enclosing a "Memorial and Resolutions, OIA, Letters Received, 7023-1881, RG 75, NA.
23. Sheldon Jackson, New York, to Hiram Price, commissioner of Indian Affairs, 31 January 1882, enclosing copy of resolutions and a memorial on Indian rights, OIA, Letters Received, 2260-1882, RG 75, NA; *Thirteenth Annual Report*, BIC, p. 8.
24. Indians (Petitions), Accompanying Papers File, House Records, 47th Cong., RG 233, NA. The endorsement on one of these petitions reads as follows: "Memorial of Rev. Campbell Fair, D.D., and others [sic] ministers citizens of Baltimore City, and of Maryland, representing about 20,000 people in favor of a new policy of the Government in its treatment of the Indians." This document, consisting of ten duplicate petition forms signed by representatives of different Protestant denominations, was referred to committee on 24 February 1883.
25. BIC Minutes, 22 January 1884, Minutebook, RG 75, NA. A copy of Dawes's speech is in the *Fifteenth Annual Report of the Board of Indian Commissioners, 1883*, printed with *Report of the Secretary of the Interior*, U.S., Congress, House, Executive Document No. 1, 48th Cong., 1st sess., Serial 2191, pp. 731–32.
26. William Hayes Ward and Shelton Jackson to Congressman Olin Wellborn, chairman of House Committee on Indian Affairs, 25 January 1884, BIC Letterbook, RG 75, NA.
27. BIC Minutes, Mohonk Lake, N.Y., 24 September 1884, Minutebook, RG 75, NA.
28. Resolutions of WNIA at meeting in Philadelphia, 17 November 1885, signed by Clinton B. Fisk, OIA Resolutions, File L28776, RG 75, NA.
29. BIC Minutes, Mohonk Lake, N.Y., 24 September 1884, and Washington,

D.C., 9 November 1885, RG 75, NA; *Sixteenth Annual Report of the Board of Indian Commissioners, 1884*, printed with *Report of the Secretary of the Interior*, U.S., Congress, House, Executive Document No. 1, 48th Cong., 2d sess., Serial 2287, pp. 726–27; *Seventeenth Annual Report of the Board of Indian Commissioners, 1885*, U.S., Congress, House, Executive Document No. 109, 49th Cong., 1st sess., Serial 2398, p. 110.
30. Sen. John T. Morgan to Alice Fletcher, 2 January 1882, Fletcher Papers, National Anthropological Archives, Smithsonian Institution; U.S., Congress, Senate, *Congressional Record*, 47th Cong., 1st sess., 11 January 1882, 13, pt. 1:342–43.
31. *Seventeenth Annual Report*, BIC, app., pp. 112–13.
32. Whittlesey to Secretary of the Interior, 20 March 1885, BIC Letterbook, RG 75, NA; J. D. C. Atkins to Clinton B. Fisk, 3 February 1886, BIC, Letters Received, RG 75, NA; C. Schurz, secretary of the interior, to William Stickney, secretary of BIC, 13 or 18 August 1879, BIC, Letters Received, RG 75, NA; Hayt, commissioner of Indian Affairs, to William B. Allison, chairman of Senate Indian Committee, 1 March 1878, Indian Division, Letters Sent (Miscellaneous), vol. 18, RG 48, NA.
33. Hayt to Secretary of the Interior, 23 May 1878, enclosed, "Bill Providing for the Consolidation of Certain Indian Tribes, and Sale of Their Lands," transmitted to A. M. Scales, chairman of House Indian Committee, 31 May 1878; William M. Leeds, acting commissioner, to Secretary of the Interior, 13 January 1879, amending bill of 23 May transmitted to A. M. Scales, 16 January 1879, Letters Received, RG 48, NA.
34. U.S., Congress, Senate, *Executive Document No. 54*, 47th Cong., 1st sess., Serial 1987, 5 pp.
35. Whittlesey to Sen. H. L. Dawes, 4 March 1882, BIC Letterbook, RG 75, NA.
36. Revised copy of S. 48, Original Bills, Senate Records, 48th Cong., RG 46, NA.
37. *Sixteenth Annual Report*, BIC, app., pp. 722–23.
38. Arthur I. Chapman (an employee of the War Department) at Walla Walla, Washington Territory, to Gen. Clinton B. Fisk, 27 November 1885, BIC, Letters Received, RG 75, NA. Chapman was responding to an interview which the Committee of Twenty-five had with Secretary of the Interior Lamar on 10 November. He said, "The reservation system should be broken up and is no longer a question among those who are well informed on the subject, and I desire to acquaint you with the fact that the time has arrived when the Indians are in condition to render practicable the putting of your plans into execution." Fisk gave the letter to Secretary Whittlesey with the penciled endorsement, "good straw for your Report! F." *Seventeenth Annual Report*, BIC, p. 9. For other evidence that the board was opposed to letting Indians hold land in common on reservations, see *Tenth Annual Report*, BIC, app., pp. 129–30. Board member Rush Roberts objected to the form of the first general land-in-severalty bill prepared by the Indian office because, "it leaves the settlement of the quantity of land remaining in those reservations to future time to determine. The period prescribed in this bill is indefinite. It may be a

hundred years before the reservations can be finally closed."
39. *Seventeenth Annual Report*, BIC, app., pp. 115–16. Compare S. 19, 47th Cong., with S. 48, 48th Cong., Original Bills, Senate Records, RG 46, NA.
40. Fifty replies to Whittlesey's questions (sent out between 23 and 27 November) dated 1 December to 22 January 1885–86, BIC, Letters Received, RG 75, NA; *Seventeenth Annual Report*, BIC, pp. 9–10.
41. *Sixteenth Annual Report*, BIC, app., pp. 722–23; *Seventeenth Annual Report*, BIC, app., pp. 838–40.
42. Dawes to E. L. Stevens, chief clerk of the Indian Office, 13 December 1884, enclosing S. 2369, OIA, Letters Received, 23907–1884, RG 75, NA.
43. *Sixteenth Annual Report*, BIC, pp. 682–87.
44. Letters Received, 20523–1886, OIA, RG 75, NA. Gates's twenty-three-page pamphlet was incorporated in the *Seventeenth Annual Report*, BIC, pp. 13–35, with a full endorsement.
45. *Twenty-fifth Annual Report of the Board of Indian Commissioners, 1893* (Washington, D.C.: Government Printing Office, 1894).

COMMENTARY

Robert F. Berkhofer, Jr.

Thanks to the perceptiveness of the two authors and their awareness of the larger issues involved in their topics, these papers exhibit several striking parallels in their overall stories. Although the papers deal with two different time periods, a single individual versus many individuals and one government official as opposed to a group of philanthropists, each paper traces a remarkably similar sequence of events in basic plot. In both cases, the people involved first try one kind of reform, consider themselves "sabotaged" by the government, and then advocate another kind of reform that falls nicely in line with the larger political trend in Indian policy at the time. McKenney favored supporting religious and philanthropic societies to educate, Christianize, and civilize the Indians according to his image of what they needed in line with his goal of assimilation. When the program seemed on the verge of doing some good, according to its ostensible goal, Congress refused to appropriate funds for its achievement. After a decade of the program's operations, McKenney became discouraged with the dearth of results and turned to the removal program as the best possible method of protecting the Indians from the blighting effects of white civilization. At the same time, he professed to believe such segregation would aid in the further assimilation of the Indians by concentrating them in the West for benevolent manipulation by philanthropic whites. In a similar sequence, the Board of Indian Commissioners began by coordinating the selection of Indian agents by religious denominations, not only for the more honest administration of the agencies but also for the better assimilation of the natives through education, religion, and other preferred means. Later the Interior Department and Congress hampered these efforts through inadequate financing and the failure to give the commissioners any real power of appointment or of administration. Subsequently, the board lobbied actively for the allotment of Indian lands in severalty and a unified system of compulsory education.

That these parallels existed raises larger questions in the analysis of nineteenth-century philanthropy and reform than the usual discussion of motives attributed to persons and policies advocating Indian assimilation into white American life. Why do persons said to possess quite different motives frequently advocate the same policy? In these two papers, benevolent, religious, and supposedly disinterested individuals supported the same policies—removal and allotment—as did the insensitive politicians and westerners interested in Indian lands. Even when philanthropic policies were applied to Indians, why did they result in much the same effect upon Native Americans' lives as the more crassly motivated programs? Why, in light of all the interest in Indian reform and assimilation, was so little financial support given to the task? Why did reformers and philanthropists pay as little attention to Indians' views of their own needs as any of the government officials, army officers, or average whites of the time? Why did the methods and aims of all of the reformers for Indian assimilation vary so little during the course of the entire century? Lastly, why were more individuals interested in and more support given to Indian reform during the nineteenth century than any previous one, and yet why was so little accomplished in the eyes of those who favored, as well as those who opposed, these reforms?

The similarity of goal and the arrogance of method among all varieties of white Americans must be ascribed, I believe, to their attitude of cultural superiority and the ethnocentrism it engendered in relation to other peoples. All whites, unless they advocated extermination, had no choice, given their fundamental outlook, but to espouse the necessity as well as the desirability of raising the Indian to those standards of progress they presumed the nineteenth-century United States represented. To those men and women dedicated to helping the Indian, as well as to the legislator, farmer, pioneer, and other white Americans, that goal was so important that force was justified in its achievement, if persuasion and example were insufficient to its accomplishment. Cultural imperialism was advocated by all white Americans, even by those who backed down from genocidal extermination or territorial aggrandizement. Reformers and philanthropists were arrogant, after all, not only towards the poor "savage" but also toward their backsliding fellow whites, for their sense of moral stewardship was as keen for their white brethren as for their red charges, as McKenney's enthusiasms listed by Viola show.[1] Such a view, as I have argued before, determined the view of the Indian, explained what needed to be done, and justified the measures necessary to turn the "savage" into the ideal American.[2] Philanthropy and Manifest Destiny, democracy and progress, and frontier expansion and Indian removal all marched westward hand-in-hand to the glory of the Republic and the uplift of the aborigine, who would perish otherwise by one means or another, and perhaps ought to, in the opinion of most whites.[3] Church, school, manual labor training, and other reform methods were all directed to the salvation of the Indian on earth as well as in the afterlife. Given this view of the general cultural premises among whites of the period, no differences in basic goals could emerge regardless of motives, occupation, or religiosity. In the end, the Indian as stereotyped had to face extermination through acculturation, if not through genocide. Either way Native Americans were to disappear without attention to their views or needs.

That the methods in the end should prove so similar for such a long period of time depends upon the nature of what is involved in assimilation and the techniques then available for its accomplishment. According to Milton Gordon, assimilation can operate upon several levels and, therefore, involves several processes. His analysis provides a checklist, so-to-speak, of what it takes to fuse one society into another:

(1) Cultural assimilation, or acculturation, refers to the change in attitudes and behavioral patterns when one society assumes the culture of another.

(2) Structural, or social, assimilation involves the mingling of the two societies throughout the network of social relationships, whether in the form of clubs, cliques, formal and informal institutions, or collectivities. Such assimilation need not take place upon equal terms, for economic and functional interdependence can lead to social stratification and inequality, with the members of the different societies clearly distinguished as higher and lower in the social hierarchy.

(3) Marital assimilation, or amalgamation, occurs through widespread intermarriage between the members of the two societies.

Gordon also argues that complete assimilation must involve four additional conditions:

(1) One society must come to feel identity with the other society, so that a feeling of peoplehood or common ethnicity develops in terms of only one of the two previous societies in contact.

(2) Discrimination must be absent from the relations between the two peoples for assimilation to be complete.

(3) Prejudice must also be absent to accomplish assimilation.

(4) Finally, Gordon suggests that value and power conflict must be eliminated, for the dominant society cannot feel that the subordinated society poses threats to its values and power. He terms this last condition "civic assimilation."[4]

If this checklist is complete, then we can immediately see what those who would reform Indian life—be they missionary, philanthropist, government agent, or legislator—had to aim at and why their programs were limited in diversity and accomplishment. Quite obviously, the efforts at education, Christianization, and language training were all directed at cultural assimilation. Speaking and reading English meant more than the acquisition of the prevailing language in American society; it also entailed the learning of the values of that society in the Indian classroom in much the same manner as it did in the Anglo-American classroom. Textbooks and lessons for red and white children alike preached the virtues esteemed by white reformers as well as the ostensible subject matter.[5] Likewise, the manual labor boarding school, so beloved by Thomas McKenney, Richard Pratt, and many others, taught young Indians the male and female roles considered appropriate in American society along with the values of industry, frugality, and sobriety—all in an environment removed from the social relationships and culture of the tribe. Ultimately, the learning of trades was meant to fit native youths into the general economic and therefore social patterns of the American society. In short, vocational preparation was essential to economic assimilation, which in turn was considered fundamental to structural and social assimilation. The aim of economic self-sufficiency could only be achieved, however, through incorporation into an economy increasingly marked by functional differentiation and interdependence as the nineteenth century passed, an economic reality many white farmers and laborers of the period also discovered to their chagrin. Thus the reformers' tasks increased in difficulty as they progressed toward its accomplishment. In fact, their efforts were made possible by the very economy that made their ends impossible of accomplishment.

At the base of social and cultural assimilation was the necessity for allotment of Indian lands in severalty because only by this action could the reformers strike two blows simultaneously at tribal cultures and their social foundations. Allotment provided the economic basis for structural assimilation, indeed forced it upon the Indian, at the same time as it destroyed the land basis for tribal solidarity and the consequent persistence of the culture through communal reinforcement. Indians would be coerced to be free individuals in an economy and society collectively and legally organized to foster that sort of individualism in outlook and in income. Allotment was essential, therefore, to change native orientations from received values to value received in the market nexus favored by crass and by philanthropic Americans alike. What looked to the latter like collectivism among Indians must be stamped out culturally and socially in favor of what they praised as INDIVIDUALISM, as they would have written it. Religion, reading, and arithmetic provided the cultural foundations for such social assimilation, just as allotment afforded the structural foundations for it. The capstone of reform was citizenship in the United States society, for full-fledged civic and identificational assimilation was the implicit, if not stated, aim of the various programs.

In the same manner as the checklist offered a guide to the ends of the reformers, so too does it call attention to what they failed to do or could not do in line with their overall goal of assimilation. The most conspicuous omission is the encouragement of marital assimilation. Although the results of amalgamation between white and Native Americans frequently afforded the best evidence of reform success—whether measured by conversion to Christianity, attendance at school, or the learning of a trade or farming—missionaries, philanthropists, and government officials generally eschewed such a practice for themselves and seldom encouraged it for other whites either.[6] Equally obvious, white prejudice and discrimination continued regardless of what an Indian might do to conform to the aims of the reformers, as the tragic tale of James McDonald in marriage and career demonstrates.[7] Although American society espoused an ethic of equality, white reformers like their compatriots did not really believe in racial equality or in cultural pluralism. Thus the dominant society's members revealed in attitude and in practice discrimination and prejudice against Native Americans, regardless of how the latter might change their ways in accord with white aims and values. Such attitudes and practices, whether conscious or not, reinforced the reverse prejudice of red peoples, confirmed their general suspicions of all white people, and undermined the reformers' efforts at assimilation. In other words, at the same time as the reformers sought the transformation of Indian cultures and social relationships in line with the values of the dominant society, they and their fellow Americans refused to follow some of the best assimilation tactics and, in effect, deliberately fostered their own failure by their actions.

Basically, though, it was the reservation policy that hampered the reformers because this policy provided the foundation for the continuance of tribal societies and therefore their cultures. Although the reservation was meant by its proponents to carry out the same goals of education, Christianization, economic training, and citizenship common to all forms of re-formation of Indian life,[8] the latent consequences of the reservation, as those seeking allotment were well aware, was to afford Indians the opportunity not to assimilate structurally in American society and therefore retain their cultures also. In Gordon's opinion, structural assimilation is the basis of the other assimilation processes, unless there exists sharp discrimination as in the case of the black experience in the United States. The reservations, although constantly whittled down by avaricious whites, still belonged to Indians legally, and there Native

Americans could maintain their traditional patterns of social relations and values in spite of white intervention. Territorial integrity as represented by the reservation, even after removal, enabled Indian political systems to survive also. The powerless politics traditional to most tribes were reinforced by the wardship policies of the federal government. The tendencies of tribes to factionalize, in turn, thwarted white actions and programs whether aimed at reform or otherwise through the dissipation of white energy or the outright defeat of white ends.

In a larger sense, the reservation produced a peculiar dependence between white reformers and Native Americans that was to defeat the ostensible goals of both groups of people. By denying Indians the "therapeutic experience of responsible democracy," to use Henry Dobyn's telling phrase,[9] the reservation policy in particular and United States policy in general failed to offer the Indians the very experience of managing their own affairs that would have made them independent in the white world or even in their own world as modified by white contact. At one and the same time, then, these policies guaranteed the continued helplessness of the Indians, defeated the reformers' ultimate ends, and insured the prolonged presence of reformers as necessary in the scheme of things Indian. In light of today's history of nineteenth-century reform movements, can we not see Indian reformers, like other philanthropists of the period, as having a vested interest in the permanent helplessness of their wards? All reformers were entering at that time what we see today as the early stages of professionalization of the reform impulse in American society. Indians, like abolition, penology, temperance, or mental health, offered positions of pay and status to unemployed lawyers creating new organizations in which to serve, ministers seeking new outlets for their talents, women frustrated in finding purposeful lives, and others discontented or worried about their world and their place in it.[10] The same economy that rendered so much of Indian vocational training meaningless during the time because of the increasing specialization of labor and the complex interdependence of the market also made possible the professionalization of philanthropy in general, including the enormous expenditure in time, personnel, and money for Indian reform.[11] Paternalism went hand-in-hand with the professionalization of reform as an occupation among Indians as among other wards, for the agents needed recipients for their benevolence as much as the recipients were presumed to need the help of the givers. The longer the wards failed to reform, the longer the professional philanthropists could offer their aid and hold their jobs and the more the rise of a new profession was justified. While it would be wrong, I believe, to accuse reformers of deliberately arranging such a state of affairs, their ideals and their actions contributed to the evolution of a new profession in the nineteenth century. In brief, philanthropy towards Indians became part of and was made possible by the increasing specialization of labor and the growing market network in the period. Thus the success of the programs might better be measured by the statistics of paid white agents than by the numbers of Indian converts to church or farm.

Once again, the moral of the story depends upon the larger historical trends of the period and upon the unanticipated consequences of actions aimed at other ostensible ends rather than upon deliberate motives and espoused goals. That the story comes out in this way results, of course, from the overall framework of contact between the two peoples. Until we have more comparative analyses of social and cultural (and racial) contact among the many peoples of the earth, we will not be able to assess for certain such factors as the numbers involved on both "sides," the types of economies in contact, and the natures of social groupings and cultural values coming together in affecting the history of white philanthropy among Indians, let alone the whole history of Native and Anglo-American relations for the nineteenth or other centuries. That whites wanted land for agriculture, that the native population could not be exploited efficiently for the economic purposes of the time but through the expropriation of their lands, and that the tribes rarely united in opposition to the white invaders, who were many in number and made larger by virtue of their social organization, all constitute important elements in the story of philanthropy as well as in the general history of white-Indian contact. Their precise importance cannot be ascertained until the study of comparative contact in the many regions of the world into which Europeans expanded is advanced considerably beyond the present studies. Until that time, the story of philanthropic activities among Indians must wait for its full analysis of intent and results.[12]

NOTES

1. A general exposition of moral stewardship in the philanthropic movements of the time is Clifford S. Griffin, *Their Brothers' Keepers: Moral Stewardship in the United States, 1800–1865* (New Brunswick: Rutgers University Press, 1960).
2. Robert F. Berkhofer, Jr., *Salvation and the Savage: Protestant Missions and American Indian Response, 1787–1862* (Lexington: University of Kentucky Press, 1965), pp. 1–15. Compare Bernard W. Sheehan, *Seeds of Extinction: Jeffersonian Philanthropy and the American Indian* (Chapel Hill: University of North Carolina Press, 1973).
3. Brian W. Dippie, "The Vanishing American: Popular Attitudes and American Indian Policy in the Nineteenth Century" (Ph.D. diss., University of Texas, 1970).

4. Milton Gordon, *Assimilation in American Life: The Role of Race, Religion, and National Origins* (New York: Oxford University Press, 1964), pp. 68–71.
5. For the moral content of American texts in the period, see among many: Richard D. Mosier, *Making the American Mind: Social and Moral Ideas in the McGuffey Readers* (New York: Kings Crown Press, 1947); J. Merton England, "The Democratic Faith in American Schoolbooks, 1783–1860," *American Quarterly* 15 (1963): 191–99; Ruth M. Elson, *Guardians of Tradition: American Schoolbooks of the Nineteenth Century* (Lincoln: University of Nebraska Press, 1964).
6. Prof. Mary Young points out that Return J. Meigs, the agent among the Cherokee in the early nineteenth century, did urge intermarriage as a specific policy. Likewise, missionary children took Indian spouses at times. In both cases, however, I feel these were the exception rather than the rule.
7. Compare Berkhofer, *Salvation and the Savage*, pp. 107–24, for the plight of the Indian convert to Christianity.
8. William T. Hagan summarizes succinctly the purpose of reservation policy in his article, "Indian Policy after the Civil War: The Reservation Experience," in *Lectures of the Indiana Historical Society, 1970–1971* (Indianapolis, 1971), pp. 20–23.
9. Henry F. Dobyns, "Therapeutic Experience of Responsible Democracy," in Stuart Levine and Nancy O. Lurie, eds., *The American Indian Today* (Baltimore: Penguin Books, Inc., 1970), pp. 268–91.
10. The history of the professionalization of occupations in the United States is not well told, but see Daniel H. Calhoun, *Professional Lives in America: Structure and Aspiration, 1750–1850* (Cambridge, Mass.: Harvard University Press, 1965).
11. The size of this expenditure is measured against that of previous centuries, not in terms of what was needed to accomplish the reformers' espoused goals in our opinion today.
12. Some indication of the work being done in race relations in general may be seen in Pierre L. van den Berghe, *Race and Racism: A Comparative Perspective* (New York: Wiley, 1967); Philip E. Mason, *Patterns of Dominance* (London: Oxford University Press, 1970).

COMMENTARY

Loring B. Priest

No area of American Indian study demands more emphasis at this moment than the history and problems of peaceful interracial adjustment. Yet few scholars have ventured to discuss the subject. Over the years, sociologists and anthropologists have described fully and competently the background and nature of a wide variety of Indian societies, but since 1934 they have almost unanimously shunned any favorable reference to assimilation proposals, past or present. At the same time, certain historians, especially those interested in whetting public attention, have recognized the superior marketability of books on interracial *conflicts* as opposed to treatments of interracial accommodation. More study of past efforts to promote Indian adjustment might be undertaken if it were not for the widely expressed opinion that such accounts would be both insignificant and perverse. It is sad that at the very moment when the two races are coming into closer contact every day, there is a dearth of information about the successes and failures of the past. Careful study of such accounts could greatly advance the goal of maintaining Indian self-respect and of preserving certain of their social institutions while continuing greater participation in other phases of white society.

Yet a more normal difficulty than academic hostility and a public lust for a recital of past sins besets the prospective scholar of assimilation—a problem of too little material or of too much. Though social change involves group adjustment, assimilation is an intensely individual matter requiring personal testimony. No recitation of law or description of events is as satisfactory as a human experience. In Dr. Viola's paper, the portrayal of McKenney's deep disillusionment over the tragic failure of James McDonald to adjust to white society as a factor in his abandonment of plans for Indian advancement, for example, makes infinitely more comprehensible, though nonetheless unfortunate, his succumbing to the demand for removal. Also, by putting oneself in McDonald's place, though there is no testimony from him, the enormous psychological problems plaguing anyone who attempted to make a transition to white life can be understood. Knowledge of such personal experience is rare in these early years. Full comprehension of the individual difficulties faced in assimilation will emerge only through consideration of other instances, recounting successes as well as failures.

Even for post-Civil War years, when pressure to assimilate was overwhelming, there is no abundance of personal information. Biographies, more numerous as successful transition took place, contribute some record of the sacrifices that were demanded.[1] The most valuable material, however, should be provided by having those responsible for current oral history projects regularly include questions on assimilation.[2] To belittle such testimony on the ground that all who made a successful transition were either racial traitors or were unique will be to ignore the gradual process by which many other individuals and tribes have in recent years accepted certain features of white life. While government records do exist involving group adjustment before the Civil War, the predominance of other matters nationally is confirmed by the relatively small space devoted to acculturation in excellent recent histories of the years before 1865.[3]

A wealth of information on assimilation is to be found in governmental documents of the period following the Civil War. Yet the very quantity of material itself presents certain difficulties. A walk through the National Archives collection, for example, will impress anyone with the immense amount of time administrators were forced to spend on details of finance and land titles and the relatively little attention that could be devoted to the Indians themselves. For the years immediately after the Civil War, the increase in available material presents fewer problems than might be expected because of a most useful classification of documents by jurisdiction. Indeed, until chronological filing was adopted in 1881, the work of anyone studying the history of a particular tribe or agency or concerned with the overall development of United States Indian policy is greatly facilitated as documents not involved with problems of a special area are readily available in a "general" file. Researchers concerned with a subject involving a variety of agencies, of course, need to examine a much larger amount of material.[4] But the problems of those working on developments before 1881 are much less, in any case, than for those doing research in the period following.

It is for the years 1881 to 1907, when Indian Bureau correspondence was filed indiscriminately by date of receipt, that students of general governmental policy will find their work most difficult. Since publication of *Uncle Sam's Stepchildren,* I have often lamented that no adequate documentary study of disillusionment with the Dawes Act and of efforts to remedy its defects in the Burke Act of 1906 has appeared. In January

Commentary

1972, pursuing the possibility of undertaking the task myself, I ascertained in only a short time that any such project would require an immense amount of labor. That valuable information can be obtained through use of agency letterbooks for these years is shown by Dr. Berthrong's excellent *Kansas Quarterly* article on Indian-white difficulties among the Cheyenne and Arapaho in the early 1890s.[5] But for in-depth analysis of the nature and deficiencies of government policies during these years, as well as for presentation of contrasting situations on different reservations, it would seem that only by first using other sources and then turning to the Archives for *particular* items can satisfactory results be achieved.[6] Since resumption of jurisdictional filing in 1907, the problems of research regarding assimilation are again less formidable. Instead, the central concern about such study has become whether it is either relevant or desirable!

Let me confess at the start that a reading of recent works on Indian-white relations often has proved deeply disturbing. Two schools apparently exist: one claiming assimilation can never succeed because Indians are incapable of achieving it, while the other states with equal determination that assimilation *should* never be demanded because Indians are irrevocably opposed to it. Seldom is it indicated that there *must* be some degree of assimilation; that the process of interadjustment takes place naturally in any event; that the only question is whether changes should take place haphazardly by an inevitable evolutionary process (William Graham Sumner) or in a more orderly manner through some degree of human intervention (Lester F. Ward).

No one today believes, as the large majority of citizens of the late 1800s hopefully expected, that Indians will vanish either by extermination or by absorption in white society. Yet very little current literature presents assimilation as a vitally important matter. Most writing about Indians either recites once again the catalog of white sins or emphasizes that Indians must be allowed to be themselves.[7] In most instances, the years 1870–1920 are presented as an evil period, which should be either forgotten or remembered with shame. Remarkably, the years before the Civil War escape relatively uncriticized in several recent histories, for what is regarded as unforgivable today is the effort to speed assimilation, *not* the disastrous removals. The removals at least, along with the accompanying reservation system, had provided a chance for the survival of Indian uniqueness and self-government as a means of avoiding absorption.

But while more research needs to be done in the field of Indian-white relations, the present situation is far from being as bleak as it once was. Several excellent scholarly books presenting the history of Indian relations have appeared recently, and a growing number of individuals are establishing themselves as specialists. Among the foremost is Dr. Fritz, with whom I have much in common. He has submitted my work to painstaking analysis, backing his statements and interpretations with full documentation. In his presentation, he has provided new information based on the records of the Board of Indian Commissioners, most of which could not be located when I was doing my original research. When I discovered them in the Archives this January, I knew they should be tapped. While I am still inclined to feel that the board was somewhat less influential than Dr. Fritz indicates, and while the ethnocentrism of the board majority is not unmentioned in *Uncle Sam's Stepchildren*, this distinguished paper is an absolutely essential addition to the literature on the Dawes Act. Few individuals are so fortunate as to have a scholar of such competence working in one's area of special interest. The very fact that we do not see eye to eye on several subjects has made our accounts complementary rather than repetitive. What particularly pleases me is that while Fritz's first book focused attention on the 1870s, he now is extending his critical and interpretative talents to the important decades of the 1880s and 1890s.

There are numerous other scholars whose work in the field of government Indian policy is outstanding, but I will mention only a few here. One of the earliest was Peter Rahill, whose account of Catholic pressure for fair treatment during the years of the peace policy must be read in conjunction with Dr. Fritz's highly critical account.[8] Frank discussion of quarrels within the church which seriously handicapped its lobbying efforts marks Rahill's book and illuminates a major problem which plagued the labor of all churches engaged in the Indian field. The new breed of military historians, of which Robert Athearn and Richard Ellis are leading members, deserves mention for emphasizing the careful attention given by many army administrators to the Indian question and to the submission of proposals for peaceful Indian advancement. One hopes the often-repeated charge that the military provoked Indian wars so they might have something to do will some day be answered by a book which does nothing else than bring together under one cover the innumerable instances when soldiers took significant stands in *behalf* of Indians. Such a volume might or might not show that control of Indian policy by the War Department was preferable after 1865, but it should at least establish the fact that the stereotype of the military ogre has been unjust to many friends of the Indian. Study of reformers and of lobbying groups also has made advances. With the publication last year of a history of post-Civil War reformers by Robert Mardock,[9] the need for a detailed treatment of the influence of individuals upon Indian policy before 1880 is met most satisfactorily. Governmental, literary, and newspaper sources are fully exploited in bringing to life people who have too often been mere names.

Mardock also refers to the work of Indian organizations; but since their greatest activity was yet to come, one anticipates eagerly studies of the 1880s employing such rich documentary sources as those of the Indian Rights Association. Following so full a presentation of earlier reformers, analysis of reform efforts during the last years of the century will cause historians to be grateful indeed.

Important accounts of the application of new government policies in the field are also available. Often in the form of articles, they show that policies are easier to devise than to administer. The wide variety of experience with government programs makes histories of different tribes most valuable to students of racial adjustment. The confusion, internal disagreements, pressure for conformity, and fear of further disillusionment which accompanied official insistence on change after 1860, for example, are unforgettably presented in the appropriately titled *History of the Santee Sioux: United States Indian Policy on Trial* by Roy Meyer.[10] At the opposite extreme from tribal histories, William Hagan's excellent summary of American Indian history is as influential as his text is brief.[11] For more detailed presentation of post-Civil War Indian policy, the second portion of Father Prucha's history of Indian policy is awaited with knowledge that its appearance will mark a high spot in interpretation of these most significant years.

But anthropologists, sociologists, and ethnologists have as much reason to be, and fortunately are, as much interested in questions of assimilation as historians.[12] Many of the best approaches to racial adjustment are, and should increasingly be, interdisciplinary. There is tremendous value in the short research articles by a variety of scholars collected in such publications as the May 1957 *Annals of the American Academy*, in the *Midcontinent American Studies Journal* for the fall of 1965 and the resulting book in 1958, and in the *Kansas Quarterly* of fall 1971. Established scholars pursuing their specialties and graduate students seeking opportunity to publish can, through such cooperative ventures, reach colleagues with material which might otherwise find no outlet. The quality of work in these publications is high and their contents relevant to students in widely diverse areas of study.[13]

Individuals in these professions have provided notable full-length volumes treating assimilation as well. It is perhaps because she is also a historian that I am so deeply impressed with the discussion of Pan-Indian movements of the early twentieth century in Hazel Hertzberg's *Search for an Indian Identity*.[14] New attitudes toward reform which resulted from Indian participation are admirably presented by employing the papers of Arthur C. Parker, of the Society of American Indians. By detailed recounting of organizational discussion and disagreement, the nature of Indian disputes over their future is clarified, and it is important to note that many more anthropologists than historians were among the Indian and white members of the society. Perhaps because of her feeling of a need for historical perspective, policies after 1934 are not discussed in any detail, but no one can deny that anthropological concern for preservation of Indian institutions plays a large part in current insistence on racial rights. At times historians may find a tendency on the part of ethnologists to overemphasize the superior virtues of Indian civilization,[15] but there is little doubt that without the constructive influence of fellow social scientists, historians might completely surrender to their belief that change is inevitable and should be allowed its way.

There is much that is encouraging about the stress upon Indian self-determination these days. While those most concerned with Indian welfare realize termination of federal jurisdiction is not the answer, more administrative matters are in the hands of tribal authorities than have been for many years. A wide variety of attitudes toward white ways results in a situation where the adoption of appropriate white customs is common among some tribes (the Navajos) and sternly opposed by others (the Zunis).[16] While Indians continue to leave reservations for life among the whites, reservation population continues to grow. Complex problems, however, still haunt Indians—the pain and frustrations of those who endeavor to lead a new life in the face of prejudice on and off the reservation, the poverty of many tribes located where little opportunity for profitable activity exists, and the strong pressure by many older Indians for conformity. Yet these and other difficulties may well be overcome if sincere efforts are made to understand why reformers of the last century were thwarted in achieving their goals.

My main fear for the future of Indian-white relations is that ignoring or indiscriminately condemning reformers of the last hundred years will greatly reduce the possibilities of future progress in interracial relations. There is need to know why the hopes of the reformers were defeated. There is need to know them as individuals. There is need to ask what the condition of Indians would be today without their having lived. For all his dogged persistence in pursuing the goal of complete absorption, would the present situation be better if there had been no Capt. Richard Pratt? Would there have been so strong a case for Indian self-determination today if a Meacham and a Bland had not supported the cause of consultation so strongly in the *Council Fire?* Would Indians now be better off if Helen Hunt Jackson had not taken up their cause? To ask such questions, I believe, is to answer them.

It is a common historical error to expect those of the past to have been like oneself. People are a product of the age in which they live. So are reformers. It is necessary to remember that following the Civil War faith

Commentary

in the melting pot and belief in the perfection of the American way of life were high. Men and women of those days, weaned on the idea of survival of the fittest, accepted readily arguments on behalf of teaching Indians the ways of white society before it was too late. That this white society included alarming evils and countless temptations which Indians had to be taught to resist did not cause reformers to question the change they demanded. Most failed to consider that the land on which many tribes lived was incapable of sustaining the individual farming upon which their plans depended. They shared the optimism of a period which believed that with God's help all would work well. By 1900, however, faith in the melting pot was on the decline, and there was a growing uncertainty about certain wonders of the American way. Some indication of the direction proposals for interracial relations would take can be sensed as T. H. Tibbles, a white veteran of the reform movement, concluded his autobiography of 1905 with comments on an encampment which had brought together Indians who "walked in the new path" with those who "clung doggedly to all of the old." "I was sincerely glad," he wrote, "that some small part of all which had been finest in the old life had been and would continue to be revived in the new. For if the new life were [is] to succeed, its keynote must be, not governmental or religious repression, but inspiration; not the old restrictive bonds of tradition, superstition, or childlike fear, but a new freedom born of a whole-souled understanding of its own rights and duties and the rights and duties of others."[17]

The papers on twentieth-century federal Indian policy present an opportunity to learn much of what remains to be accomplished if the hopes which Tibbles so eloquently expressed are to be realized. Considerable improvement in Indian-white relations has already resulted from increased insistence upon the right of Indians to reach their own decisions, both corporately and individually. Without adequate appreciation and knowledge of the achievements and defects of early reform measures, however, gains will be limited. Only as the importance of past experience is recognized and its lessons applied will the full potential of today's goals be attained. Then, and only then, will the efforts of post-Civil War reformers prove not to have been in vain.

NOTES

1. There are interesting possibilities in contrasting accounts of a single individual such as those of the Cheyenne, Roman Nose, by Ellsworth Collings and Karen Peterson in *Chronicles of Oklahoma* 42, no. 4 (Winter 1964–65): 429–78.
2. Most immediately those working under the Duke Projects in Oral History, of whom one is Floyd O'Neil at the University of Utah.

3. Francis Paul Prucha's *American Indian Policy in the Formative Years,* for example. Records of adjustments during the colonial and early national years by scattered eastern tribes, portions of the Six Nations, and the Five Civilized Tribes are quite extensive in colonial, state, and tribal archives.
4. It may be that a joint project in which each scholar works on a limited area and the total output is analyzed before publication will prove useful.
5. Donald J. Berthrong, "White Neighbors Come among the Southern Cheyenne and Arapaho," *Kansas Quarterly* 3, no. 4 (Fall 1971): 105–13.
6. In retrospect it becomes clear that my research on the background of the Dawes Act from 1881–87 was made possible primarily by using congressional documents, contemporary literature, scattered letters of the Board of Indian Commissioners, the extensive material of reform organizations, the *Council Fire,* and the timely bequest of Senator Dawes's papers to the Library of Congress by Anna L. Dawes. Recently I have noticed that several very fine histories of post-Civil War Indian affairs concentrate on the period before 1880 and treat quite sketchily the years following. What can be accomplished without use of detailed archival materials is admirably evident in a history of allotment to 1900 by D. S. Otis written for the Indian Office in 1934 (*Hearings on H. R. 7902,* before the House Committee on Indian Affairs, pt. 9, pp. 428–89). This invaluable report, brought to light in a 1973 reprint, is a tribute to its author, its editor, and its publisher, the University of Oklahoma Press. See D. S. Otis, *The Dawes Act and the Allotment of Indian Lands,* ed. and with introduction by Francis Paul Prucha (Norman: University of Oklahoma Press, 1973).
7. There seems to exist a considerable amount of understandable, but not fully justifiable, professional hostility stirred by the success of the best-sellers: Vine Deloria, Jr., *Custer Died for Your Sins: An Indian Manifesto* (New York: Macmillan, 1969), and Dee Brown, *Bury My Heart at Wounded Knee: An Indian History of the American West* (New York: Holt, Rinehart & Winston, 1970).
8. Peter J. Rahill, *The Catholic Indian Missions and Grant's Peace Policy, 1870–1884* (Washington: Catholic University of America Press, 1953).
9. Robert Winston Mardock, *The Reformers and the American Indian* (Columbia: University of Missouri Press, 1971).
10. Roy Willard Meyer, *History of the Santee Sioux: United States Indian Policy on Trial* (Lincoln: University of Nebraska Press, 1967).
11. William T. Hagan, *American Indians* (Chicago: University of Chicago Press, 1961).
12. An excellent move in the right direction is the paper by Robert M. Utley, "The Frontier Army: John Ford or Arthur Penn," in the section "The Role of the Military" in this volume (pp. 133–45).
13. One would hope that psychologists might soon be included in such a list, for their contributions toward understanding individual pressures resulting from interracial adjustment would be of immense value.
14. Hazel W. Hertzberg, *The Search for an American Indian Identity: Modern Pan-Indian Movements* (Syracuse: Syracuse University Press, 1971).
15. Most historians, I believe, will find difficulty in accepting the emphasis or

conclusions of chapter 14 of Peter Farb's *Man's Rise to Civilization* (London: Paladin Books, 1971).
16. For the contrasting attitudes of these tribes toward World War II veterans, see Farb, *Man's Rise to Civilization*, pp. 271–74.
17. Thomas Henry Tibbles, *Buckskin and Blanket Days* (Lincoln: University of Nebraska Press, 1969), p. 335.

DISCUSSION NOTE

Angie Debo of Marshall, Oklahoma, opened the discussion by asserting her belief that the actual selection of Indian agents by religious denominations lasted for only a short period. The Baptist Church, which was assigned the Creek Agency, was responsible for only one appointment at that agency. Thereafter, all Baptist appointees for that agency were selected for political reasons and their religious affiliations were incidental. The church had no real voice in the selections, and after 1871 not a single appointment originated with the Baptist Church. John Bret Harte of the University of Arizona stated that the Dutch Reform Society of Foreign Missions was responsible for appointments of agents for all the Indian agencies in Arizona. His research on the San Carlos Indian Reservation showed that even under the most urgent of circumstances the Committee of the Dutch Reform Church often delayed making nominations for as much as five or six months. This kind of a situation was an open invitation to political pressures, such as those applied by Commissioner of Indian Affairs Ezra A. Hayt at the beginning of 1877.

Henry Fritz said that he had no doubt that a continuous effort was made to bring the agencies under political influence during the period of the peace policy. But in 1878 the churches and missionary associations still thought that there had been a high degree of adherence to the theory of nominations by religious groups. Between 1878 and 1882, however, political influence became more important, and thereafter the religious denominations were unwilling to be associated with the appointment of Indian agents.

Ronald Satz of the University of Tennessee at Martin, Tennessee, questioned McKenney's motives in advocating the Indian removal policy. He pointed out that McKenney wished to retain his position in the Office of Indian Affairs during the administration of Andrew Jackson, whose election he had actively opposed in 1828. Was his motivation, therefore, perhaps political and in a sense economic as well as humanitarian?

Herman Viola replied that McKenney was a professional reformer, fully aware of the political implications of removal. He began to favor removal as early as 1824, well before Jackson's campaign and election, and his experience with James McDonald convinced him that the civilization program was a failure. McDonald was a very able and articulate young Choctaw on whose education thousands of dollars in government funds had been expended, and McKenney pointed to him as an example of the achievements of the civilization program. Hired by the Choctaws as their lawyer, McDonald returned to Washington in 1826 after an absence of several years to represent this tribe in treaty negotiations. His demands prolonged the negotiations and he drank constantly. Due to the nature of their former relationship, McDonald became a public embarrassment to McKenney, and they never met again after this occurrence. Therefore, McKenney's attitude changed drastically and his support of the civilization program waned. His interest in removal increased steadily, and when Jackson took office, he fully supported Jackson's removal policy.

Muriel Wright, editor of the *Chronicles of Oklahoma*, asked Viola why he omitted mention of the Choctaw Academy in Kentucky, which was administered by Richard Johnson, a Congressman affiliated with the Baptist Church. With a student body composed of both Indians and whites, it was one good example of a school founded on the principle of education to assimilate and bring the Indian people into the mainstream of white civilization. She pointed out that James McDonald's cousin, Robert M. McDonald Jones, graduated from the Academy a well-educated and cultivated man. He became one of the wealthiest men in the Southwest and was active in the establishment of the Choctaw Nation in Indian Territory. He remained prominent in Choctaw affairs down to the Civil War, when he favored joining the Confederacy.

Viola agreed that the Choctaw Academy was a remarkable institution. He did not mention it because it was outside the Indian country, as McKenney outlined it in his program, and it was completely atypical of the schools that were established. It served almost as a college, since those boys who completed the Choctaw mission schools went on to the academy. James McDonald was opposed to the academy, because the boys were taken from their homes and placed in a foreign environment. Viola also noted that Robert McD. Jones inherited McDonald's allotment after McDonald committed suicide.

Senapaw of the Creek Nation objected to what he understood to be Father Prucha's theory of writing history, namely, that history can be neutral and that the historian practices a science. He asserted that in his opinion the historian practices an art. He considered Viola's presentation to be a racist statement because of an underlying assumption that native people had to be civilized. In refutation he noted that the Creek Nation had a civilization long before white people arrived in America. Senapaw was also disturbed about what he felt was insufficient Indian participation in the conference and charged that the National Archives essentially was training white historians and anthropologists to study Indians. The Indians were not being given the opportunity to learn about the holdings of the National Archives so that they could present their own interpretation of events. He then reiterated his view that history is not a science, it is an interpretation.

In defense of Viola's paper, Robert Berkhofer noted that much of the paper was composed of quotations from McKenney's writings. Consequently, the sentiments attributed to Viola were actually those of Thomas L. McKenney. He acknowledged the fact that the dominant influence in the writing of Indian history has been white. This is a matter of great concern to all of the panel members, and the prospect of having more Indian historians has excited a great deal of interest in the profession. American Indians have already moved into the field of law and are gradually moving into other areas. As they become active in the historical field, they will be welcomed into the profession.

III

Indian Collections Outside the National Archives and Records Service

INTRODUCTION
Thurman Wilkins

The first paper on Indian collections outside the Archives is by John C. Ewers who has been engaged for nearly forty years in the study of historic artifacts made by or for Indians. The majority of his publications have been concerned at least in part with the significance of artifacts or pictures or both. His research has been primarily in the history and mythology of the Plains Indians, documenting the findings of his fieldwork with library, archival, and museum sources. He and Mrs. Ewers lived for three and a half years on the Blackfeet Reservation in Montana at a time when many veterans of the Indian tribal wars and buffalo hunts were still living. In addition, he has done fieldwork among the Flathead and Assiniboin tribes of Montana, the Sioux of South Dakota, and the Kiowa of Oklahoma.

The second essay is by Angie Debo. Debo was born on a farm near Beatty, Kansas, in January 1890. In 1899 she was brought by her parents to Marshall, Oklahoma, her present home. She taught in rural schools and high schools of Oklahoma and served on history faculties of colleges in Texas and Oklahoma. She has written numerous articles and reviews and twelve books, all except one about Indian and western history.

The final paper is by C. Gregory Crampton who is professor of history at the University of Utah in Salt Lake City. His teaching fields are the United States and Latin American history, with emphasis respectively on the American West and Mexico. He has taught American history in Panama, England, France, and Germany, and has served the scholarly public as editor, historical archaeologist, and oral historian. He has published widely in a number of fields but is perhaps best known for his prize-winning *Standing Up Country*.

Artifacts and Pictures as Documents in the History of Indian-White Relations

John C. Ewers

When Indians and whites met at a wilderness trading post they exchanged more than words.

When colonial authorities negotiated peaceful alliances with influential Indian chiefs they gave more than promises.

When Christian missionaries lived among the Indians they taught them to do things other than to say their prayers.

When the Sioux and their Allies confronted Custer's soldiers on the Little Big Horn they did not talk them to death.

These are some ways of reminding us that the history of Indian-white relations was not really *written*, it was *acted;* and that artifacts played important roles in that acting. Call them trade goods, Indian presents, annuity payments, or weapons (Indian handicrafts, if you will), they were all artifacts.

In an effort to reconstruct and interpret the history of these relations as clearly and as truthfully as possible, the historian should not overlook or minimize the roles played by artifacts. The whites who helped to make that history did not, nor did the Indians.

Anthropologists tell us that when peoples of different cultural backgrounds meet they exchange both ideas and things, and that as a result of this exchange *both* cultures are enriched. Certainly, that was the case when the Indians met whites from the several colonizing nations of Europe. Furthermore, these contacts stimulated ingenuity on both sides. Ingenuity was channeled into the design and making of artifacts which would appeal to the receiver. If the Hudson's Bay Company point blanket was invented during the eighteenth century to please the Indians, so was the beaded rabbit's foot made by Zuni Indians for sale to suspicious white tourists more recently. The members of the receiving group determined how the objects they received would be used. If Indians could not foresee that many of their artifacts would be preserved for educational and study purposes in white museums, white manufacturers could not anticipate many of the Indian uses for their products.

Cultural borrowing was a two-way process on the Indian frontier. I shall not attempt to call the role of the many contributions Indians have made to American and world culture, but will mention just a few that date back to an early period in Indian-white relations and were of particular importance during the frontier period.

In 1669 René de Brahant de Galinee traveled westward by canoe from Montreal in search of unknown tribes to convert to Christianity. His party made the earliest recorded ascent of the Great Lakes to Sault Sainte Marie. After he described the birchbark canoe in detail, he commented, "I see no handiwork of the Indians that appears to me to merit the attention of Europeans, except their canoes and their rackets for walking on snow."[1]

Snowshoes have been much used by whites for winter travel overland in the northern latitudes, but the bark canoe played a much greater role in American history. By paddling and portaging, whites first explored a considerable portion of the interior of this country and Canada, and canoes became indispensable to the wide-ranging fur trade that extended westward from Montreal to beyond the Rockies.

Buckskin clothing and moccasins adopted from, if not actually made by, Indians became the clothing of the white pioneers. In 1885 an observant army officer, Capt. W. P. Clark, wrote, "The moccasin is the last thing an Indian gives up as he travels toward civilization, and the first thing adopted by whites who, as hunters, trappers, traders, or 'squaw men' mix, mingle, and live with Indians."[2]

The Indians' partiality to moccasins persists in the second half of the twentieth century. As recently as 1968, Pauline Dempsey informed me that among her people, the Blood Indians of Alberta, who occupy the largest Indian reserve in Canada and are considered one of the most prosperous tribes in the Dominion, one hundred or more Indians still wear moccasins daily, except in winter.

This suggests another factor in Indian-white relations. Indians were selective in what they obtained from the whites—they took what they thought they could use and rejected what they did not want.

Let us examine the matter of clothing from the Indian side of the frontier. There is evidence that the body clothing whites wore had a great fascination for Indians virtually from the time of first contacts between the races on the seacoast of North America.

On May 14, 1602, Gilbert and Gosnold anchored off the coast of Maine.

Soon they were visited by six Indians, whose leader wore a "waistcoat and breeches of black serdge, made after our sea-fashion, hose and shoes on his feet. The rest (saving one that had a pair of breeches of blue cloth) were all naked."[3] This was proof enough to the Englishmen that some Basque fishermen had been the Kilroys who had preceded them to the rugged coasts of Maine.

On the far side of the continent, Capt. James Colnett may have been the first white man to meet the Tsimshian Indians in Calamity Bay, on September 16, 1787. During his first meeting with the tribe, Chief Seax offered Colnett his own clothes in exchange for a coat of European cut. The Englishman gave the chief a coat, shirt, and pair of trousers but would accept no exchange for them.[4]

During the colonial period, French, Spanish, and English authorities commonly presented handsomely decorated coats to prominent Indian chiefs, who coveted them as symbols of their rank. The Hudson's Bay Company employed tailors at its wilderness posts to make clothing for Indians, as well as for company employees. The United States followed colonial precedent in presenting coats to prominent Indians, and the term "chief coat," for a colorful garment of military or semimilitary style, liberally embellished with metal lace, was familiar to Indian agents on the frontier until the Civil War.

Many more cloth garments, as well as quantities of yard goods for making clothing, reached the Indians through trade and in the annuity payments that followed treatymaking. It is noteworthy that although historians tend to remember the important 1851 Treaty of Fort Laramie as a *document,* which was intended to keep that important lifeline through the Indian country—the Oregon Trail—open to whites, the powerful Sioux Indians who were party to that treaty tended to remember the year 1851–52 in their pictographic winter counts as the year of the first distribution of annuities. That year is depicted in one winter count as a blanket spread on the ground, with goods on it, surrounded by marks representing Indians.[5]

In the Indian War of 1867, Red Cloud's Sioux humiliated the whites and gained a second Treaty of Fort Laramie in 1868, which was very favorable to his people. In 1870 Red Cloud, in the presence of some five thousand of his people, receipted for annuities that included more than thirteen and a half miles of yard goods, much of which may have been intended for making tepee covers, even though buffalo were still plentiful in Montana.[6]

Every treaty negotiated with the western tribes from 1867 on contained an article providing "each male person over fourteen years of age, [with] a suit of good substantial clothing, consisting of coat, pantaloons, flannel shirt, hat, and a pair of home-made socks."[7]

The flooding of the western Indian country with manufactured clothing and yard goods occurred more than a decade before the buffalo were exterminated and several years before the nomadic tribes of the High Plains were confined to reservations. Much of the material was shoddy, and the principal beneficiaries of the government's payments to Indians may have been the New England millowners. Certainly ethnologists should not wonder why many old medicine objects from the Plains Indians are wrapped in a half dozen or more layers of colorful cloth. Cloth was something those Indians had plenty of.

The fur trade—the most important business of whites in the American wilderness—was essentially an Indian trade.

When the mountaineers tried to trap beaver on their own in the country of the warlike Blackfoot, they soon encountered armed resistance and paid for their neglect of the Indian trade with their lives. Indian cooperation was a prime requisite to the continued expansion of the fur trade.

To go a step further, the Indians were not only cooperative, they were eager to take part in a trade that would furnish them with manufactured goods and materials they wanted. They had been traders before the whites arrived, and after they began to obtain horses from whites, they became astute horse traders, with all of the shrewdness that term implies.

Archaeologists working in the heartland of this continent, the Great Plains, are becoming increasingly aware of the antiquity and the importance, long before the appearance of Coronado, of intertribal trade in this region. Findings of artifacts, such as shells from distant seacoasts in prehistoric villages on the Missouri River in the Dakotas, imply lengthy trade routes into and from this region before the Indians acquired horses. Artifacts of iron, brass, and glass found in seventeenth-century sites of this same region reveal that these Indians were obtaining artifacts of white manufacture through Indian intermediaries before they themselves had met whites. The written observations of eighteenth-century and early nineteenth-century explorers and traders tell of these Indians' eagerness to acquire firearms, tomahawks, knives, axes, and other metal tools and weapons.

Historians should resist the temptation to think of some of the smaller items in the traders' inventory, such as glass beads, mirrors, metal bracelets, or rolled metal jinglers as "mere trinkets" simply because they were of little monetary value to whites. During the early years of white contact such items may have served as status symbols to the Indians who acquired them. Even after trade goods became more plentiful, Indians found ways to use the more common artifacts they received in trade so as to reflect their prestige among their fellows. As recently as a century ago, members of poorer families among the Plains Indians did not display themselves on ceremonial occasions in heavily beaded shirts and dresses, any more than they posed as owners of large horseherds or as possessors of the most complex and sacred medicine bundles.

Artifacts and Pictures as Documents

No object of white manufacture was more coveted by India[n] tribes than was the gun, an alien weapon which they did no[t] managed to make peculiarly their own. A Birmingham gunsmit[h] have anticipated the Indians' peculiar regard and some of the[ir uses for] this product. He could not have known that the seventeenth-century Sioux, believing there must be a spirit within the muzzle-loading flintlock, would call it "medicine iron"; that the Mandans, the most sophisticated Indians on the Upper Missouri, would consecrate their guns in elaborate religious rituals; that the Cheyenne, Arapaho, and Sioux would raise their guns skyward and fire them to drive away thunder and lightning, which they feared might bring some dreadful calamity to their people; or that the Crow Indians would come to think of the thunder as an immense bird that carried a gun in its talons and would discharge it to cause lightning. Nor would he have known that Indians sometimes lightened the weight of their guns by cutting off several inches of the barrel, making arrowheads or tools from the removed sections, and converted old gun barrels into skindressing tools, tobacco pipes, and courting flutes. Historians should be aware that the gun had meanings to and uses for Indians that were unknown to the white culture.

The demand for trade goods in the Indian trade was met not only by large manufacturers in this country and abroad, but it also gave employment to such household industries as the making of shell wampum, hairpipes, and moons in New Jersey; of clay tobacco pipes in Virginia and North Carolina; and of tomahawks by blacksmiths in various localities on the frontier.

Of course, Indians had smoked tobacco long before the time of Columbus, but they came to prefer the tobacco offered by whites to their own. Perhaps, too, the high-bowled, inverted T-shaped pipe we commonly refer to as a "Siouan calumet" was popularized among the Indians of the northern Plains through the fur trade. Many of these pipes were made by whites. Using the attractive red catlinite from the sacred pipestone quarry in Minnesota, whites began to turn thousands of these "Indian pipes" on lathes during the mid-1860s for use by Indians.

Indian missions long have been regarded as one of the most potent and persistent agencies for introducing white civilization to the Indians. Surely, the missionaries did much more than teach the Indians how to pray to their God. In mission schools and in the Indian communities where they resided, missionaries also taught children and adults how to make new things with their hands. Some of the handicrafts we formerly considered "typically Indian" bear the marks of mission influence, such as porcupine-quilled bark boxes and belts of loom-woven beadwork. And some missionized Indians became skilled in crafts which had long been regarded as "typically European." For example, the making of lace of Italian-renaissance type among the Oneida Indian women in Wisconsin was introduced to them by the Sisters of the Nativity of the Catholic Church in 1898. During the first decade of this century, Oneida-made Italian lace doilies, pillow covers, and bedspreads were marketed on Fifth Avenue in New York City. At the same time, this Oneida-Italian lace was winning gold medals in international expositions, one of them in Milan, Italy, in 1906. The best proofs of the Indian women's skill in this work are not in written records, but in the examples of their handicrafts that have been preserved.[8]

Renaissance-type lace square made by a twelve-year-old Oneida Indian girl. Early twentieth century. (Cat. No. T12794-A, National Museum of History and Technology, Smithsonian Institution.)

Lewis Henry Morgan, often termed the "father of American anthropology," liked to refer to Indian artifacts as "silent memorials." In 1850 he wrote, "These memorials unlock the social history of the past; and although silent, they speak more eloquently than all human description."[9]

I would go a step further and include among the artifacts that can serve as primary sources in the study of Indian history and the history of Indian-white relations in this country those artifacts made by non-Indians for Indian use. Indian-made artifacts are particularly valuable as concrete testimony of the kinds of objects Indians made and used at particular stages of Indian-white contacts. Indian religious objects testify to the survival of traditional beliefs long after Christian missionaries came among them, even to the present day.

The Blackfoot medicine pipe was mentioned by an English fur trader who was among those Indians more than one hundred seventy years ago. Yet there is a published description of a medicine pipe ceremony observed in the living room of a conservative family on the Blackfeet Reservation in Montana as recently as 1971. There were framed diplomas on the walls and the television set was pushed into a corner before the age-old Indian ritual was begun.[10]

Artifacts and Pictures as Documents

Many thousands of Indian artifacts are preserved in hundreds of museums, large and small, in this country and abroad. No single museum, however large, has a complete representation of the objects made by Indians at different periods in history. Many small museums possess some excellent examples. Some once-common artifacts have not been preserved at all. Unfortunately, too, we know little about the history of many artifacts because museum records are incomplete. It is paradoxical, but true, that an artifact is of little value as a *historical document* unless it is documented by a written record of who (or what tribe) made it, when, and for what purpose. An unidentified artifact may be of no more historical value than an unsigned letter.

Undoubtedly, the preservation in museums of many undocumented artifacts of Indian origin, and of others of questionable dating or tribal attribution, has been a deterrent to the study of artifacts. But so is the fact that few scholars are willing to devote the time and thought to their study that is necessary to make the most effective use of artifacts as historical and cultural documents.

There are many documented artifacts that can shed light upon the history of Indian cultures and of Indian-white relations. Archaeologists have been adding to their numbers through scientific excavations at sites of historic Indian villages, trading posts, mission stations, Indian agencies, frontier military posts, and battlefields. The imperishable materials they obtain from the ground provide much valuable information on the kinds of artifacts made by or for Indians. But perishable materials, such as skins, textiles, wood, or feathers, are rarely found in archaeological contexts. We must look for them in museums.

I believe that as fieldwork with living informants yields less and less of unquestionable value to the study of traditional Indian cultures—even as recently as the end of the nineteenth century—ethnologists will turn more appreciatively to museum collections in search for primary source materials.

Even so, the absence of readily usable finding aids may deter all, save the most dedicated and persistent students. And the question of how finding aids can be developed most effectively and economically still remains unsolved. Some advocate putting all the specimens on computers. This would mean cluttering the record, at a tremendous cost, with many undocumented or erroneously attributed pieces.

I am inclined to believe it may be more useful to study the history of collecting in each of the cultural areas, with particular emphasis upon those better documented collections preserved in museums. My studies of the history of collecting among the Plains Indians to date convince me that a history of collecting might also be a contribution to the understanding of an aspect of Indian-white relations in itself. Perhaps we may never know the entire history of collecting in this region, but I am impressed by the number of known collectors between Coronado and the end of the nineteenth century, as well as the information that can be found on why, how, and what they collected.

I have found, for example, that many of the artists who drew or painted Plains Indians in their own country during the nineteenth century made collections of Indian artifacts, which they referred to in developing and detailing their more elaborate works in their studios after they returned home. These studio collections, therefore, must be factors to consider in appraising the works of artists who pictured Indians.

Drawings, paintings, and photographs can be important documents to the history of the Indians and of Indian-white relations. Yet I agree wholeheartedly with the late Robert Taft's statement that "most of us, whether authors or publishers, fail to treat pictures as an integral part of the record of the past and to subject these sources to the same scholarly identification, explanation, and determination of authenticity as we do more familiar materials."[11] Many pictures of Indians cannot stand such scrutiny without revealing the very substantial imaginative element involved in their creation. Yet some of them continue to appear as illustrations for the writings of very reputable historians.[12]

The number and variety of *authentic* pictures of Indians is much greater than most of us know. There were at least one hundred fifty artists who pictured Plains Indians from life before the end of the nineteenth century. Photographers began to catch likenesses of some of these Indians before 1850. Many pictures by little-known artists and photographers depict prominent chiefs and aspects of Indian life not portrayed by their more famous contemporaries.

As is the case with artifacts, the collections of original and authentic drawings, paintings, and photographs of Indians are widely scattered in this country and abroad. Many of these artworks are in private hands and are little known to scholars. Others are in museums of history, science, or art, or in libraries or archives.

During the second half of the nineteenth century the pictorial press in this country and abroad sent competent artist-reporters into the western Indian country to make on-the-spot sketches, which were reworked in the home offices for publication. Some of the originals have been preserved. These talented artists pictured important treaty and council scenes, some aspects of the Indian wars, and scenes of Indian life before and after the Indians were placed upon reservations. They represented not only such popular American magazines as *Harpers* and *Leslies* but also the *Illustrated* London News, the *Graphic* of London, and *Die Gartenlaube* of Munich. These revealing works should remind us that foreigners continued to make contributions to the historic record of the Indians long after the close of the colonial period, and that Americans were not the only people who were fascinated by Indians in more recent times.[13]

Artifacts and Pictures as Documents

C. M. Bell photographing a delegation of Omaha, Ponca, Sioux, and Winnebago Indians for the government in Washington, D.C. From a sketch by A. B. Shults, published in Frank Leslie's Illustrated Weekly, *September 10, 1881, p. 26. (Neg. No. 2860-zz-16, National Museum of Natural History, Smithsonian Institution.)*

If pictorial documents are to become more useful sources for historians, we must have finding aids that reveal what pictures are available and where they may be seen. The Museum of the American Indian, Heye Foundation in New York, has led the way in this direction with its publication of Jeanne O. Snodgrass's very useful compilation of biographical data on more than eleven hundred American Indian artists, with references to the collections in which their works are preserved. Not a few of those artists were active during the nineteenth century. Some of them were employed by anthropologists to picture sacred artifacts that were never collected or ceremonies and other scenes that were never recorded by white artists or photographers.[14]

As yet we have nothing comparable for the many white artists and photographers who pictured Indians, although the task of collecting, compiling, and publishing information on them should be no more complicated than that performed by Snodgrass and the Museum of the American

Indian for the Indian artists, except for the photographers. After the Civil War, nearly every frontier town had its photographer, and many city photographers traveled extensively in the Indian country. The sheer volume of their contribution to the historic record was immense. Much good work has been done on individual artists and photographers. Perhaps the compilation of finding lists could proceed most effectively by region and by period. This task should not be left to one person, but lack of a coordinated effort may lead to much duplication as well as to individual and institutional frustrations.

Artifacts, pictures, and words are the stuff of history left to us long after the deeds have been done and the participants have died. Too many word-minded historians have neglected the artifacts and pictures. Others have been less critical of these documents than they have been of published or unpublished words. It is my hope that in the future all three of these media can be employed constructively in fashioning a history of the American Indians and their relations with non-Indians that will be more inclusive and more insightful as well as more interesting and more comprehensible to everyone.

NOTES

1. René de Brahant de Galinee, "The Journey of Dollier and Galinee, 1669–1670," in *Early Narratives of the Northwest,* ed. Louise Phelps Kellog (New York: Scribner's, 1917), pp. 171–73.
2. W. P. Clark, *The Indian Sign Language* (Philadelphia: L. R. Hammersly & Co., 1885), p. 257.
3. John Brereton, "Briefe and True Relation of the Discoverie of the North Part of Virginia," in *Early English and French Voyages, 1534–1608,* ed. Henry S. Burrage (New York: Scribner's, 1932), pp. 330–31.
4. Beverly B. Moeller, "Captain James Colnett and the Tsimshian Indians, 1787," *Pacific Northwest Quarterly* 57, no. 1 (January 1966): 14–15.
5. Garrick Mallery, "Picture-Writing of the American Indians," *Tenth Annual Report of the Bureau of American Ethnology* (Washington, D.C.: Government Printing Office, 1893), pp. 323, 569.
6. *Second Annual Report of the Commissioner of Indian Affairs for the Year 1870* (Washington, D.C.: Government Printing Office, 1871), pp. 69–70.
7. Charles J. Kappler, *Indian Affairs, Laws and Treaties* 2 (Washington, D.C.: Government Printing Office, 1903), p. 755 ff.
8. Emily Noyes Vanderpoel, *American Lace and Lace-Makers* (New Haven: Yale University Press, 1924), p. 2, plates 10–13.
9. *Third Annual Report of the Regents of the University on the Condition of the State Cabinet of Natural History* (Albany, N.Y.: Weed, Parsons and Co., 1850), p. 94.
10. Alice B. Kehoe, "The Blackfoot Medicine Pipe Ceremony," *Lore* 21, no. 4 (Milwaukee, Wisc.: Milwaukee Public Museum, 1971): 119–25.

11. Quoted in John C. Ewers, "Fact and Fiction in the Documentary Art of the American West," in *The Frontier Re-examined,* ed. John Francis McDermott (Urbana: University of Illinois Press, 1967), p. 81. Taft's own book, *Artists and Illustrators of the Old West, 1850–1900* (New York: Scribner's, 1953), is a model of historical scholarship applied to the study of pictures.
12. For a criticism of the Indian pictures by America's leading nineteenth-century illustrator, see John C. Ewers, "Not Quite Redmen: The Plains Indian Illustrations of Felix O. C. Darley," *American Art Journal* 3, no. 2 (1971): 88–98.
13. Paul Hogarth's *Artists on Horseback* (New York: Watson-Guptill, 1972), is a well-illustrated account of English special artists in the American West between 1870 and 1895.
14. Jeanne O. Snodgrass, *American Indian Painters, A Biographical Dictionary* (New York: Museum of the American Indian, 1968).

Major Indian Record Collections in Oklahoma

Angie Debo

The importance of the Indian record collections in Oklahoma is due to the fact that the state was once an Indian territory, and its history begins not with the "first white settlement" but with the history of the sixty-five or more tribes and fragments of tribes that were settled there from various parts of the United States. The Cherokees, Choctaws, Chickasaws, Creeks, and Seminoles—known as the Five Civilized Tribes to distinguish them from their buffalo-hunting neighbors of the Plains—set up self-governing republics with written constitutions, laws, and courts; comprehensive educational systems; well-defined "foreign" policies; and other institutions that are the stuff of history, and the records were kept in their national archives. The other tribes settled in the Indian Territory had no such official documents, but the files of the federal agencies constituted the story of their development. Thus much history had been recorded in Oklahoma before the first tract was opened to white settlement in 1889.

Typically, the first little Oklahoma history text introduced in the public schools immediately after statehood in 1907 began with the Indian period, and scholarly research and writing followed the same sequence. By the same pattern, every local historical society has collected Indian records but the major collections are at the University of Oklahoma at Norman, the Oklahoma Historical Society at Oklahoma City, and the Thomas Gilcrease Institute of American History and Art at Tulsa.

When James Shannon Buchanan and Edward Everett Dale of the history department of the University of Oklahoma wrote a one-volume history of the state in 1924, they devoted one-third of their space (121 of its 357 pages) to Indian history. Dr. Dale had come to the department in 1914, and it was chiefly through his leadership that the university began systematically to build up its Indian collections. Even before his time it had acquired, from a source now forgotten, the manuscript acts of the General Council (legislature) of the Choctaw Nation. One of Dale's early finds was the discovery of three big trunkfuls of letters (more than two thousand) of the Watie-Ridge-Boudinot family in the garret of a farmhouse in the Cherokee hills. These letters date from 1828 to 1907 and give an inside picture of Cherokee history through the removal period, the ensuing tribal feud, the Civil War, and the white encroachment that finally engulfed the Cherokee Nation. About two hundred of the letters were published by Dale and Gaston Litton under the title *Cherokee Cavaliers*, but the others remain as an unexplored treasure trove of Indian history.

The University of Oklahoma now has approximately forty important collections of Indian records. Most of them are the personal papers of individual chiefs and leaders of the Five Civilized Tribes. They begin with the Reconstruction period following the Civil War and continue down to the liquidation of their governments at the turn of the century. The chiefs' papers include their messages to the councils, official correspondence, proclamations, and directives issued in their losing fight to maintain the tribal integrity. Every one of the Creek chiefs is represented, and all but two or three of the executives of the Cherokees, Choctaws, and Chickasaws. Of the conservative Seminoles, less well known to historians, are the papers of John Jumper, long influential in the government and briefly recognized as principal chief; John F. Brown, son-in-law of Jumper, who was elected chief in 1877 and except for one term served throughout the rest of the tribal period, while at the same time operating an extensive trading house; and Hulbutta Micco, who defeated Brown in 1901 and served as chief until his death in 1905. These papers of chiefs and others refer not only to governmental affairs, but to their personal and business relationships, thus forming a composite picture of tribal society.

There are also the papers of some outstanding missionaries who identified themselves with Indian interests. Other collections consist of letters and letterbooks from military posts in the Indian Territory giving details of the relationship of the federal government with the Plains tribes.

Meanwhile, as the university collections were growing, Grant Foreman, of Muskogee, was writing his scholarly books on the early Indian period in Oklahoma, using original sources at Washington, the Public Record Office in London, and other places. In 1924 he became a member of the board of directors of the Oklahoma Historical Society and began a patient and tireless campaign to make it an official depository of Indian records.

The archives of the Five Civilized Tribes had been kept in their capitols. These consisted of the acts of their councils, messages of their principal chiefs, proceedings of their courts, ballots and election returns (in which the candidates courteously voted for their opponents), county records, census reports, marriage licenses, school reports—all the acts of functioning governments. When these governments were terminated, their papers were deposited with the Union Agency at Muskogee, where they were stored in the attic, outdated for current Indian administration and unavailable to historians.

The accumulated records of the agencies for the other Indian tribes of Oklahoma had also become outdated, and no facilities existed for pre-

A graduating class of the Cherokee Female Seminary, Park Hill, Cherokee Nation, Indian Territory. The school was built by the Cherokee at a cost exceeding $45,000. John Ross, chief of the Cherokee, laid the cornerstone on June 21, 1847. The school opened on May 7, 1851, and burned to the ground on April 10, 1887. (RG 75, No. 75-IP-1-47)

serving them. They were put away in various places—an abandoned barn, the loft of an old warehouse, a coal bin, on top of furnace pipes—and worried agents and superintendents were anxious to have them deposited in a safe place.

Through Foreman's leadership the directors of the Oklahoma Historical Society persuaded the legislature to construct a fireproof building with facilities for storage. Then, mainly through his influence, Congress enacted legislation in 1934 authorizing the removal of the Five Tribes records and the various agency records not in current use to this depository. Thus long before the enactment of the law of 1951 establishing the federal records centers, these official papers found a place in Oklahoma, where they have remained. Only the papers of the Osage Agency are not included.

All of the papers have been expertly organized and calendared. There are approximately 430,000 loose pages and 740 manuscript volumes of Cherokee records, 54,083 pages and 499 volumes of Choctaw records, 17,510 pages and 106 volumes of Chickasaw records, and 55,973 pages and 88 volumes of Creek records. The Seminole records are largely missing—only 228 pages and 12 volumes survive. It is believed that they had been stored in the trading post owned by the Brown family and were lost when the building burned. There are also nineteen filing case drawers of loose papers and 242 volumes of records of the Dawes Commission, which liquidated the affairs of the Five Tribes. There are 2,230,343 pages and 4,505 volumes of the agency records of the other tribes. This makes a total of approximately 2,797,137 pages and 6,169 volumes, plus the nineteen filing case drawers of uncounted pages.

The Five Tribes papers, in particular, give an inside view of these societies. One intriguing item listed in the Cherokee tribal census of 1880 is "Col. W. P. Rogers, native Cherokee, 7 months old, living in the Cooweescoowee District." (Will Rogers was named for Col. William Penn Adair, and according to Indian custom received the title along with the name.) When a Creek man or woman died, the estate, no matter how small, was partitioned by the courts. The judge and two disinterested neighbors rounded up the livestock; counted the fruit trees; listed the cultivated fields, the fence rails, and the buildings; and made an inventory of every dish, chair, hoe, hammer, and farm implement—all the possessions of the deceased. Thus the Creek court records give a complete cross section of social and economic development.

The agency records of the other tribes antedate in some cases their Oklahoma settlement. The Sauk and Fox records begin in Iowa in 1840, then record their experiences in Kansas before they were brought to the Indian Territory in 1867. In the Shawnee Agency files is a letterbook kept at the Tonkawa Agency at Fort Griffin, Texas, from 1873 to 1881 concerning the Lipan Apaches.

Also, like the University of Oklahoma, the Oklahoma Historical Society has many papers of individuals—chiefs and other officials and leaders of the Five Tribes, missionaries, and traders. Often the two collections supplement each other—each may contain a portion of the papers of a given person. This is not as inconvenient as it may seem, for the two institutions are only about twenty miles apart.

One important collection is common to both. In 1937 the Historical Society initiated and sponsored a WPA project using unemployed white collar workers to record the reminiscences of aged Oklahomans. (This was long before Allan Nevins at Columbia started the movement to preserve local history through the memories of living witnesses.) Grant Fore-

Sauk and Fox Day School, Indian Territory [ca. 1880], as identified by the Office of Indian Affairs. (RG 75, No. 75-1P-3-2)

man served as director, and capable interviewers collected the stories. Two copies were made, one for each institution. They comprise 112 volumes of 500 typewritten pages each, and they have been adequately indexed and cross indexed. Many of the informants were Indians, former citizens of the Five Tribes and buffalo hunters of the Plains.

It became strikingly apparent that Indian memory is accurate for a century. (Beyond that period it dissolves into hazy tradition.) Elderly men and women unfamiliar with written history related incidents that accorded exactly with Foreman's scholarly *Indian Removal.* For example, in this book, relying on official documents, he described the Arkansas swamps; an old Indian told of the swamp as his father saw it. "He said it wasn't anything like crossing a small sized swamp for it took them six days before they ever set a step on dry ground. Knolls, higher levels of ground . . . were sought out for sleeping places. . . . My father even told of the time that he once had the luck to find a bone which was the large shoulder blade of some large animal and this he used for a rest for his head." Aged Blacks described the easy servitude of Indian slavery: "I've heard of a slave owner borrowing money from his slave."

The Historical Society also has an extensive collection of newspapers, and several of these periodicals were published by Indians or contain much Indian material. These have also been indexed. And recently a great mass of new material has been acquired by the society—the federal court records of the Indian Territory, beginning in 1889 when the first court was established there and ending with statehood in 1907. Somehow they were dumped in the basement of the county courthouse at Muskogee, where they became water soaked, and then carried to the attic. Early in 1971, through the initiative of some Muskogee attorneys, these records were rescued and given to the Historical Society. They consist of more than two hundred ledgers and probably two hundred fifty separate items, divided into criminal, civil, and probate cases. Some of the criminal and civil cases involved Indians. It is known that one famous trial—of the perpetrators of a lynching where white settlers burned two Seminole youths to death for a crime of which they were clearly innocent—is documented in the records. And it is certain that nearly all the probate cases involve the property of Indian minors, for when the tribal estates were broken up by the Dawes Commission, all the citizens shared equally in the division, and the robbery of Indian children by white guardians became a major racket. These records are not available at present, but in time they will be organized and classified.

The third major Indian record collection in Oklahoma, at the Gilcrease Institute, grew directly out of Indian experience. When the Five Tribes were liquidated and their land holdings were divided, young Thomas Gilcrease, a Creek citizen of one-eighth Indian blood, happened to receive his 160-acre allotment in the area soon to become famous as the Glenn Pool oil field. By the time he was seventeen, there were thirty-two producing wells on his land. Soon he started his own oil operations. This required an office in Europe, and there he began collecting paintings, rare books, and manuscripts, concentrating on Indians and the American West. Eventually, he gave the collection and the building that housed it to the city of Tulsa.

Nearly three-fourths of the manuscript collections relate to Indians. To a certain extent these reflect the interests of the antiquarian rather than those of the archivist. Included are, for example, three priceless copies of Sequoyah's syllabary written by the hand of the Cherokee Cadmus himself. But there are many rare documents depicting Indian history and culture. Unlike the other Oklahoma collections, these are not concentrated on tribes of the area but relate to the changing frontier from Columbus on.

There are reports and letters of English colonial administrators throughout the seventeenth and eighteenth centuries. These include correspondence from Sir William Johnson concerning his dealings with the Iroquois and letters from Sir John Johnson written during the Revolution. There are also records concerning the relations of the new American government with the Indian tribes of the Old Northwest and with the Creeks, beginning in 1782 and continuing through the time of Alexander

McGillivray. Other accounts depict the life and customs of the Cherokees from the early eighteenth century on and the events of the Seminole wars and removal. Letters from Zachary Taylor deal with Indian affairs as he observed them on the frontier; writing from Prairie du Chien in 1836, he expressed his strong sympathy for the Indians and his objections to their removal.

In general these collections are not basic, although they cast light on situations obscurely known and would be useful to scholars doing research in a given period. But some are extensive. In this class are the Foreman papers. These fill eighty-four boxes and contain thousands of pages of transcripts copied by Grant Foreman and his wife, Carolyn Thomas Foreman, a historian in her own right, as they searched through 113 major collections and archives in the United States and foreign countries. They are mainly from the eighteenth- and nineteenth-century records relating to the Indian tribes that were eventually removed to the Indian Territory and constituted the sources of the Foremans' own writing. A vast quantity of the material, however, has never been used.

A few Gilcrease collections form the most important source for a particular field. This is graphically expressed by W. David Baird in his recent biography of Peter P. Pitchlynn, leader in Choctaw affairs throughout much of the nineteenth century. Dr. Baird said, after seeing the twenty-one feet of Pitchlynn papers, "For a historian to locate such a wealth of untapped materials was analogous to [the] discovery of the Comstock Lode," and "I made a resolution then to do a biographical study of the man." His research carried him to many other collections, but the Gilcrease records served as his fundamental source. Another important collection is the John Ross papers, comprising eleven feet of space. They contain the correspondence and proclamations of Ross, who served the Cherokees as principal chief from 1828 to his death in 1866, and many other records of the tribal government. Especially significant are the reports of the various removal detachments on their sorrowful trail from their eastern homeland to the Indian Territory.

The location of the Ross collection at Gilcrease is typical of the division of the major record collections in Oklahoma. The Ross papers and the Watie-Ridge-Boudinot papers, representing the opposing factions in the Cherokee Nation, are in separate depositories at Gilcrease and the University of Oklahoma, respectively, and the bulk of the tribal records is at the Oklahoma Historical Society. In this, as in many other fields of research, the scholar must consult all three collections. But in spite of this inconvenience the Oklahoma collections are rewarding beyond the scope of this brief summary. Not for all aspects of Indian history, but in a surprising number, they must be consulted before a study can be classed as definitive.

The Archives of the Duke Projects in American Indian Oral History

C. Gregory Crampton

For six years seven state universities—Arizona, Florida, Illinois, New Mexico, Oklahoma, South Dakota, and Utah—collected unwritten history from the American Indians. Each of these schools labored as a partner in a coordinated operation funded by Doris Duke of New York. The program, initiated in the last days of 1966, terminated before the end of 1972. The overall objective was to record on tape what the Indians know of their own past and of their relations with whites and other Indians and to assemble their views on American history in general. It is surely obvious to anyone familiar with the sources of American history that projects wherein the Indians have been permitted to reveal their own history have been all too few and too long in coming.

Of course, we do have documents based upon information supplied first hand by the Indians. Sahagun, writing soon after the Spanish conquest of Mexico, based his great multivolume *General History . . . of New Spain* entirely on the oral recitations of the conquered Aztecs. Much original material coming from the Indians of Canada appears in the *Jesuit Relations*. Since the English colonials generated few documents of this sort, we may conclude that they were less interested in the New World natives than their neighbors to the north and south.

The outlines of Indian-white relations in the United States are well known. The Indians were shouldered aside and dispossessed of their land by treaties and otherwise. Many of the tribes were uprooted and moved to reservations at great distances from their ancestral homes. By about 1860, there were only small pockets of Indians living east of the Mississippi River.

The same tragic story was repeated west of the Mississippi. American expansion, stimulated by the gold rush to California, was so rapid that the frontier of free land was all but gone by 1900. The Indians lost out to the miners, farmers, ranchers, and railroads. At times the tribes rose in armed opposition but, seldom able to work out enduring alliances, they were overwhelmed by superior power. The Indians were crowded onto reservations, usually in areas devoid of natural resources, and some of the best of these areas were lost to them under an allotment system where reservation lands were parceled out to individuals and often alienated by them. At least in the western United States the tribes were not removed long distances from their original homes.

Until the 1920s and 1930s, federal policy was predicated on the assumption that the Indians were a doomed people and would disappear eventually. The "vanishing Americans," however, have demonstrated an amazing capacity for survival, and their voice today, among the other "ethnic minorities" in the United States, is clamoring for audience and recognition.

Coming back to the matter of sources bearing on the history of Indian-white relations, the American Indian has always had a small, but appreciative, audience. There are those who have valued the cultural and historical legacy of the tribes and have recognized how much they have enriched the American language, economy, menu, folklore, medicine, dress, music, literature, and the study of anthropology. To Europeans at large the American Indian has been the most interesting of races. Travelers, observers, and scientists have written many papers and books, and a number of important museum collections are found on the Continent.

Indeed, writers have produced voluminous published literature about the American Indians. An examination of the card catalog of any large general library will disclose that holdings on Indians always outnumber those of other minorities. For example, the New York Public Library requires twenty-three drawers to list its holdings on American Indians and only seven to list those on blacks.

The unpublished material relating to the Indians of the United States is equally large. The dimensions of that bulk in the National Archives have been discussed here. Adding to this the holdings of private parties, historical societies, museums, and state archives, it would seem that we have all the basic materials needed to write a complete Indian history of the United States.

But do we? How many titles in the card catalogs were written by Indians? One can find a great deal of miscellany and quite a few biographies. And in the nation's archives rarely are found documents coming first hand from the Indians. By and large, the works are the products of the dominant culture. Much of the bulk of the vast literature focuses on war rather than culture and contributions and lives lived in peace. Much of it is romantic in tone and even mystical, and precious little of it comes from the heart and mind of the Indians.

The writers working with primary material taken at first hand from the Indians were free to read into the facts their own interpretations and to place on them judgments in accord with their own value systems, and more often than not they did so, since adverse criticism could hardly be expected from a generally illiterate minority. Perhaps it was in the nature of things that the views of the victors should prevail in the literature of the conquest. The trouble is, as many Indians will tell you, that the biases of the earlier writers usually show up in the writings of later writers.

But now in the United States the Indians are demanding recognition, a better life, a larger place in the sun, and, appropriately enough, a more balanced treatment in the pages of history. Whites may be able to write a history of the Indians of the United States but that would not be an Indian history of the United States. Where, the historian will ask, are the documents to redress these imbalances? It is in the mountains of material already mentioned, of course, but the revisionists should bring more critical standards to bear on these sources. They will certainly have difficulty in locating collections made systematically on a large scale for the purpose of documenting the Indians' viewpoint.

In this connection one thinks at once of the anthropologists who have long been at work and who have published an astonishing number of monographs based on field studies. We know, however, that many anthropologists persist in ignoring history altogether, and historians may find little of value for their own research in the works of anthropologists. On the other hand, historians have been slow to leave the libraries and the archives and go to the field. They have been content to use the documents others have collected.

Thus the chronicling of Indian-white relations, for example, largely rests upon the documents generated by whites. We have John Smith's side of the affair but not Pocahontas's. One who writes of the anguished hegira of the Delawares must use mainly the white society's sources. Indian authors, I would guess, have contributed less than 5 percent of the titles to the ever-lengthening bibliography on the affair at Little Big Horn. The condition is not altogether one-sided. I am mindful that within the National Archives the historian will find much Indian testimony taken before members of federal investigating committees and commissions. Two examples are the investigations carried out after the Meeker massacre in Colorado and the testimony collected by the Dawes Commission in Oklahoma. But where can one point to any archive of substantial proportions where the Indian is other than a peripheral figure?

The Duke program in Indian oral history is an endeavor in some measure to fill in the serious and lamentable blanks in the documentation of the American past. Located mainly in Indian country, each of the seven Duke projects collected data primarily from the tribes nearby, but in some instances operations have been extended far afield, though not beyond the borders of the United States. Unfortunately, we have not been able to blanket the entire country; in a number of areas—broadly speaking, the northeast and northwest—we have undertaken practically no collecting. A comprehensive national program in Indian oral history, one which the federal government might well undertake, has not been possible with the funds provided. However, the Indian public and the scholarly world will be lastingly indebted to Doris Duke for the generous support of a program of lasting national significance.

The magnitude of the collections will be reflected in a few statistics. These totals include the collections of the seven projects and they are closely approximate: 9,500 hours of tape have been recorded, representing 5,400 interviews (25 percent of which are in native languages) and 130 tribes, bands, and groups, which are listed at the end of this paper as Table B. Reservations and rural Indians account for most of these figures, but substantial collections were made in the cities—notably Los Angeles, San Francisco, Denver, and Chicago—and on some college and university campuses.

The first question one might ask is of what value this mass of material will be to historians and other researchers. This can only be determined as the documents are used by serious students, at which time their value will become apparent. In general, we have found that there are few long discourses on historical matters, but there are occasional nuggets that reveal valuable bits and pieces not known before. Little information is precisely stated, especially when the subject matters extend beyond the lifetime of the informant.

Subject matter coverage of the projects varies widely. Much of the material is heavily autobiographical, but this is a characteristic of most collections of oral history. While we have sought historical information, both old and young—particularly the young—informants are inclined to dwell upon the problems faced by Indians living in American society. We recognize this as important contemporary history, and we also recognize that the most valuable, and most easily verifiable, information is obtained when individuals speak from their own experiences. We regard the Utah project tapes cut by urban and college Indians as some of our best.

Legends, stories, tales, traditions, and ceremonies are very large in bulk, and family histories are common. A wide variety of ethnological information, ranging from drying blueberries to scalp dancing, appears prominently in all the collections. The historian of the future, the sociologist, social worker, educator, government employee, and the Indians themselves will find much specific information on tribal government, intertribal affairs, factionalism, education, matters of health, problems of acculturation and adjustment, and of relations with non-Indians.

What of validity? Oral history is the raw source, the primary document. And it is the obligation of scholars to apply the accepted standards of criticism to any documents they use. Fieldworkers on the Duke projects, for the most part, have been trained in the art of oral history, and they have been concerned primarily with the collection of significant documents, not with the utilization of the documents. Verification of factual data must rest with the scholarly investigator, difficult as this may be coming as it does mostly from unknown authors.

For those who may be interested in using the Duke collections in Indian oral history, each archive will remain in the custody of the collecting institution—usually in the university library. The formation of a central archive is not contemplated. In the near future it is quite likely that some portions (those where adequate releases have been obtained) will be brought into the *New York Times* Oral History Program and published on microfilm. Preliminary catalogs have been issued for nearly all of the projects, and it is contemplated that a complete analytical catalog will be published for each project. Furthermore, to facilitate use of the collections, taped material is being fully translated and transcribed. As a general guide, the material collected is primarily from the tribes living within the region of each project.

Scholars, the Indian public, and others are beginning to use the collections. A book edited by Joseph H. Cash and Herbert T. Hoover, *To Be an Indian* (1971), was the first to appear based wholly on the Duke materials. Those of us who have labored in the program know that, although collecting has now stopped, we have scarcely begun a work long overdue. But even so, the archives now at hand constitute an unparalleled source of American Indian history of enduring significance to the world of scholarship.

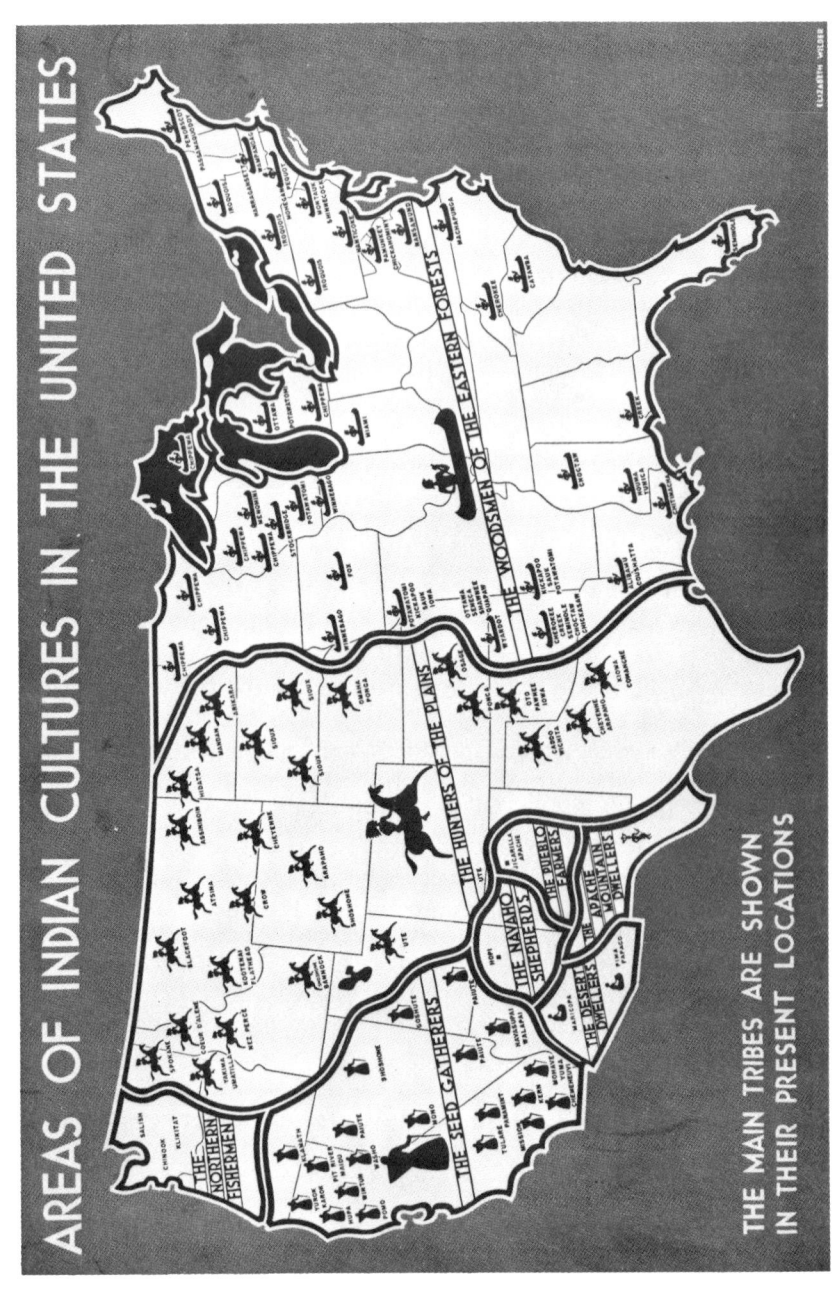

Map prepared for the Indian Exhibit at the Golden Gate International Exposition held in San Francisco, California, in 1939. (Records of the Indian Arts and Crafts Board, RG 435)

Table A

The Duke Archives in American Indian Oral History

The materials collected by the several Duke projects in Indian oral history will remain permanently in the custody of the universities involved. Inquiry concerning the use of these archives should be addressed to the departments listed below.

ARIZONA	Curator, Arizona State Museum University of Arizona Tucson, Arizona 85721
FLORIDA	Chairman, Department of History University of Florida Gainesville, Florida 32601
ILLINOIS	Chairman, Department of Anthropology University of Illinois 109 Davenport Hall Urbana, Illionis 61801
NEW MEXICO	Chairman, Department of History University of New Mexico Albuquerque, New Mexico 87106

OKLAHOMA	Director, Indian Programs The American Indian Institute University of Oklahoma Norman, Oklahoma 73069
SOUTH DAKOTA	Director, American Indian Research Project University of South Dakota Vermillion, South Dakota 57069
UTAH	Curator, Western Americana Division Marriott Library The University of Utah Salt Lake City, Utah 84112

Table B

The Duke Projects in Indian Oral History Collections: Tribes Represented

Acoma
Aleut
  East
  West
Apache
Arapaho
Arikara
Atna
Bannock

Blackfoot
Caddo
Cahuilla
Cayuga
Chemehuevi
Cherokee
Cheyenne
Chickasaw

Chippewa
  Leech Lake
  Mille Lacs
  Red Lake
  White Earth
Choctaw
Clallam
  Elwah
  Jamestown

Little Boston
Cochiti
Cocopa
Coeur d'Alène
Comanche
Cree
Crow
Cuna
Delaware
Diegueno
Eastern Cherokee
Flathead
Florida Indian
Fox
Fort Sill Apache
Genizaro
Gosiute
Gros Ventre
Haida
Halchidome
Havasupai
Hidatsa
Highland Chontal
Hitchiti
Hopi
Hopi-Tewa
Hualapai
Iowa
Isleta
Jemez
Jemez-Santa Clara
Kalispel
Keres
Kickapoo
Kiowa
Kiowa Apache

Koyukon
Kwakiutl
Laguna
Luiseno
Lumbees
Makah
Mandan
Maricopa
Miami
Mojave
Muskogee
   Creek
Nambe
Narragansett
Navajo
Northern Cheyenne
Northern Eskimo
Nunamiut
Osage
Oto
Ottawa
Paiute
Papago
Pawnee
Peoria
Picuris
Pima
   Alto
   Bajo
Plains Cree
Point Barrow Eskimo
Pojoaque
Ponca
Potawatomi
Quapaw
Salish
Sandia

San Felipe
San Juan
Santa Ana
Santa Clara
Santo Domingo
Sauk
Seneca
Shawnee
Shoshoni
Sioux
   Hunkpapa
   Oglala
   Rosebud
   Santee
   Standing Rock
   Yankton
Spokan
Swinomish
Taos
Tesuque
Tigua
Tillamook
Tiwa
Tlingit
Towa
Tutchone
Ute
Western Apache
Western Eskimo
Wichita
Winnebago
Wyandot
Yakima
Yaqui
Yavapai
Zia
Zuñi

DISCUSSION NOTE

David L. Shaul, a Smithsonian Institution fellow, asked Angie Debo if the Oklahoma depositories contained extensive linguistic collections for tribes other than those of the Five Civilized Tribes. Debo replied that her knowledge of records in tribal languages was relatively limited, but she knew from personal research that some of the records relating to the Creek Nation were written in the Creek language. Omer C. Stewart, University of Colorado, commented that he had recently done research at the three institutions mentioned in Debo's paper. They were most cooperative, and he found many documents that, so far as he could determine, had not been used by other scholars.

IV

The Role of the Military

INTRODUCTION
Robert G. Athearn

The following essay is by Robert Utley of the National Park Service who, over the years, has written a considerable amount of material concerning Indian-military relationships on the Plains. The commentary is by Richard Ellis of the University of New Mexico. He is also involved in this particular aspect of Plains history and has written a fine book on General Pope dealing with the subject.

We have had so much written about bugles and cavalry charges that we tend to forget that frontier warfare consisted to a large extent of much waiting and little fighting. There must have been many, many people on the frontier who never heard a shot fired in anger or malice or under battle conditions. From my own study of the forts of the Upper Missouri, I learned of the boredom of garrison duty. The soldiers were more or less marooned. They worried about scurvy, and they worried about trying to stay alive under Plains conditions. Much of garrison life was just boredom and staying inside, away from the Indians. Of course, they worried about Indians, but they did not go out and hunt very hard for them. I imagine that many of the soldiers rarely saw an Indian.

I think there is a great deal yet to be done on the army's nonfighting role on the frontier. It accomplished a number of things in a noncombatant role, not all of which concerned the Indians. But with regard to the Indians, often the post doctor or some of the officers were very much interested in anthropology and ethnology and the collecting of artifacts. And the soldiers were curious about the Indians—I was surprised to find a general lack of animus on their part toward the Indians. It is this view of the military that is presented in these papers.

The Frontier Army: John Ford or Arthur Penn?

Robert M. Utley

In the climactic scene of John Ford's motion picture "Fort Apache," a 1947 release, cavalry officer John Wayne philosophizes on the courage, stamina, skill, and carefree, jocular nature of the regular army troopers who conquered the American West and opened it to civilization. A cavalry column with banners flying marches in silhouette against a desert sunrise as swelling music proclaims the majesty and grandeur of their contribution to the epic of America. With such stirring scenes Ford shaped a whole generation's conception of the frontier army. In a recent television tribute to Ford, John Wayne conceded that the master was not above perpetuating legends, consoling himself that if this was not exactly the way it happened, it was the way it ought to have happened.

Arthur Penn admits no such distortion in the portrayal of the frontier army that unfolds in his 1971 film "Little Big Man." Brutish soldiers rampage about the West gleefully slaughtering peaceable Indians and taking special delight in shooting down helpless women and children. This and similar films, such as "Soldier Blue," perpetuate a characterization increasingly evident in the growing body of literature that expresses the white society's guilt over its historic treatment of the Indian. For modern America, this ugly stereotype has all but replaced the heroic stereotype of John Ford's generation.

Both stereotypes sprang from nineteenth-century origins. In large measure Ford's view is the frontier army's self-image. It is to be found in the writings of officers such as Miles, Custer, Forsyth, Bourke, Price, Rodenbough, Parker, and Carter;[1] of officers' wives such as Elizabeth Custer, Ellen McG. Biddle, Martha Summerhayes, and Mrs. Orsemus B.

Boyd;[2] and of friendly newsmen such as John F. Finerty.[3] It is to be glimpsed in the art of Frederic Remington and Charles Schreyvogel. Above all, it is to be credited to Capt. Charles King, who in dozens of novels reinforced the army's view of itself. King summed it up years later in an address to Indian war veterans:

> It is all a memory now, but what a memory, to cherish! . . . A more thankless task, a more perilous service, a more exacting test of leadership, morale and discipline no army in Christendom has ever been called upon to undertake than that which for eighty years was the lot of the little fighting force of regulars who cleared the way across the continent for the emigrant and settler.[4]

Similarly, Arthur Penn's vision in "Little Big Man" conveys to modern audiences the picture of the army seen by much of the humanitarian community in the last half of the nineteenth century. Antislavery leaders such as Wendell Phillips and William Lloyd Garrison turned energies liberated by the Emancipation Proclamation to a crusade in behalf of the Native Americans, and the army felt the sting of rhetoric sharpened in the long war against the slavocracy. "I only know the names of three savages upon the Plains," declared Phillips in 1870, "Colonel Baker, General Custer, and at the head of all, General Sheridan." Baker's assault on a Piegan village in 1870 inspired a verse that typified the humanitarian stereotype of the army:

> Women and babes shrieking awoke
> To perish 'mid the battle smoke,
> Murdered, or turned out there to die
> Beneath the stern, gray, wintry sky.[5]

Evidence can be marshaled to support or contradict both of these extreme interpretations. Neither faithfully represents the whole. Just as campaigning troopers sported both black hats and white hats, and any other hue that suited their fancy, so a fair appraisal of the Indian-fighting army must acknowledge a mix of wisdom and stupidity, of humanity and barbarism, of selfless dedication and mindless indifference, of achievement and failure, of triumph and tragedy, but above all—as in most human institutions—of contradictions and ambiguities. To give the frontier army a characterization that strikes a proper balance between John Ford and Arthur Penn is the purpose of this paper.

Central to such an assessment is a basic truth that is rarely emphasized in modern literature and that eluded most of the nation's top soldiers of the nineteenth century. The United States Army was not so much a little

The Frontier Army

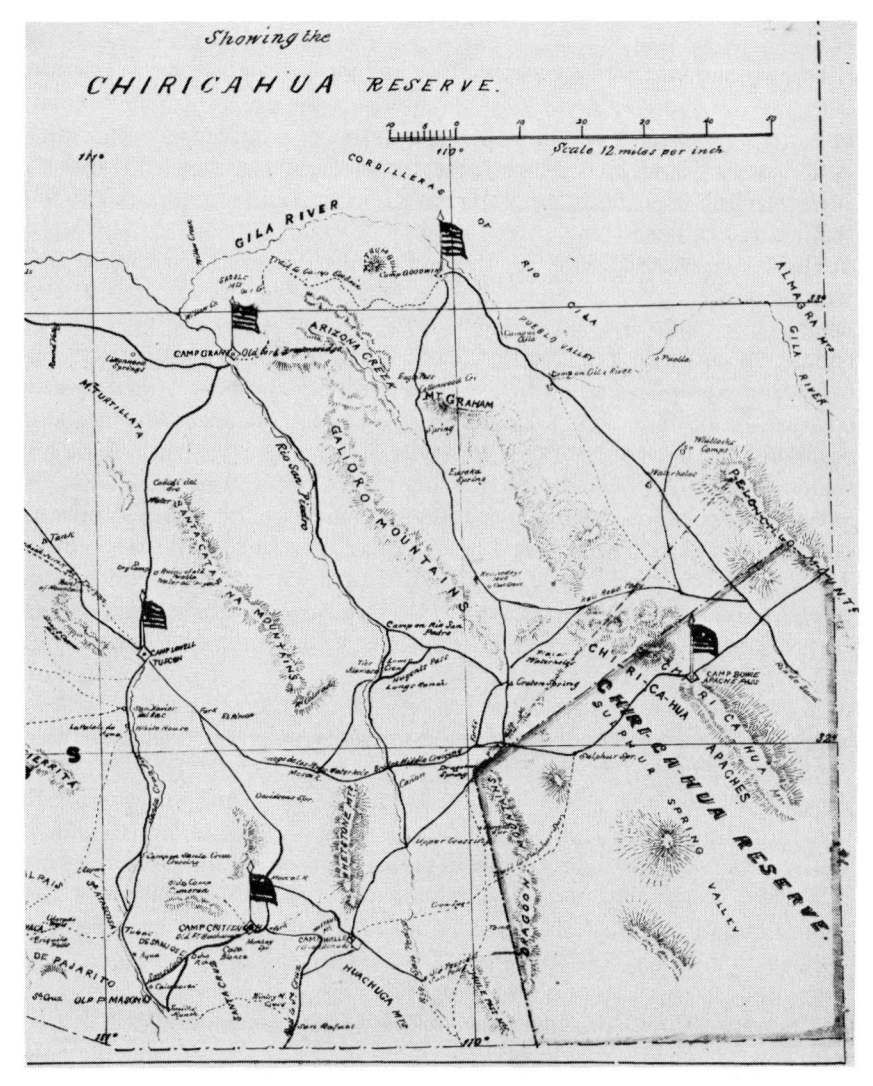

Detail of a map of the southeastern corner of Arizona Territory showing the reservation created in 1872 for Cochise and his band of Chiricahua Apache. The number of military establishments located in this relatively small area clearly indicates the unsettled conditions in the territory. Gen. Oliver Otis Howard ended thirteen years of intermittent warfare with the Chiricahua when he and Cochise's trusted friend, Tom Jeffords, persuaded the chief to settle on the reserve. With Jeffords as their agent, the Chiricahua kept the peace with their Arizona neighbors until 1876 when the Office of Indian Affairs decided to remove them to the San Carlos Reservation to join the other groups of Apaches concentrated there. Two-thirds of the Chiricahua resisted the move, some seeking refuge with Apaches in New Mexico Territory, others fleeing into the Mexican state of Sonora. Among the latter group was Geronimo. (RG 75, Central Map File, 392)

army as a big police force. Scattered in tiny contingents through the frontier regions, it was charged with watching over the Indians and punishing those who declined to do the Great Father's bidding. The regulars had other missions too, such as coast defense, wilderness exploration, public works, and civil disturbance, but except for four conventional wars it found its principal employment for more than a century in policing the Indian frontier.

Three special conditions set this police mission apart from more conventional military assignments. First, it pitted the army against an enemy who did not fight in conventional ways. Second, it was directed at an enemy who usually could not be clearly identified and differentiated from tribesmen not disposed at the moment to be enemies. And third, it charged the soldiers with policing a native people that aroused conflicting emotions. Such considerations, it may be noted parenthetically, were not the unique burden of the United States Army in the American West. In varying proportion, the military forces of most of the imperial powers encountered like complications in fixing colonial rule on the peoples of Africa, Asia, and the Pacific, and there are parallels in the recent American experience in Vietnam. In the army's response to these three conditions of its western assignment may be discerned its distinctive character.

As a first condition of its police mission, the army confronted a militarily unconventional enemy. Most officers clearly recognized their foe as unconventional both in the techniques and aims of warfare. Their writings abound in admiring descriptions of his cunning, stealth, horsemanship, agility and endurance, skill with weapons, mobility, and exploitation of the natural habitat for military advantage.[6] Characterization of the Plains warriors as the finest light cavalry in the world attained the proportions of a cliché.[7] Some officers also perceived the military implications of the value system that gave motivation and direction to Indian warfare. The Indians' reluctance to fight unless favored by overwhelming odds, for example, or the part that plundering raids played in their scheme of military honors, prompted frequent mention by army commentators.[8]

Yet if the officers recognized the Indian as a master of guerrilla warfare, the army as an institution never acted on that recognition. It remained throughout the nineteenth century a conventional army awaiting the next conventional war. No military school or training program, no tactics manual, and very little professional literature provided guidance on how to fight or treat with Indians. Indeed, the senior major general advised a congressional committee in 1876 that the Indian service of the army was "entitled to no weight" in determining the proper strength, composition, and organization of the peacetime army.[9]

Designed for one task and assigned another, the army performed neither with outstanding success. Indian service, scattering units widely in little one- and two-company forts, unfitted the army for conventional war, as became painfully evident in 1812, 1846, 1861, and 1898. Lacking a formal body of doctrine for unconventional war, moreover, the army waged conventional war against the Indians. Heavy columns of infantry and cavalry, locked to slow-moving supply trains, crawled about the vast western distances in search of Indians who could scatter and vanish almost instantly. One officer compared such an expedition to a dog fastened by a chain: "within the length of chain irresistible, beyond it powerless. The chain was its wagon train and supplies."[10] Conventional tactics sometimes worked, by smashing a village whose inhabitants had grown careless or by wearing out a quarry with persistent campaigning that made surrender preferable to constant fatigue and insecurity. Such tactics, commanders quickly discovered, succeeded more readily in the winter, when Indians could not move easily or rapidly and when they were less alert to danger. But most offensives of this character merely broke down the grain-fed cavalry horses and ended with the troops devoting as much effort to keeping themselves supplied as to chasing Indians. The campaign of 1876 following the Custer disaster is a classic example.

That the army as an institution never elaborated and applied a doctrine of Indian warfare does not mean that it contained no officers capable of breaking free of conventional thought. The most original thinker was Gen. George Crook, who advocated heavy reliance on mule trains as the means of achieving mobility and who saw the conquest of the Indian as ultimately dependent upon pitting Indian against Indian. Army organization provided for Indian scouts, but Crook's concept went considerably beyond their use as guides and trailers. "To polish a diamond there is nothing like its own dust," he explained to a reporter in 1886:

> It is the same with these fellows. Nothing breaks them up like turning their own people against them. They don't fear the white soldiers, whom they easily surpass in the peculiar style of warfare which they force upon us, but put upon their trail an enemy of their own blood, an enemy as tireless, as foxy, and as stealthy and familiar with the country as they themselves, and it breaks them all up. It is not merely a question of catching them better with Indians, but of a broader and more enduring aim—their disintegration.[11]

Although Indian auxiliaries were occasionally employed in strong force with good effect, the idea never won wide acceptance or official support.

Much of the army's bad press sprang from the second condition of the police mission—the bewildering rapidity with which Indians changed from friend to foe to neutral, and the near impossibility of distinguishing one from another. The common response to the problem was to declare all Indians on a reservation or other designated tract of territory peaceful and all off it hostile. This seldom worked, since for any of a variety of causes hostiles might be within the safe zone and peacefuls outside it. Further complicating the problem, both kinds were often mixed together in the same group.

Thus the army suffered the torments of warring on people that some said were peaceful and others said were hostile but that in truth could almost never be neatly categorized as either. Custer's attack on Black Kettle's Cheyenne village at the Washita in 1868 is a case in point. Black Kettle and his associates wanted peace and were making sincere efforts to comply with government directives. But the young men favored war; a war party had returned from a raid on Kansas settlements only the night before, and the village contained four white captives. Was it peaceful or hostile?[12] The Washita set off an explosion of humanitarian protests. Yet to have spared Black Kettle's village would have provoked a comparable protest from settlers whose neighbors had been robbed and killed by his young men. As General Sherman complained in 1867: "It is a grievous wrong to force our soldiers into the unnatural attitude in which they now stand, when the people of the frontier universally declare the Indians to be at war, and the Indian commissioners and agents pronounce them at peace, leaving us in the gap to be abused by both parties."[13]

Closely related problems grew out of the differing relationships in which the police mission cast soldier and Indian. Soldiers who had witnessed the plunder, rape, torture, and mutilation of Indian hostilities had no difficulty viewing the adversary as a savage beast. Yet between conflicts, troops and Indians mingled with enough familiarity to reveal dimensions of Indian character that a white man could find fascinating and even admirable and to disclose something of the injustice, deceit, fraud, and cruelty the Indian endured from government officials and frontier citizens.

Ambivalence, therefore, marked military attitudes toward the Indians —fear, distrust, loathing, contempt, and condescension on the one hand; curiosity, admiration, sympathy, and even friendship on the other. Most of the officers who wrote for publication, and the wives too, apparently recognized no inconsistency in characterizing the Indians as ferocious wild animals bereft of any human emotion and in the same book describing their customs as well as individual personalities in sympathetic, if patronizing, terms.

The memoirs of a veteran of Apache service afford a revealing glimpse of this ambivalence. "Exasperated, our senses blunted by Indian atrocities," he wrote, "we hunted and killed them as we hunted and killed wolves." Yet after serving for a time with Apache scouts, he confessed: "My feelings toward them began to change. That ill-defined impression

GENERAL ORDER, }
No. 2.   Fort Washakie Wyo., February 22, 1900.

1. With sorrow is announced the death of WASHAKIE. For fifty years, as Chief of the Shoshones, he has held the confidence and love of his tribe. His friendship for the whites began with their earliest settlements in this section almost that long ago. WASHAKIE was born in the early years of 1800, so his life covered almost a century with its changes. His great influence preserved his tribe not only a friend but an ally of our people in their struggles here. It was his pride that he had never allowed a white man's blood to be shed when he could prevent it.

WASHAKIE was of commanding presence and his resemblance in face to Washington often remarked. His countenance was one of rugged strength mingled with kindness. His military service is an unbroken record for gallantry, and officers now wearing a star fought with him in their subaltern days. The respect and friendship of these former commanders was prized to the day of his death. WASHAKIE was a great man, for he was a brave man and a good man. The spirit of his loyalty and courage will speak to soldiers; the memory of his love for his own people will linger to assist them in their troubles, and he will never be forgotten so long as the mountains and streams of Wyoming which were his home, bear his name.

His last request was a Christian burial in the Post Cemetery with the soldiers who were his friends.

The Post Commander directs that WASHAKIE be buried with military honors in the Post Cemetery at 2:00 P. M. to morrow and that a copy of this order announcing his death be mailed to officers under whom he served the government.

BY ORDER OF
CLOUGH OVERTON,
1st. Lieutenant 1st Cavalry, Commanding Post.

AUBREY LIPPINCOTT,
2nd, Lieutenant 1st Cavalry Adjutant.

A "General Order" commemorating the long and close friendship between Washakie, chief of the Shoshoni, inset, and the military establishment. The agent for the Shoshoni reported that Washakie's funeral was attended by "a large concourse of people—the largest ever seen in this country." (RG 75, 13725-1900; photograph 111-SC-83537) that they were something a little better than animals but not quite human; . . . the feeling that there could be no possible ground upon which we could meet as man to man, passed away."[14]

Against the familiar picture of cavalry storming through a village cutting down fleeing Indians must be balanced the army's long and creditable record as defender of the Indian. A memorable illustration is the battle of Generals Howard and Crook against the deportation of the Chiricahua Apaches to Florida after the surrender of Geronimo in 1886.[15] Another is Gen. Nelson A. Miles's advocacy of Chief Joseph's cause after the Nez Percé surrender in 1877.[16] General Pope eloquently, if verbosely, assailed the inequities of federal Indian policy for more than three decades.[17] The performance as Indian agents of such officers as Adna R. Chaffee, Ezra P. Ewers, and George M. Randall revealed the army in a notably humanitarian stance. "Oh, where is my friend Randall—the captain with the big mustache which he always pulled?" an Apache chief asked about a former agent. "When he promised a thing he did it."[18]

A generalization that acknowledges such contradictions is difficult, but it seems fair to characterize the attitude of the officer corps toward the Indian as dominantly one of qualified humanitarianism. Most of the officers were humanitarians in viewing the Indians as human beings, in understanding at least the surface manifestations of the ethnic disaster overtaking them, in seeking ways to ameliorate their suffering, and in striving to deal with them honorably and justly. But their humanitarianism was always limited by ethnocentrism. Indians were indeed humans, but inferior humans. Their culture was interesting to study but—except in occasional flashes of nostalgia—unworthy of preservation. They must yield to the extent necessary for the higher purpose of peopling the continent with a race that could fully exploit its treasures. Their salvation lay in becoming part of that race by adopting its values, institutions, and technology—in short, by transforming themselves into Christian tillers of the soil.

It was this impulse to civilize, not an impulse to exterminate, that dominated military attitudes in the nineteenth century as it dominated public sentiment and government policy, and that belies the modern conventional wisdom that the United States pursued a policy of genocide toward the Indians. Certain pronouncements of military leaders, notably Sherman and Sheridan, sound like exterminationism.[19] But closer examination reveals most such assertions to have been addressed not to the Indian race as a whole but only to those portions of it that defied the government's will. Genocide is the systematic obliteration of a whole people. Many officers, it is true, believed extinction to be the Indians' ordained fate;[20] but few advocated or attempted to bring it about by any means other than those implicit in programs aimed at assimilation. Genocide was not the result either. There are now twice as many Indians as a century ago.

But against those tribes or bands that resisted, the army undeniably practiced total war. Warriors rarely allowed themselves to be drawn into battle unless caught in their villages, and in such encounters women and children were nearly always present. They mingled with the fighting men, often themselves fought, and in the confusion and excitement of battle were difficult to identify as noncombatants. Bluewater, Sand Creek, Washita, the Baker Battle, and Wounded Knee yielded especially graphic scenes of slaughter and are often characterized as massacres. In dozens of other engagements as well, women and children fell victim to army bullets.

A judgment of the army's record in this regard must take account of intent as well as result. In at least two instances, the killing of women and children seems to have been a matter of planned, deliberate intent by the commander—Sand Creek and Remolino. Sand Creek, in 1864, was the work of short-term volunteers with exterminationist attitudes led by a fanatical militia colonel. Remolino, climax of Ranald Mackenzie's famed "raid" of 1873 into Mexico to crush Kickapoo marauders, was mounted upon receipt of intelligence that most of the fighting men had left their village.[21] Conceding a few such instances of purposeful slaughter, conceding instances of deliberate or careless killing of noncombatants by individual soldiers, and conceding instances in which commanders failed to take proper precautions, it is still clear that most officers tried hard to spare women and children. Even Wounded Knee, which took the lives of at least sixty-two women and children, discloses extraordinary efforts to avoid harming them.[22] The officer corps subscribed to a Sir Walter Scott code of chivalry that exalted womanhood. Although perhaps not embracing Indian womanhood, it nevertheless held in contempt the mistreatment of any women. In the overwhelming majority of actions, the army shot noncombatants incidentally and accidentally, not purposefully. The result is to be abhorred, but the contrary intent should be noted.

But what of the morality of a strategy aimed at finding and destroying Indian villages where women and children would unquestionably be present and suffer death or injury? This is a question not to be asked of the Indian wars alone but of all the conflicts in which war has been waged on whole populations. Whether, as General Sherman contended, such warfare is in the end more humane because more speedily and definitively ended may be argued at length. The significant point in the present context is that Sherman's strategy for the conquest of the Indians was as moral, or immoral, as his march across Georgia in the Civil War or as the leveling of cities from ground and air in World War II and Vietnam. The frontier army cannot properly be singled out for special condemnation.

The ethical questions implicit in the style of war against the Indians are less appropriate to a characterization of the frontier army than to a discussion of the whole sweep of the nation's military history and tradition.

The frontier army was not, as it saw itself, the heroic vanguard of civilization, crushing the savages and opening the West to settlers. For the most part, the settlers managed that task themselves. Still less was the frontier army the barbaric band of butchers, eternally waging unjust war against unoffending Indians, that is depicted in the humanitarian literature of the nineteenth century and the atonement literature of the twentieth. Both John Ford and Arthur Penn transformed a few small truths about the frontier army into the whole truth, and both, thereby, perpetuated a falsehood.

Rather, the frontier army was a conventional military force trying to control, by conventional military methods, a people that did not behave like conventional enemies and, indeed, quite often were not enemies at all. Usually, the situation did not call for warfare, merely for policing. That is, offending individuals needed to be separated from the innocent and punished. But this the conventional force was unable to do. As a result, punishment often fell, when it fell at all, on guilty and innocent alike.

Had the nation's leadership understood and acted on the lessons of General Crook's experience, the army might have played a more significant role in the westward movement, and one less vulnerable to criticism. An Indian auxiliary force might have been developed with a capability of differentiating between guilty and innocent and, employing the Indian's own fighting style, of effectively contending with the guilty. Indian units were indeed developed, but never on a scale and with a continuity to permit the full effect to be demonstrated. Such an Indian force would have differed from the reservation police, which in fact did remarkably well considering their limitations.[23] It would have been larger, better equipped, and less influenced by the vagaries of the partisan and patronage politics that afflicted the Indian Bureau. Above all, it would have been led by a cadre of carefully chosen officers imbued with a sense of mission and experienced in Indian relations—the kind of officers artist Fredric Remington said were not so much "Indian-fighters" as "Indian-thinkers."[24] How different might have been the history of the westward movement had such a paramilitary force been created and employed in place of the regular army line.

Instead, the regular army composed but one of those groups of pioneers that an observer like Frederick Jackson Turner, taking an imaginary station at South Pass, might have watched pushing the frontier westward. (Actually, Turner did not even mention the bluecoats in the procession that passed before his mind's eye.) Although the army may be credited with precipitating the final collapse of most of the Indian tribes, other frontier settlers—trappers, traders, miners, ranchers, farmers, railroad builders, and merchants—share largely in the process that led to the collapse. They, rather than the soliders, deprived the Indians of the land and the sustenance that left them no alternative to collapse. In this perspective, and divested of John Ford's romanticism and Arthur Penn's grotesque perversion, the frontier army finds its proper character.

NOTES

1. Nelson A. Miles, *Personal Recollections and Observations* (Chicago: Werner Co., 1896); idem, *Serving the Republic* (New York: Harper & Bros., 1911); George A. Custer, *My Life on the Plains, or Personal Experiences with Indians* (New York: Sheldon and Co., 1874); George A. Forsyth, *The Story of the Soldier* (New York: D. Appleton and Co., 1900); idem, *Thrilling Days of Army Life* (New York: Harper & Bros., 1902); John G. Bourke, *On the Border with Crook* (Chicago: Scribner's, 1891); George F. Price, *Across the Continent with the Fifth Cavalry* (1883; reprint ed., New York: Antiquarian Press, 1959); Theo. F. Rodenbough, comp., *From Everglade to Cañon with the Second Dragoons . . . . 1836-1875* (New York: D. Van Nostrand, 1875); Rodenbough and William L. Haskins, eds., *The Army of the United States* (New York: Maynard, Merrill & Co., 1896); James Parker, *The Old Army Memories, 1872-1918* (Philadelphia: Dorrance & Co., 1929); William H. Carter, *Old Army Sketches* (Baltimore: The Lord Baltimore Press, 1906); idem, *From Yorktown to Santiago with the Sixth U.S. Cavalry* (Baltimore: The Friedenwald Co., 1900).
2. Elizabeth B. Custer, *Boots and Saddles, or, Life in Dakota with General Custer* (New York: Harper & Bros., 1885); idem, *Following the Guidon* (New York: Harper & Bros., 1890); idem, *Tenting on the Plains, or, Gen'l Custer in Kansas and Texas* (New York: C. L. Webster & Co., 1893); Ellen McG. Biddle, *Reminiscences of a Soldier's Wife* (Philadelphia: Press of J.B. Lippincott Co., 1907); Martha Summerhayes, *Vanished Arizona: Recollections of the Army Life of a New England Woman* (Salem, Mass.: The Salem Press, 1911); Mrs. Orsemus B. Boyd, *Cavalry Life in Tent and Field* (New York: J. S. Tait & Sons, 1894).
3. John F. Finerty, *War-Path and Bivouac, or the Conquest of the Sioux* (1890; reprint ed., Norman: University of Oklahoma Press, 1962).
4. Quoted in Robert G. Carter, *On the Border with Mackenzie* (1935; reprint ed., New York: Antiquarian Press, 1961), pp. 46–47. For a sketch of King see Don Russell's introduction to King's *Campaigning with Crook* (Western Frontier Library ed., Norman: University of Oklahoma Press, 1964), pp. vii-xxii. See also Russell's *Captain Charles King, Chronicler of the Frontier,* Westerners Brand Book 9 (Chicago, March 1952): 1-3, 7-8, which lists all sixty-nine of King's books.
5. Quoted in Robert Winston Mardock, *The Reformers and the American Indian*

(Columbia: University of Missouri Press, 1971), p. 69. This study admirably describes the humanitarian viewpoint and the literature expressing it.
6. See especially Custer, *Life on the Plains;* and George Crook, "The Apache Problem," *Journal of the Military Service Institution of the United States* 7 (1886): 257–69.
7. See for example Col. Wesley Merritt in *Army and Navy Journal* 15 (4 May 1878): 628.
8. Especially notable insights appear in John C. Cremony, *Life among the Apaches* (San Francisco: A. Roman & Co., 1868); and Lucille M. Kane, trans. and ed., *Military Life in Dakota: The Journal of Philippe Régis De Trobriand* (St. Paul, Minn.: Alvord Memorial Commission, 1951).
9. Maj. Gen. Winfield Scott Hancock to Secretary of War, 19 October 1876, U.S., Congress, House, *Miscellaneous Document No. 56,* 45th Cong., 2d sess., Serial 1818, p. 5.
10. Maj. G. W. Baird, "General Miles's Indian Campaigns," *Century Magazine* 42 (July 1891): 351.
11. Charles F. Lummis, *General Crook and the Apache Wars* (Flagstaff, Ariz.: Northland Press, 1966), p. 17. This is a series of articles correspondent Lummis wrote for the *Los Angeles Times* during the Geronimo campaign of 1886.
12. See especially William H. Leckie, *The Military Conquest of the Southern Plains* (Norman: University of Oklahoma Press, 1963), chap. 4; Donald J. Berthrong, *The Southern Cheyennes* (Norman: University of Oklahoma Press, 1963), chaps. 13–14; and W. S. Nye, *Carbine and Lance: The Story of Old Fort Sill* (Norman: University of Oklahoma Press, 1937), chaps. 4–5.
13. U.S., Congress, House, *Annual Report of the Secretary of War, 1867,* Executive Document No. 1, 40th Cong., 2d sess., Serial 1324, p. 67.
14. Britton Davis, *The Truth about Geronimo* (New Haven: Yale University Press, 1929), pp. 50, 111.
15. Martin F. Schmitt, ed., *General George Crook: His Autobiography* (Norman: University of Oklahoma Press, 1946), pp. 289–300. See also Herbert Welsh, *The Apache Prisoners at Fort Marion, St. Augustine, Florida* (Philadelphia: Indian Rights Association, 1887).
16. Alvin Josephy, *The Nez Percé Indians and the Opening of the Northwest* (New Haven: Yale University Press, 1965), p. 634 ff.
17. Richard N. Ellis, *General Pope and U.S. Indian Policy* (Albuquerque: University of New Mexico Press, 1970).
18. Bourke, *On the Border with Crook,* p. 436. See also William H. Carter, *The Life of Lieutenant General Chaffee* (Chicago: University of Chicago Press, 1917), chap. 12.
19. See for example Sherman to Sheridan, 15 October 1868, U.S., Congress, Senate, *Executive Document No. 18,* 40th Cong., 3d sess., Serial 1360, pt. 1: 3–5.
20. See especially Gen. J. H. Carleton's remarks in 1865 about the unfathomable design of the Almighty that the red man, like the mastadon and great sloth, disappear from the earth (U.S., Congress, Senate, *Condition of the Indian Tribes,* Report No. 156, 39th Cong., 2d sess., Serial 1279, p. 433); Colonel Philippe De Trobriand's declaration in 1867 that "The destiny of the white

race in America is to destroy the red race" (Kane, ed., *Military Life in Dakota*, p. 18); and Sheridan's characterization of a "fading-out people" (U.S., Congress, House, Report No. 384, 43d Cong., 1st sess., Serial 1624, pp. 220–21).
21. For Sand Creek, see Stan Hoig, *The Sand Creek Massacre* (Norman: University of Oklahoma Press, 1961). For Remolino, see Ernest Wallace, *Ranald S. Mackenzie on the Texas Frontier* (Lubbock, Tex.: West Texas Museum Association, 1965), chap. 6.
22. Robert M. Utley, *The Last Days of the Sioux Nation* (New Haven: Yale University Press, 1963), chap. 12.
23. See William T. Hagan, *Indian Police and Judges* (New Haven: Yale University Press, 1966).
24. "How an Apache War Was Won," in Harold McCracken, ed., *Frederic Remington's Own West* (New York: Dial Press, 1961), p. 49.

COMMENTARY
Richard N. Ellis

Historians have explored the history of the Indian campaigns in considerable detail, but all too often they have written straight narrative histories. Only occasionally have they attempted to evaluate the place of the Indian campaigns in American military history or to assess the impact or lack of impact of frontier service in the development of military organizations, tactics, or strategy. Robert Utley's paper is important for providing an evaluation of the army and its role on the frontier and for describing the changing attitudes toward that role. He has reminded us that the army was a conventional force confronted by an unconventional enemy and that it was "not so much a little army as a big police force" employed in policing the Indian frontier. It is also important for emphasizing the fact that the army resisted change and failed to adapt to western conditions.

Modeled after European armies and trained in the European tradition, the United States Army never adjusted to guerrilla warfare and the limited nature of the Indian campaigns despite the fact that its primary duty during most of the nineteenth century was on the frontier. When army officers thought about the impact of frontier service on the army as an institution, they were concerned that service in the Indian country ill prepared the army for a conventional war; they feared that by scattering companies in small posts, morale and efficiency would be reduced and soldiers would perform ineffectively as larger units.[1]

While the army did occasionally enlist Indian soldiers, the number was limited and the largest experiments actually occurred in the late 1880s and 1890s near the conclusion of the Indian campaigns. The United States Army therefore provides a marked contrast to the British military establishment in India where in 1857, on the eve of the great Indian Mutiny, only 19 percent of the army was European and to the German army in German East Africa in the early 1900s where less than 1 percent of the army was European.[2] We can only speculate on the possible impact of the employment of a large native force by the United States Army.

The attitude of army officers toward the American Indians is also an important question. Were they a group of brutal, unfeeling exterminationists who eagerly sought combat for career advancement; were they unsympathetic men, trained for war and hardened by Civil War experiences to the destruction and suffering caused by battle; or did they, as Utley argues, exhibit an attitude of qualified humanitarianism? A perusal of the memoirs of frontier officers and a careful study of the military records in the National Archives and of personal papers located in other depositories indicates that the latter portrayal is more accurate.[3]

Few would describe George Crook or O. O. Howard as exterminationists, and the list of officers who demonstrated humane attitudes while serving as Indian agents could be expanded. A Crook, a Howard, or a Grierson, a Chaffee or a Randall (whose departure caused an Apache chief to lament, "O, where is my friend Randall"), and many others did seek humane, honorable, and just treatment for the Indians.

There is no doubt, however, that their humanitarianism was limited by ethnocentrism. While some officers might have had a partial understanding of Indian cultures and values, they did not appreciate them. Most officers were in general agreement that the American Indians must be civilized and that they must be prepared to take their place in American society. In this belief, they were in obvious agreement with officials of the Office of Indian Affairs and with the reform groups in the East that so often criticized military activity in the West.

The officer corps and reformers shared the same basic goal—that of assimilation. Army officers, therefore, were in the mainstream of American thought regarding Indian policy. Americans then, and to a lesser degree now, assumed that their system was best and that minority groups must conform. White America was determined to remake the Indians into its own image. Efforts were made to destroy the power of the chiefs, break up tribal organizations, treat Indians as individuals, outlaw religious observances, and eventually allot land in severalty. The correspondence of army officers indicates that they gave support to these efforts.

Despite the commonality of goals for reformers and officers, the late nineteenth century was often marked by bitter dissent regarding the conduct of the military in the West. The institution of the regular army had always been regarded with suspicion by those who saw a standing army as a threat to democracy. The tiny post-Civil War army gave no indication of presenting such a danger, but the legacy of distrust existed. Furthermore, the very nature of the Indian wars, which should more properly be called campaigns, encouraged conflicting attitudes.

Although westerners on occasion might disagree, North American Indian tribes presented no distinctive threat to the security of the nation. Hostile warriors might have retarded or driven back the line of settlement temporarily, and they might have won occasional victories on the field of battle, but they were doomed to ultimate defeat. No one seriously believed that the Indian tribes could do any more than delay the progress of settlement across the continent, and the tiny size of the army, about twenty-five thousand men in this period, indicates the lack of a clear and present danger. This factor, along with the limited and intermittent nature of conflict with the Indians, permitted the nation to debate Indian policy and military activity. It should be remembered that Americans have often engaged in such debate in time of war. Indeed, the United States has rarely gone to war without some kind of dissent.[4] Rarely, however, has the army been singled out so effectively as during the Indian campaigns. Under normal circumstances the debate was over the policy rather than the instrument of that policy—the military establishment.

After the Civil War the debate did center on the role of the army, and undoubtedly the controversy was heightened by efforts to transfer or retransfer the control of Indian affairs back to the War Department. Such a move threatened the maintenance of a policy of peace toward the Indians, reformers thought. The rhetoric at times became quite heated. Many of the humanitarian reformers had learned the techniques of public debate in the abolition movement, and at times army officers must have concluded that they carefully avoided moderation. How much the pronouncements of Wendell Phillips and others reflected the attitude of the rank and file of the reform movement is difficult to judge, despite the recent publication of Robert Mardock's fine study, *The Reformers and the American Indian*. Certainly when Phillips announced in 1869 that Indians had begun to tear up the rails and shoot trainmen and passengers on the Pacific road and stated, "We see great good in this," he was not stating the views of most Americans.[5]

The army can be criticized for a reliance on and an occasional misuse of force, for overreaction, for ambivalent attitudes toward the Indian people, and for an oversimplified view of Indian-white relations. No one, for example, can defend a Sand Creek. However, if we judge the army, should we not also judge its critics? How realistic were the humanitarians; how understanding were they of Indian cultures, attitudes, and needs; how humane were the policies they proposed; and how oversimplified was their view of Indian-white relations?

I think that most of us will agree that given the inability or unwillingness of the government to regulate frontier expansion and protect Indian lives, rights, and property, and that given the failure of Congress to fulfill treaty provisions, the most extreme attacks upon the army, including a recommendation to abolish it, were ridiculous. Few Americans believed that the West should remain in the hands of the Native Americans, and the constant demand for new areas for white development virtually guaranteed trouble.

It is the consensus also of scholars that late nineteenth-century reformers had little understanding or appreciation of or sympathy for Indian culture and values. The humanitarians were dedicated to the eradication of Indian culture, and many expected that they could civilize the Indians within the space of a decade. Moreover, the reformers were determined to convert the Indians into farmers, completely disregarding the nature of the country where most reservations were located. They did not study the western environment, nor did they take cognizance of the repeated agricultural failures on western reservations in preceding decades. Instead they were convinced land allotment was both good and necessary. As a result of the Dawes Act and the failure to protect Indian property after its passage, the Indian land base was dramatically reduced.

Equally serious was the approval by reformers of federal treatment of the Five Civilized Tribes. If the goal of the humanitarians and of federal policy was the civilization of the Indians, the Five Civilized Tribes had done the most to attain these goals. They had constitutions, democratic governments, police forces, courts, schools, newspapers, and a written language. But land allotment was forced upon them and tribal governments were destroyed. This policy, approved by the reformers and enforced in part by their leading political spokesman, former Senator Henry Dawes of Massachusetts, has been soundly condemned by historians.[6]

If we look then at the activities of the army and of the reformers and evaluate them from the perspective of the twentieth century, which group deserves the most condemnation or praise: the reformers, who were responsible in part for the establishment of policies that constituted a brutal attack on Indian land holdings, culture, and livelihood, or the army, which enforced rather than made policy and which occasionally did use more force than necessary?

The conflicting views regarding the Indian fighting army that were so evident in the nineteenth century exist in the twentieth century as well. The images of John Ford and Arthur Penn provide dramatic examples of these views and of the changing mood of the nation. Ford's heroic soldiers were appropriate figures in a patriotic era, an era that had seen the nation united in defense against an easily definable foe, an era of victory for American arms against the Axis powers, and the beginning of a new era that would be called the Cold War. The decades of the 1940s and 1950s were also a time of declining interest in New Deal Indian reforms and of transition to the policy of termination.

More than a score of years later when audiences watched United States soldiers brutally massacre the Cheyennes in Arthur Penn's "Little Big Man," national attitudes had changed. No longer were the issues so sharply defined; no longer was the nation united against an immediate danger. In the 1970s the nation is in no mood for war heroes. The war in Vietnam dragged on, causing growing discontent. Vietnam is far away, and the danger to national security seems slight to many Americans. It is possible, therefore, to criticize the use of B-52s and napalm and to discuss the morality of war and the impact of the conflict upon the civilian population of Vietnam. How different this is from World War II when such issues were rarely raised. The peace movement of the 1960s and 1970s—large-scale antiwar demonstrations, etc.—indicates that vast segments of the population are receptive to antiwar messages. This factor, combined with the impact of the civil rights movement and the current interest in American Indians and guilt feelings regarding their treatment in the past, helps explain recent criticisms on screen and printed page of the frontier army.

It is perhaps appropriate at this time for us to attempt to evaluate the role of the Indian fighting army and to place it in a broad perspective as Bob Utley has done. His descriptions of the strengths and weaknesses and successes and failures of the army and his label of qualified humanitarianism for army officers may not appeal to those holding more extreme views, but his thesis is eminently reasonable and is based upon years of research. Army officers assuredly offered a wide range of views, but among them were a large number of humane men. Their humanitarianism unquestionably was modified by ethnocentrism, but we must remember that so too was the humanitarianism of the reformers.

NOTES

1. U.S., Congress, Senate, *Annual Report of the Secretary of War, 1876*, Executive Document No. 1, 44th Cong., 2d sess., Serial 1742, pt. 2:452-53, is an example.
2. Ernst Gerhard Jacob, ed., *Deutsche Kolonialpolitik in Dokumenten* (Leipzig: Dieterich sche Verlagsbachhandlung, 1938), p. 217. The figures for German East Africa show 260 Europeans and 2,470 natives; for Cameroon there were 200 Europeans and 1,600 natives; in Togo there was only a police force with five Europeans and 200 natives. Percival Spear, *India: A Modern History* (Ann Arbor: University of Michigan Press, 1961), p. 271.
3. See sources listed in Richard N. Ellis, "The Humanitarian Generals," *Western Historical Quarterly* 3, no. 2 (April 1972): 167-78.
4. Samuel E. Morison, Frederick Merk, and Frank Freidel, *Dissent in Three*

American Wars (Cambridge: Harvard University Press, 1970), provides examples of wartime dissent.
5. *New York Times*, 11 June 1869.
6. See, for example, Angie Debo, *And Still the Waters Run* (Princeton: Princeton University Press, 1940); and Wilcomb E. Washburn, *Red Man's Land—White Man's Law* (New York: Scribner's, 1971).

DISCUSSION NOTE

Bruce White of the University of Toronto opened the discussion by asking Robert Utley if he felt that Indian policy would have been significantly or even slightly different had the War Department regained control of Indian affairs. Utley replied that he was convinced that the attitudes and goals represented in the officer corps were essentially those professed by the Indian administrators and would have been the ones sought. The army felt that it was eminently qualified to administer the reservation program, and experience proved that some of the army officers who were detailed as Indian agents made very good agents. Much of the corruption attached to the Indian administration would have been eliminated under the military since the army was composed of career people rather than political appointees whose tenure was uncertain. It was undeniably true, however, that substantial bodies of troops living in close proximity to the Indians proved to be a definite corrupting influence on the Indians.

An observation was made that the experience the army gained from campaigning against the Indians proved useful in terminating the Philippine insurrection. This point was illustrated by a story in which a veteran of the Indian wars counseled a young soldier to cease firing at the insurgents who were retreating. From the regular's point of view, the objective had been achieved with the rout of the insurgents. The objective was not necessarily to kill people. Support for this statement came from John C. Ewers, Smithsonian Institution, who pointed out that the army frequently was criticized by friendly Indians as being too lenient with the hostiles.

Utley was then asked if he believed that the military developed the policy of exterminating the buffalo as a means of subjugating the Indians. He rejected the idea that such a policy was officially pursued although some evidence does exist indicating that certain army officers did use the extermination of buffalo as one means of conquering the Indians. Robert G. Athearn stated that he thought there was good evidence to show that the Indians themselves were responsible for a rather wasteful destruction

Role of the Military

of the buffalo. He then asked John Ewers if his research supported this belief. Ewers agreed and mentioned the Red River mixed bloods who trafficked in buffalo meat. They continued to follow the buffalo as its range became smaller and joined with the white hide hunters in the last kill. He believed that they were fully as destructive as the whites. Utley enlarged upon this point by saying that he did not believe that the Indians realized until near the very end that the resources that supported their distinctive way of life were disappearing. Consequently, he does not think that they consciously practiced conservation in the modern sense of the word. A reference was then made to a study by William T. Hornaday of the Smithsonian Institution who estimated that the Indians themselves were responsible for killing a minimum of four hundred thousand buffalo a year. ("The Extermination of the American Bison with a Sketch of Its Discovery and Life History," Report of the United States Museum, 1887, *Annual Report of the Board of Regents of the Smithsonian Institution* [Washington, D.C.: Government Printing Office, 1889], pp. 367–548.) By 1865 the buffalo already were headed for extinction, as they were being killed much more rapidly than they could breed. It was also noted that any group of people whose favorite method of hunting was to stampede the buffalo over a cliff and to take only as much meat as they needed from the slaughtered animals could not be called conservationists.

V
Recent Research on Indian Reservation Policy

INTRODUCTION
Donald J. Berthrong

The first paper on recent research on Indian reservation policy is by William T. Hagan of the State University College, Fredonia, New York. I met Tom Hagan some twenty-five years ago and knew him when he was working on *The Sac and Fox Indians*. He has since authored two other volumes on Indian history—a general history of the American Indian and a study of Indian police and judges. Currently, he is writing a history of the Comanche in the reservation era.

The second paper is by Kenneth R. Philp of the University of Texas at Arlington. He has developed his research in the area of recent Indian policy concentrating on John Collier and Indian policy in the 1920s. At present, he is assembling his research for a biography of John Collier.

The commentaries following these papers are by Roy W. Meyer of Mankato State University, Mary E. Young of Ohio State University, and W. David Baird of the University of Arkansas. Roy Meyer did his graduate work at the University of Iowa, completing his Ph.D. in 1957 in English but within the department plan of American civilization. He has written significant studies on the middlewestern farm novel and the Santee Sioux. Mary Young received her Ph.D. from Cornell University where she worked with Paul Wallace Gates. Her book on Indian allotments in Alabama and Mississippi is well known in the field, and she also has written a number of articles on Indian leaders. The concluding commentary is by David Baird who received his graduate degrees from the University of Oklahoma and was awarded his Ph.D. in 1969. He has published a number of articles on Indian history and a biography of Peter Pitchlynn, a Choctaw leader. He is now completing a study on the Quapaw of Oklahoma.

The Reservation Policy: Too Little and Too Late

William T. Hagan

"The nation having now triumphed over the gigantic rebellion . . . the President deems the present an auspicious and fitting time for the renewal of efforts to impress upon the Indians . . . the rapidly increasing and pressing necessity for the abandonment of their wild and roving habits, and the adoption . . . of the more peaceful and industrial arts of life."[1] Thus wrote Secretary of the Interior James Harlan to his commissioner of Indian Affairs in June 1865, less than a month after the surrender of the Confederate forces west of the Mississippi.

Behind this ponderous prose lay recognition of a very real problem. American expansion had not ceased during the Civil War, and either the government must seize control of affairs in the West, or a war of annihilation would ensue as the whites penetrated the territory of the nomadic warrior tribes. These Indians, ranging from the Blackfeet and Dakota in the North to the Kiowas and Comanches in the South, had acquired and held their lands by force. That a greater force generated by 40 million people would continue a supplanting process begun two and a half centuries earlier, admits of little doubt. The only question was how the deed was to be done.

By 1865, twenty-five years before the census of 1890 signaled the end of the American frontier, the ring had closed on the American Indian. With the exception of what is now Oklahoma, Congress had established states and organized territories over every foot of the West, and, in Secretary Harlan's words, "invited their settlement by civilized people."[2]

Bypassed Indians, the bedraggled remnants of once proud tribes, were wasting away on reservations to which they had been moved to make way for previous migrations. But the debate on Indian policy in the post-Civil War years did not center on these tribes. Their day had passed and they merited little consideration. It was the still vigorous nomadic tribes whose principal dependence was on the buffalo who were the challenge. It was Indians like the Dakota and the Kiowas who would dominate discussion of the Indian problem for the next quarter century.

The broad outline of the approach the government would follow on the problem of these Indians was made clear by Secretary Harlan before the end of 1865.[3] As the secretary spelled it out, the Indians must give up their nomadic ways and accept location on reservations of sufficient size to permit them to partially support themselves by hunting. There the Indians would be introduced to farming and stockraising as a way of life. During the difficult transition period, the government would supply the difference between the needs of the Indians and what they could produce as hunters and farmers. Then, as the Indians became self-supporting farmers and stockraisers, the government would cease rationing them and they would give up their surplus acres to the expanding white population. Concurrently, young Indians would be educated in manual labor schools for their new way of life. Hopefully, church and charity groups could be drawn into the education work, at once easing the financial burden on the government and exposing the Indians, in the secretary's words, to people "whose lives conform to a higher standard of morals than that which is recognized as obligatory by too many of the present employés of the government."[4]

The big question in 1865 was not the objective of Indian policy, which was to facilitate American occupation of the West, but how to achieve it. The Plains Indians had developed what was for them a very satisfying way of life. With their horses and their firearms they had been able to stake out claims to vast hunting grounds and hold them from all intruders until the white invasions got underway in the fifties. For the men especially, it was an exciting, satisfying way of life, and they would not give it up willingly. Not only would they resist white efforts to subdue them, they would seize the initiative where the opportunity presented itself, taking the scalps of whites as trophies, running off their horses, and capturing white women and children. The Kiowas and Comanches, for example, worked the Texas frontier as industriously in the sixties and early seventies as the New England farmers tilled their stony acres.

The solution was to crush the nomadic warriors. Whites preferred that this be done by the army, but if that was not possible, state or territorial troops could be raised for the purpose. The Chivington Massacre and the indiscriminate ferocity of Texas irregulars already had disillusioned people, who were at a more comfortable distance from the frontier, with the use of state or territorial troops. Moreover, there was no general enthusiasm for the use of the army. The Plains Indians were such elusive targets that it appeared prohibitively expensive to a nation exhausted by a terrible civil war. Secretary Harlan pointed out that it cost $2 million a year to maintain a regiment on the Plains, and that all the marching and countermarching of the summer of 1865 had inflicted few casualties on the hostile Indians.[5] Diplomacy must first be resorted to, and a number of treaties were arranged in the years 1865-68.

The 1865 series accomplished little.[6] The treaties did bind the Indians to acknowledge the jurisdiction and authority of the United States and to stay away from the main emigrant routes. In exchange, annuities were promised the Indians and, in the case of the southern tribes, reservations were assigned them. But this was rather meaningless as the Kiowa and Comanche Reservation included a substantial section of western Texas, which that state was unlikely to surrender, and the Cheyennes and Arapahos could hunt anywhere between the Platte and the Arkansas. But the government now had documents it claimed pledged the Indians not to interfere with the emigrant trails and to remain at peace. Interpreted unilaterally by the United States the treaties could be the basis for punitive action.

The whole treaty process must have made little sense to these Indians. The prospect of a distribution of presents and food attracted them to the council grounds. Given the problems of translation and the Indian unfamiliarity with the legal concepts embodied in the treaties, tribal leaders could not have comprehended much of what they were being committed to. Certainly their political structure did not provide the machinery for enforcing compliance on the individual Kiowa or Teton Dakota.

The events of 1866 bore this out as a new wave of hostilities followed further encroachments of the whites on Indian land. Although brute force had its advocates, the argument prevailed again that for humanitarian as well as economic reasons another try should be made at negotiating the Indians onto reservations.

In July of 1867, Congress created a Peace Commission to do the job, with the provision that if it were unsuccessful the army would be brought in. The commission produced another series of treaties with the nomadic tribes by which they agreed to take up residence on reservations.[7] In line with the views expounded by Secretary Harlan in 1865, provisions were made for schools, instruction in farming, and temporary support in the form of clothing and food. A main objective of the reservation system was suggested in the stipulations for individual allotments for Indians who would be willing to cultivate them.

It is impossible that the Indians realized to what they were being committed. They were drawn to the treaty councils by the promise of food and gifts and after the distribution of these goods returned to a life of buffalo hunting interspersed with raids on their white and red enemies. Indeed, there were bands that were completely unrepresented at the so-called negotiations,[8] yet the government would hold responsible every member of every tribe for which a purported treaty had been drafted.[9] It remained to be seen whether the United States would be as faithful to its obligations. But first the Indians must be gathered on the reservations.

One gets the impression that a generation was the time span to be required to produce the desired changes in the Indians' lifestyle—about twenty-five years.[10] With the policy decided upon and the treaties written to provide the framework of the operation, this should have meant that by 1892 or 1893 the job would be done.

Actually, about ten of those twenty-five years were consumed in getting all of the Indians on the reservations. It was achieved ultimately by the tactic the Peace Commission had been conceived to render unnecessary—force.[11] Force in the form of Texas rangers or Montana miners who shot down Indians found off the reservation, without waiting to discover whether they were hunters driven by hunger or some of the raiders who made a spring or summer full moon a time of fear for frontier settlers. Force also in the form of army columns crisscrossing the plains, seldom able to more than keep the Indian villages moving, except when the Indians were immobilized by winter. Force finally in the form of white hunters who were making steady inroads on the buffalo herds on which these Indians depended. Without force the whites could not have imposed their will upon the nomadic warriors. There was no more incongruous spectacle than that of a Quaker agent preaching the virtues of peace and agriculture to a plains warrior, treating this man, rightfully proud of his highly developed skills as a horseman, hunter, and fighter, as a simple, misguided soul who could be brought to see the error of his ways by compassion and sweet reason.

Nor were the conditions on the reservations likely to attract and hold the Indian populations assigned to them. All of the treaties specified an annual issue of clothing, tools, and other useful articles. Twenty-five years after the western Dakota had been committed to reservations, they were receiving, in lieu of the "suit of good substantial woolen clothing" the treaty promised, suits of ten-ounce canvas described by inspectors as "devoid of appearance, warmth and durability."[12] The Indians refused to wear them, indeed they could not wear the pants as they were cut so poorly that no place was left for the hips and they split as soon as the man tried to sit down. The issue shoes were equally useless, very stiff and with soles attached with nails poorly hammered down. When the undersized blankets, of "wool shoddy apparently mixed with a cheaper adulterant,"[13] are added to the picture, the plight of the Dakota, living in a country of terrible winter weather and unable any longer to procure deerskins and buffalo robes, is painfully apparent.

Nor was the government providing the Dakota with the quality of farm implements needed. Inspection of these revealed spades, shovels, hayforks, and posthole diggers of a soft iron so poorly finished that they were virtually unusable. A check of a warehouse of this junk at Pine Ridge disclosed that, with one exception, the tools carried no manufacturer's labels, suggesting they had been made specifically for the Indian Service contract.[14] And these were conditions uncovered in 1892, so they could not be explained away in terms of the inevitable problems that plague the early days of any program.

The architects of the reservation system for the nomadic tribes recognized that they would require rationing, at least partially, for several years. Some of the 1867 and 1868 treaties called for rations for four years, but most did not, and it was simply taken for granted. The idea had been to supplement the food the Indians obtained by hunting until they could subsist completely by farming. Clauses in the treaties permitted hunting outside the strict boundaries of the reservations, but the inevitable clashes between off-reservation hunting parties and whites led this privilege to be first restricted and then eliminated. The Indians became dependent upon government rations more quickly than had been anticipated, while their conversion to agriculture lagged behind schedule.

The quantity of food supplied by the government was never sufficient for a full ration, and the quality was frequently poor. But in view of the fact that most treaties carried no provision for rations at all, and for others they were limited to four years,[15] the members of Congress tended to look upon rations as a gratuity that should be terminated as quickly as possible.[16] The Indian Service and military personnel generally agreed that it was better to feed than to fight, but to the typical late nineteenth-century member of Congress, not yet exposed to doctrines of social welfare, there was something obscene about grown men and women drawing free rations. Appropriations for subsistence consequently fell below the levels requested by the secretary of the interior.

That starvation and near-starvation conditions were present on some of the sixty-odd reservations every year for the quarter century after the Civil War is manifest. Conditions were usually worse in late winter when the beef cattle, that had been purchased the previous fall and held on pasture, were in their poorest state. Cattle were issued in February and March that were little more than skin and bones and so weak they could not be driven to Indian camps. Nevertheless, officials found time to be horrified by Indian slaughtering practices. They tried humanely to have the meat issued only after being properly butchered by agency employees,[17] eliminating the exciting chase the Indians engaged in when the cattle were just turned over to them—that is if the cattle were not too weak to run. One young eastern woman teaching at Standing Rock suggested the SPCA might be brought in to eliminate the practice there.[18]

She, and a host of other whites, were equally repelled by the sight of Indians eating raw meat. At a time when some Indians were starving, orders went out forbidding Indian consumption of beef blood and intestines: "This savage and filthy practice . . . serves to nourish brutal instincts, and is . . . a fruitful source of disease."[19]

The issue of rations had been envisioned as a stopgap measure of probably four years duration. But it took more than twice that long to force all the Indians onto the reservations. Then it had become apparent that, with exceptions, the land they occupied was unfit for agriculture. Some of it would require irrigation and this meant outlays of cash that Congress was reluctant to provide.

Nor were these hunters and fighters exhibiting any enthusiasm for harnessing their best war ponies and putting their own hand to the plow. During that first decade, there were buffalo to be chased, and a man could still do the things that brought power and status in a warrior's society. Even if the Indian had been willing to learn, the one farming instructor assigned to agencies at this time would have been unable to guide several hundred neophyte agriculturalists scattered over areas the size of small states.[20]

Although dedication to the ideal of the tiller of the soil prevailed in Washington throughout the period, it soon became apparent to most officials acquainted with reservation conditions that stockraising was a better answer. The tribes that were the principal concern had possessed large pony herds and most Indians continued to hold many more than they had any real use for, despite seizures by the army and large-scale thefts by white rustlers. If they could be persuaded to exchange most of their ponies for cattle or sheep, and exhibit the same interest in caring for them that they had for their ponies, they should soon have a basis for self-support. That this was not such a wild theory was evidenced by the success of the Navajos in the 1870s in developing an economy based on sheep. Nevertheless, it did not work for the Blackfeet and similar tribes. Between 1867 and 1893 scores of thousands of stock cattle were issued to these Indians, but by the end of the reservation period few had many. The principal reason for the failure of the effort was the hunger that was endemic in Indian camps. An Indian with a herd of cattle would not let his relatives and friends go hungry.

But officials in Washington, a thousand or two thousand miles from this dismal scene, could not comprehend why it was taking the Indians so long to become self-supporting. They found it perplexing that as late as 1900 nearly sixty thousand Indians were, to some degree, being fed by the government.[21] It gave rise by the end of the century to the complaint that Indians were "driving into the agency . . . in buggies and carriages to receive a gratuitous distribution of supplies from an indulgent government."[22]

Reservation Policy 163

Throughout the reservation period vigorous efforts were made to wean the Indians from this support. The directives that flowed from Washington increasingly stressed the necessity for Indians to support themselves. The Indian Service appropriation bill passed in 1874 was the first to specify that male able-bodied adults must be engaged in some type of labor to receive rations.[23] For several years this was flouted in practice as agents sought and received blanket exemptions for their Indians because it was impossible to enforce the act without precipitating outbreaks.[24] Similarly, orders to ban the issue of sugar, coffee, tea, or tobacco—luxuries—to Indians who would not work,[25] were evaded or ignored. Other directives warned of the impending refusal of Congress to continue to appropriate funds for subsistence of Indians,[26] demanded that agents double the amount of land under cultivation,[27] and ordered agents to distribute supplies equally throughout the year.[28] This last element was designed to prevent desperate agents from issuing full rations as long as they would last and then pleading for emergency grants to keep their people from starving.[29]

Congress did gradually curtail the sums it was providing. For the Crows, for example, the amount available dropped from $100,000 in 1877 to $38,000 in 1883, and for the Dakota from $1,325,000 in 1884 to $900,000 in 1890.[30] But by the mid 1880s the northern buffalo herd had disappeared and deficiency appropriations had to be obtained to prevent even more Indians from starving. Complicating the situation for the administrators was the fact that Congress appropriated for the Indian Service under specific headings—350 in 1888[31]—and it was very difficult to shift funds from one tribe to another. Thus the Crows might be in desperate circumstances and the Northern Cheyennes relatively well off, but Northern Cheyenne funds could not easily be diverted to the relief of the Crows. In 1885 Congress did create a $50,000 fund to aid nontreaty Indians in distress.[32] While helpful, it was the usual too little and too late.

The government's record in meeting its other obligations was no better. With the exception of an occasional western member of Congress, everyone in Washington agreed on the necessity of education for Indians. Nevertheless, at no time in the reservation period did the government even approach meeting the need, despite the fact that many of the tribes had treaties that bound the Indians to keep their children enrolled in schools and bound the government to provide the education. Few Indian parents showed any enthusiasm for the schools. This is hardly unexpected, but the government's failure to meet its obligations is indefensible. By 1878 the Indians were located on the reservations, but school facilities to accommodate only about 20 percent of the children were available.[33] By 1893, at which time the Indians were supposed to be ready for assimilation, less than 65 percent of the school population could be accommodated.[34] This was a sorry record for a government that placed so much emphasis on education in preparing the Indians for absorption by the greater society.

The one area in which the reservation system was made to perform up to expectations was in the reduction of the Indian's land base. The policy had been clear from the 1860s. First locate the Indians on reservations held in common and sufficiently large to permit them to partially support themselves by hunting. Then gradually reduce the reservation until the Indians were located on their own individual holdings approximating in size the farms of the frontier settlers. The proceeds from the sale of reservation land would be placed to the tribe's credit and be used instead of tax monies to further civilization programs.

But even while the reservation was intact the Indians' use of it was restricted. In 1873 a federal court ruled (*United States v. Cook*, 19 Wall. 591) that the Indians could use the grass, the minerals, and the timber only to satisfy their own needs; they could not sell these items, although laws eventually were enacted to permit Indians to lease grazing rights[35] and to sell down and dead timber.[36] However, in the application of the latter law to Chippewa reservations, a secretary of the interior restricted the privilege of selling down and dead timber to those Indians who sent their children to school.[37]

There also were restrictions on the Indian's choice of allotment when that day arrived. Only agricultural lands were open for entry of Indians. Under no circumstances could they elect the easy road to wealth and civilization by choosing allotments in an area suspected of containing minerals or valuable for its towering pines.[38] The Indian would make the transition to the white society's way by following the furrow.

The government's timing for allotment, despite statements to the contrary, was determined not by the degree to which the Indians were prepared for it but rather by the pressure brought to bear by the encroaching white population. These were the people referred to by their representatives in Congress and their servants in the Department of the Interior by such phrases as "the most energetic and fearless men in the world,"[39] "the adventurous, grasping Anglo-Saxon race,"[40] and "our own race . . . [who] have carried the flag of our nationality upon the Plains . . . our brothers and friends."[41]

These people helped inspire and finally frustrate efforts to concentrate the Indian population in a few locations. The desire of white Kansans to get rid of their Indian population helped swell the population of Indian Territory in the 1860s and early 1870s. These same Kansans helped bring political pressure to bear a few years later to block locating Indians from other regions in Indian Territory. They wanted Indians neither as fellow Kansans nor as inhabitants of an adjoining territory.[42]

For about two decades the Indian population was kept on the move by the needs and fears of whites, prejudicing any efforts to convert them into farmers. In the interest of saving money by locating an agency nearer a railhead or steamboat landing, it would be moved forty or fifty miles, forcing the Indians to follow or consume most of their time and energy in traveling to the agency weekly to draw rations. Sometimes entire tribes were shifted to other regions, but, as indicated, the most ambitious plans of this nature were frustrated by whites adjacent to the proposed new locations. Despite this record, the advantage to the Indians of having white neighbors was stressed by proponents of allotment in severalty.[43]

Aside from the belief almost universally held by whites that allotment in severalty was an absolute essential in the civilizing process, it was supported by friends of the Indian as a means of combatting demands for Indian removal. By giving the individual Indian title to 160 or 320 acres, the remaining land of the reservation would be available to satisfy the demands of the white settler. Thus the guiding force of the Indian Rights Association, Herbert Welsh, defended allotment of the great Dakota reservation on the grounds that it was impossible to keep it intact for the Indians.[44] This same man could solicit a pass from a railroad by arguing that such legislation "is beneficial to western railways and to the country at large."[45] Herbert Welsh was no hypocrite; he was convinced the Dakota would have to give up most of their land to retain title to any. Eighty years later it is not obvious that he was wrong.

The process of reducing the Indians' land base, and at the same time dismantling the reservation system, was well underway by 1887. It probably would have run the same course if the celebrated Dawes Act had never been passed.[46] Under some circumstances, the president could authorize allotment by executive order, and Congress had the power to legislate for the purpose.[47] Despite the Dawes Act, Congress continued to have to legislate when the government purchased the Indians' land, since the Interior Department had no funds to finance such negotiations.

By the early 1890s Interior Department officials were issuing box scores on the amount of land obtained from the Indians: the Harrison administration claimed 13 million acres by 1890,[48] 23 million acres by 1891,[49] and over 30 million acres by 1892.[50] If there were treaties specifying procedures by which the government could acquire tribal land, as for example requiring the consent of three-fourths of the adult males, a gesture of compliance was made. The price the Indians set for relinquishing their use of the land also was negotiated, but as anyone can testify who has examined these transactions, rarely did they depart from the form of a settlement dictated by the government.

By the early 1890s the reservation experience was ending for the tribes for which it had been offered as a panacea a quarter century earlier. The objective of gradually reducing Indian land holdings had been achieved brilliantly.[51] But the congresses that were always willing to entertain bills to open negotiations for Indian land had failed miserably to provide Indians the rations, farm equipment, and education either clearly promised them in treaties or explicit in the civilization programs of which the government officials talked so much. It was consistently a matter of too little and too late.

Given the realities of the 1860s and 1870s, the original concept of the reservation system is difficult to fault. It was far better than leaving the job to Texas rangers and Montana miners. And we can dismiss the idea that the American people would have permitted Indians to enjoy most of the West undisturbed. Further, we should not forget that the reservation system did have as an ultimate objective not apartheid or benign neglect but the absorption of the Indian population on the basis of complete equality.[52] That the magnitude of the task, and Indian resistance, was badly underestimated is patent. That the government abused its role of guardian in order to meet the more pressing demands of the already enfranchised is beyond question.

Nevertheless, it could have been worse. A situation involving a landrich alien minority—and these Native Americans were just that—in a society as responsive to popular desires as late nineteenth-century United States, could not be productive of much that is pleasant to behold. Congress did consider proposals that would have rendered the reservation system even worse, proposals such as turning reservations over to private administration,[53] opening all reservations to entry by miners,[54] and giving a state power to remove restrictions on the alienation of Indian land.[55]

Probably the gulf between the treaty promises and the government's performance is best explained not as deliberate deception but by reference to the structure of our government that permits one branch to promise that which requires the cooperation of another to deliver. Finally, a generation of middle-aged liberals who have seen such panaceas as public housing, trade unionism, and welfare programs lose their glamour should be able to understand how another generation could have been mistaken about the reservation system.

NOTES

1. Harlan to Commissioner of Indian Affairs Dole, 22 June 1865, Indian Division, Letters Sent 5:262, Records of the Office of the Secretary of the Interior, Record Group 48, National Archives Building. (Hereafter records in the National Archives are cited as RG—, NA.)
2. Harlan to Maj. Gen. John Pope, 6 July 1865, Indian Division, Letters Sent 5:378, RG 48, NA.
3. In addition to the letters to Dole and Pope cited above, see also: Harlan to

Commissioners, 16 August 1865, Indian Division, Letters Sent 5:335; and U.S., Congress, House, *Report of the Secretary of the Interior, 1865*, Executive Document No. 1, 39th Cong., 1st sess., Serial 1248, pp. viii–ix.
4. *Report of the Secretary, 1865*, p. ix.
5. Ibid., p. viii.
6. These were with the Cheyennes, Arapahos, Kiowas, Comanches, Kiowa-Apaches, and nine western Dakota bands. With the exception of the Lower Brulés, the Dakota were not assigned reservations.
7. These treaties were with the western Dakota, Blackfeet, Gros Ventres, Shoshones, Crows, Kiowas, Comanches, Kiowa-Apaches, Cheyennes, Arapahos, Utes, Navajos, and Bannocks.
8. An example would be the Quahada Band of Comanches that included a higher proportion of raiders than any other Comanche band.
9. The 1865 series of treaties with the Dakota authorized the Senate to amend them without securing Dakota approval of the amendments.
10. In their report of 7 January 1868, the Peace Commission suggested the figure of twenty-five years. See U.S., Congress, House, "Report of the Commissioner of Indian Affairs," in *Report of the Secretary of the Interior, 1868*, Executive Document No. 1, 40th Cong., 3d sess., Serial 1366, p. 505.
11. By October 1868, even the Peace Commission was taking a hard line. See N. G. Taylor to the President, 9 October 1868, ibid., p. 831.
12. Secretary of the Interior Noble to Commissioner of Indian Affairs Morgan, 27 October 1891, Indian Division, Letters Sent 74:41, RG 48, NA.
13. Ibid.
14. Ibid.; see also Cyrus Bussey to Secretary Noble, 18 July 1891, Indian Division, Letters Sent 73:112, RG 48, NA.
15. To facilitate acquisition of the Black Hills in 1876, the United States agreed to ration the western Dakota until they could support themselves.
16. For example, see Sen. Preston B. Plumb's comment: "The Indians will never do a thing for their self-support so long as we concede to them every single thing which their distended stomachs demand . . . ," U.S., Congress, Senate, *Congressional Record*, 47th Cong., 1st sess., 6 April 1882, 13, pt. 3:2638–39.
17. Circular (undated, 1876[?]), Circulars, vol. 1, Records of the Bureau of Indian Affairs, RG 75, NA.
18. Jennie B. Dickson to Herbert Welsh, 9 July 1888, Indian Rights Association Papers, Microfilm Copy (Wilmington, Del.: Scholarly Resources, Inc., n.d.), Roll 13. (Hereafter Indian Rights Association Papers, Roll—)
19. Commissioner Morgan to Agents, 21 July 1890, U.S., Congress, House, *Report of the Commissioner of Indian Affairs*, Executive Document No. 1, 51st Cong., 2d sess., Serial 2841, pt. 5:clxvi.
20. An agent for the Kiowas and Comanches asked, in vain, for eighty farmers to do the job properly. See Lawrie Tatum to Enoch Hoag, 21 August 1869, enclosure in Hoag to Parker, File H408–1869, Kiowa Agency, Letters Received, 1824–80, RG 75, NA, Microfilm Publication M234, roll 376, frame 307.
21. U.S., Congress, House, *Report of the Commissioner of Indian Affairs, 1900*, Document No. 5, 56th Cong., 2d sess., Serial 4101, p. 7.
22. Ibid., *Report of the Commissioner of Indian Affairs, 1901*, Document No. 5, 57th Cong., 1st sess., Serial 4290, p. 6.

23. 18 Stat. 146, 22 June 1874, chap. 389.
24. It became law in June 1874, and in September 1874 the Crows, Blackfeet, Assiniboins, Gros Ventres, western Dakota, Utes, Apaches, Kiowas, and Comanches were exempted. See Acting Secretary of the Interior to Commissioner of Indian Affairs, 28 September 1874, Indian Division, Letters Sent 13:241, RG 48, NA.
25. Circular no. 10, 1 March 1878, Circulars, vol. 1, RG 75, NA.
26. Circular no. 102, 27 September 1882, Circulars, vol. 3, RG 75, NA.
27. Circular no. 30, 14 July 1879, Circulars, vol. 2, RG 75, NA.
28. U.S., Congress, House, *Report of the Commissioner of Indian Affairs, 1882*, Executive Document No. 1, 47th Cong., 2d sess., Serial 2100, pt. 5:7.
29. An effort was also made, beginning in 1875, to limit the salaries of employees, excluding the agent, to a total of $10,000 per agency. But as Secretary of the Interior Schurz pointed out in 1879, the army received more for transportation than the Indian Service did to support Indians. See Schurz to the Secretary of War, 6 January 1879, Indian Division, Letters Sent 20:248, RG 48, NA.
30. Commissioner of Indian Affairs Price to the Secretary of the Interior, 15 December 1883, Report Book 46:565, RG 75, NA; Secretary Noble to the Chairman of the Senate Committee on Indian Affairs, 5 December 1890, Indian Division, Letter Sent, RG 48, NA.
31. U.S., Congress, House, *Annual Report of the Commissioner of Indian Affairs, 1888*, Executive Document No. 1, 50th Cong., 2d sess., Serial 2637, pt. 5:x.
32. Secretary of the Interior Lamar to Commissioner of Indian Affairs, 4 March 1886, Indian Division, Letters Sent 44:204, RG 48, NA.
33. U.S., Congress, House, "Report of the Commissioner of Indian Affairs," in *Report of the Secretary of the Interior, 1878*, Executive Document No. 1, 45th Cong., 3d sess., Serial 1850, pt. 5:458. One estimate was that the United States had fallen $2,429,350 short in meeting specific treaty obligations in education in the period 1877–81. See, *Report of the Commissioner, 1882*, p. 34.
34. This is based on a school age population, exclusive of the Five Civilized Tribes, of about 33,000, with 20,976 enrolled. See *Annual Report of the Secretary of the Interior, 1892* (Washington, D.C.: Government Printing Office, 1892), p. xxxv.
35. 26 Stat. 794, 28 February 1891, chap 383.
36. 25 Stat. 673, 16 February 1889, chap. 172.
37. Secretary Noble to the President, 10 October 1889, Indian Division, Letters Sent 62:29, RG 48, NA.
38. Secretary Vilas to the President, 2 March 1889, Indian Division, Letters Sent 59:117, RG 48, NA.
39. U.S., Congress, Senate, *Report of Joint Special Committee, Condition of the Indian Tribes*, 39th Cong., 2d sess., Senate Report No. 156, 26 January 1867, Serial 1279, p. 6.
40. Ibid., House, "Report of the Commissioner of Indian Affairs," in *Report of the Secretary of the Interior, 1876*, Executive Document No. 1, 44th Cong., 2d sess., Serial 1749, pt. 5:384.

41. Ibid., Senate, Sen. E. G. Ross, *Congressional Globe and Appendixes,* 40th Cong., 1st sess., 18 July 1867, p. 706.
42. Commissioner of Indian Affairs Atkins spoke of the "fierce and uncompromising opposition" of citizens of Kansas, Missouri, Texas, and Arkansas to further concentrations of Indians in Indian Territory. See, U.S., Congress, House, *Report of the Commissioner of Indian Affairs,* Executive Document No. 1, 49th Cong., 1st sess., Serial 2379, pt. 5:10.
43. For example, Herbert Welsh. See Welsh to R. T. Woods, 3 February 1890, Indian Rights Association Papers, Roll 4.
44. For good statements of the position of the Indian Rights Association and Welsh, see Welsh to W. A. Linn, 18 December 1886, Indian Rights Association Papers, Roll 1; Welsh to the Editor, *Boston Herald,* 24 December 1888, ibid.
45. Welsh to John L. Gardner, 27 April 1886, ibid.
46. For example, the Northwest Indian Commission, created by Congress in 1886, negotiated agreements by which the government quieted the Indian title to over 17.5 million acres. See Secretary of the Interior Lamar to the President, 30 December 1887, Indian Division, Letters Sent 53:300, RG 48, NA.
47. Senator Dawes preferred seeing the western Dakota reservation opened through special legislation he introduced, rather than by the act bearing his name, because he felt the rights of the Dakota would be better protected. See Dawes to Welsh, 19 February 1888, Indian Rights Association Papers, Roll 13.
48. U.S., Congress, House, *Annual Report of the Secretary of the Interior, 1890,* Executive Document No. 1, 51st Cong., 2d sess., Serial 2840, pt. 5:xxiv.
49. Ibid., 1891, Executive Document No. 1, 52d Cong., 1st sess., Serial 2933, pt. 5:vi.
50. Ibid., 1892, Executive Document No. 1, 52d Cong., 2d sess., Serial 3087, pt. 5:xxxiii.
51. Secretary of the Interior Delano once claimed success for the government's Indian policy because, "it has secured the largest and freest extension and development of our railways and frontier settlements which was possible under the circumstances, with far less loss of life and property than would have been suffered under any other plan of dealing with the hostile and roving tribes beyond the Missouri River." See U.S., Congress, House, *Report of the Secretary of the Interior, 1872,* Executive Document No. 1, 42d Cong., 3d sess., Serial 1560, pt. 5:3.
52. As Secretary Lamar, a southerner, put it—rather crudely—"After incorporating into our body politic four millions of blacks in a state of slavery and investing them with citizenship and suffrage we need not strain at the gnat of 260,000 Indians." See *Annual Report of the Secretary of the Interior, 1885,* vol. 1 (Washington, D.C.: Government Printing Office, 1885), p. 25.
53. U.S., Congress, Senate, *Congressional Record,* 43d Cong., 2d sess., 14 January 1875, 3:470.
54. Secretary Vilas to the Chairman of the Senate Committee on Indian Affairs, 3 March 1888, Indian Division, Letters Sent 54:178, RG 48, NA.
55. Secretary Noble to the chairman of the Senate Committee on Indian Affairs, 23 April 1892, ibid., 75:310, RG 48, NA.

John Collier, commissioner of Indian Affairs, 1933–45. (RG 208, No. 208-PU-408B-1)

John Collier and the Controversy over the Wheeler-Howard Bill

Kenneth R. Philp

Back of all this in his (Commissioner Collier's) mind, is to build up the pride of our people; that we feel that we have got a great history and great thoughts and great ideas and inspirations in our hearts, so that we can walk away with our heads up instead of looking down all the time.

Henry Roe Cloud, WINNEBAGO EDUCATOR

On April 21, 1933, President Franklin D. Roosevelt confirmed the appointment of John Collier as Indian commissioner. One of the New Deal's foremost social planners, Collier tried to fundamentally alter Indian reservation policy by formulating radically new legislation to replace the Dawes Severalty Act of 1887. Known as the Wheeler-Howard bill, the commissioner's proposal attempted to revitalize the whole range of native values centering around autonomous Indian communities, collective ownership of land, education that promoted Indian culture, and a separate Federal Court of Indian Affairs. Collier hoped that this bill would create a utopia where tribal communities could offer a model of communal living for individualist-oriented American society.

The commissioner's interest in tribal institutions stemmed from his previous background. Devoted to the task of creating a sense of community life in an industrialized society, Collier had become a social worker in 1907 at the People's Institute, an organization in New York City which attempted to give immigrant masses a sense of solidarity in local neighborhood communities. Seeing his social work negated by the Americanization drive of World War I, Collier moved to California in 1919 to undertake leadership of that state's adult educational program. One year later, under surveillance by Department of Justice agents during the Red Scare because of his lectures concerning the development of community life and the Russian Revolution, he resigned his California position to visit the wilderness of Mexico. But his trip became permanently interrupted when Mabel Dodge, a bohemian whose prewar salon in Greenwich Village he had attended, successfully persuaded him to join her near the Indian pueblo at Taos, New Mexico.[1]

Collier's fascination with Indian culture stemmed from his sojourn at Taos Pueblo during 1920. There he discovered a "Red Atlantis," which held secrets desperately needed by the white world. Living in a golden age, the Pueblo Indians had integrated social structures offering an example of community life. Collier believed they possessed the lost attribute of communal and cooperative experience, had a profound sense of living found in primary social groups, and discovered how to become both communists and individualists at the same time.[2] Collier thought that Pueblo culture, and perhaps tribal life in general, offered a model for the redemption of white society because it concerned itself very little with the material aspects of life. Instead, its goals were beauty, joy, adventure, comradeship, and the union of people with God.[3] He hoped that the tribal communities created by the Wheeler-Howard bill would follow the example of Taos and build a Red Atlantis, which offered an alternative to the excessive materialism and shallow individualism of American society.

Collier wanted to encourage tribal or communal life because he rejected the laissez-faire tenets of Social Darwinism, which portrayed the human world as an aggregation of persons controlled by universal economic laws. Instead, Collier was a Reform Darwinist who focused upon subjective and spiritual motivations in history. He accepted Lester Ward's notion that the individual through psychic forces of mind and spirit could control the evolutionary process, while he argued that people must mold society through deliberate innovation and individual creativity.[4]

The commissioner believed that community life offered a meaningful alternative to "the atomizing intellectual and moral aims" brought about by industrialism and urbanization such as hostility to human diversity, the isolation of individuals, and the supremacy of machines over humans.[5] He realized that the *gesellschaft* mode of life, where individuals lived isolated from each other, must be replaced by *gemeinschaft* relationships, where people in communal life were motivated by shared purposes. Collier thought that only organized groups of people, joined together in tasks of cooperative self-expression, could discover a new state of social consciousness to prevent the negative consequences of the Industrial Revolution.[6]

The Wheeler-Howard Bill Controversy

Because of his interest in restoring a sense of community to the modern world, Commissioner Collier called a conference on January 7, 1934, at the Cosmos Club in Washington, D.C. He wanted to unite various groups such as the American Indian Defense Association, the Indian Rights Association, and the National Association on Indian Affairs behind a program of legislation to replace the Dawes Severalty Act. Lewis Meriam, who had directed a private investigation of the bureau during 1926, under the auspices of the Institute for Government Research, chaired this session. Other notable guests included Anna Ickes, wife of the secretary of the interior; Henry Scattergood, former assistant Indian commissioner; and Dr. Moises Saenz, educator and scholar on Indian life from Mexico.[7]

Following many of the suggestions in Meriam's published report, *The Problem of Indian Administration*, the delegates at the Cosmos Club reached a "unanimous conclusion" concerning what reforms ought to be introduced into Congress. They favored repealing the land allotment law, the consolidation of Indian heirship and trust lands, and the acquisition of additional land for landless Indians. Other proposals suggested that the government provide a system of credit to promote Indian economic development, gradually transferring the powers exercised by the Indian Bureau into organized Indian communities. Finally, the delegates indicated that Congress should return the Five Civilized Tribes in Oklahoma to federal control and settle all claims arising from broken treaties.[8]

Delighted with the recommendations offered at this conference, Collier pushed forward with his plans to end the land allotment system. He had already sent a "Questionnaire" to various superintendents and anthropologists, asking them to survey the economic and political conditions on the reservations. The commissioner was particularly interested in finding the potential for cooperative economic activity that existed in tribal social structures because he wanted to enlarge "tribal ownership of land in lieu of the present system of allotments."[9]

The response to this questionnaire varied from extreme pessimism to guarded optimism. Ralph Linton, an anthropologist from the University of Wisconsin, who had studied the Comanches in southwestern Oklahoma, warned Collier that any plans to resurrect tribal political and economic life among these Indians was "foredoomed to failure" because they seemed quite content with their "present individualistic arrangement, fearing only the loss of land to white sharpers." Linton concluded that the Comanches were adjusting well to white culture and if their land rights were protected for another fifteen years, they would be "quite capable of taking care of themselves as members of the white community."[10]

Oliver La Farge, the president of the National Association on Indian Affairs and an expert on Indians in the southwestern part of the United States, also answered Collier's questionnaire with candor. He pointed out that many Navajos favored individual ownership of property, such as sheep and allotments on the public domain, but they needed large blocks of communal land for grazing purposes. La Farge then indicated that the Navajo Tribal Council was "effective and well established," but sectionalism might develop in the future between older conservatives and the younger progressives. As far as the Hopi were concerned, they favored collective ownership of land, but he doubted whether these Indians could develop a viable tribal government because authority rested in separate villages.[11]

Finally, La Farge commented on the economic and political situation among the New Mexico Pueblos. He believed that they favored any plan concerning the collective ownership of land because the ultimate title to their property already was vested in the tribe. Nevertheless, La Farge had qualms about the viability of Pueblo self-government. These Indians had traditionally run their own affairs, but their government was a "curious mixture of democracy and absolutism," which often worked very badly. Ultimate authority in each Pueblo rested with a priest called a cacique, while the people elected a governor and counselors who handled civil matters. In theory, the governors and their advisors were selected alternately from two groups called Summer and Winter People. If a dispute started between these two moieties, the matter was supposed to be thrashed out in a meeting of the whole Pueblo. What had happened in practice, however, was the growth of factionalism and hostility that led to the breakdown of Pueblo self-government. At Santa Clara, for example, the alternating system of government had disintegrated to the level where each moiety simultaneously elected its own governor.[12]

In spite of these warnings that his plans for a revival of tribal authority might prove difficult, Collier sent a lengthy circular entitled "Indian Self-Government" to superintendents, tribal councils, and individual Indians.[13] Dated January 20, 1934, it stressed that the government planned to reorganize its Indian administration and suggested that the superintendents and tribal councils engage in a "free and frank" discussion of alternatives to the land allotment policy and consider plans for enlarged self-government. Within three weeks they were to send their recommendations to the bureau so it could draw up appropriate legislation.[14]

Collier then offered a guideline of the changes that the government favored. First, the Indians needed to alter their system of land tenure to "assure to all Indians born on the reservation a fair share of land." This could be accomplished by transferring individual control over their property to a tribal corporation. In return, they would receive "a proportionate interest in the entire land holdings of the community." Such a system would permit them to establish proper timber, grazing, and farm units. Collier also pointed out that they should discuss the possibility of increasing their powers of self-government by organizing chartered municipal corporations with the powers of a "village or county government," which would gradually assume the powers exercised by the Indian Bureau. These autonomous Indian communities would elect their own officers, control the expenditure of tribal funds, assume responsibility for law and order, and engage in "cooperative marketing and purchasing." Furthermore, it might be necessary for the Indian community to "require all its members to take part in common labor such as irrigation and the construction of homes."[15]

Expecting general approval of his plan for "Indian Self-Government," Collier must have been dismayed by the negative response from many Indian tribes and their superintendents. Opposition proved especially strong on reservations where land allotment had broken down tribal life. Americanized Indians, who had become assimilated, proved especially hostile to his circular. They objected to relinquishing individual allotments for community ownership and feared that the creation of self-governing communities would restore outdated traditions. Many superintendents also opposed the measure because it might eliminate their jobs.

W. O. Roberts, superintendent of the Rosebud Indian Agency in South Dakota, told Collier that he had "never seen a situation among the Sioux such as your circular created." Roberts indicated that it would be a fatal error to treat the Sioux in the same manner as the southwestern Indians, and he suggested that the restoration of self-governing tribal communities might apply to the Navajo but not to the Sioux because "jealousy and hatred existed between the full and mixed bloods." The superintendent further warned that the possibility of returning restricted allotted land to tribal ownership upset the fullbloods who had kept their land. They believed that he was "selling out to the mixed bloods" who had lost their property to the whites. Finally, Roberts pointed out that the preservation of Sioux culture would prove difficult because these Indians had forgotten most of their cultural heritage, and they looked to the missionaries for guidance.[16]

Two other superintendents who wrote Collier also doubted if his plan would work in their jurisdiction. O. H. Lipps, superintendent at the Sacramento Indian Agency in California, stressed that the California Indians lived in small groups on rancherias, public domain homesteads, and allotments in over forty counties. Never a united people, these Indians constantly engaged in family feuds, petty jealousies, and tribal factions that would make it difficult for them "to work together for the common welfare of the community."[17] In a similar vein, Superintendent P. W. Danielson warned Collier that the tribal business committees representing the Five Civilized Tribes in eastern Oklahoma, who owned land, had rejected his proposal because they had little interest in sharing property with those who had dissipated their holdings.[18]

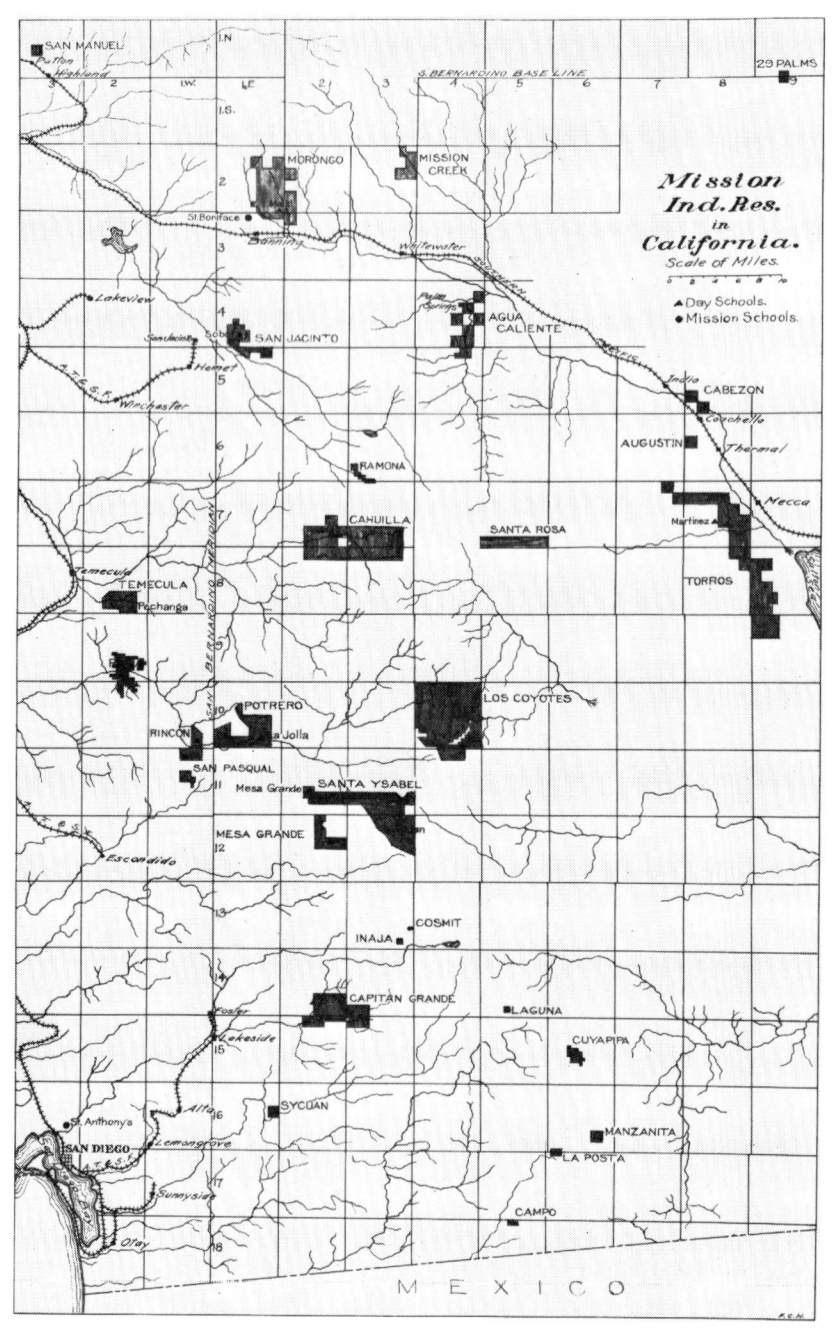

Map showing the location of the Mission Indian reservations in the southern part of California. Not shown are the many rancherias scattered throughout the central and northern parts of the state. (RG 75, Central Map File, 6462)

The Wheeler-Howard Bill Controversy 177

Extremely interested in Collier's circular, many tribes wrote him directly and voiced conflicting opinions over his plan for Indian self-government. Carpio Martinez, the governor of San Juan Pueblo, reported that his tribe favored the proposed changes as long as they did not interfere with their traditional form of self-government.[19] The Eastern Band of Cherokees in North Carolina offered a more sophisticated reply. They agreed "in principle" to a larger degree of self-government and control of their land, but reminded the commissioner that they had already managed their own affairs by incorporation under the laws of the state of North Carolina. The Cherokees saw little need to modify this charter, which had worked "in a satisfactory manner," but they believed that it would be advantageous to operate in the future under a federal charter because most of their business concentrated at the national level.[20]

Finally, the Eastern Cherokees offered other objections to Collier's reform program. They favored continued enforcement of law and order by the state and stressed that voluntary organizations such as their handicraft guild undertake the purchasing and selling of community products. They also recommended that individual members keep their heirship rights even though the land ultimately belonged to the tribe. Furthermore, the Eastern Cherokees saw little reason for changing the present method of controlling the expenditure of tribal funds, which depended upon a congressional authorization.[21]

Other Indians who had undergone land allotment offered more opposition. Fifty-two members of the Arapaho Tribe on the Wind River Reservation in Wyoming indicated that the time was not ripe "for drastic change." They thought that the idea of community government was "foreign to the Plains Indians" and opposed communal ownership of property as "unsuited" to their tribe.[22] They were joined by several Sioux at the Cheyenne Agency in South Dakota, who claimed that the era for community organization had passed and they expressed "no desire to be segregated from the state and local government."[23] The Assiniboin and Atsina Indians at the Fort Belknap Reservation in Montana agreed that allotments should not be relinquished without suitable financial reimbursement, but they favored the establishment of some form of community government.[24] Other tribes such as the Blackfeet in Montana, the Shawnee in Oklahoma, the Southern Utes in Colorado, and the Colville in Washington also registered various objections to Collier's circular.[25]

These warnings worried Collier but he was convinced that the Indians could become "pioneers" in President Roosevelt's effort to sustitute "conscious planning" for aimless drifting.[26] Consequently, he united the recommendations made at the Cosmos Club with some of his own ideas and ordered the solicitor's office to draw up an omnibus bill incorporating a new Indian policy to replace the land allotment system. Collier knew that the Indians were "unacquainted with its most essential provisions," but he hoped that a single legislative measure "would have a massive and dramatic nature, commanding the imagination of Indians and Congressmen alike."[27]

Introduced in mid-February 1934 by Edgar Howard of Nebraska and Sen. Burton K. Wheeler of Montana, as an administration measure, this bill made up a forty-eight-page document containing four major sections. It reflected Collier's ideas concerning democratic colonial administration. Deeply influenced by Julian Huxley's *African View*, the commissioner rejected the existing policy of "direct rule" where the central government imposed its will through a large bureaucracy. Instead, he favored Huxley's concept of "indirect rule" as the way into the future for the American Indian. Collier believed that the federal government should use native institutions as the vehicle for progressive social change. He hoped that the bill would encourage local pride and initiative, while blocking white "predatory exploitation," through the technique of "democratic communal organization."[28]

Title I of the Wheeler-Howard bill, called "Indian Self-Government," provided for the renewal of Indian political and social structures destroyed by the Dawes Severalty Act. It reaffirmed the right of tribal societies to control their lives and property by establishing a system of home rule under federal guidance. When twenty-five percent of the adult population on any reservation asked for home rule, subject to ratification by three-fifths of the adult population that participated in the election, tribal communities would receive charters of incorporation. These charters allowed tribal societies to establish federal agencies, exempt from taxation, with the powers to operate property of every description. They could also borrow money for economic development from a revolving $5 million credit fund and exercise all powers "not inconsistent with the Constitution of the United States."[29]

According to Collier, these Indian communities could eventually assume the powers of the Interior Department relating to Indians. He pointed out that the bill authorized the government to turn over to chartered communities the lands, buildings, and equipment of the Indian Service and to spend an annual sum of $500,000 for the construction of new municipal facilities. These chartered communities had the authority to compel the transfer of undesirable federal employees after receiving approval from the commissioner. In order to prevent the construction of useless irrigation and other public projects, no chartered tribe could be charged a reimbursable debt without its consent or have its tribal funds spent without authorization from a community official. Finally, the Indians were to receive copies of all bills affecting them and they could offer suggestions concerning Interior Department appropriation requests sent to Congress and the Bureau of the Budget. Any persons who left a chartered community would receive compensation for their assets.[30]

The Wheeler-Howard Bill Controversy 179

Title II of the Wheeler-Howard bill, entitled "Special Education for Indians," reflected Collier's view that the government must preserve the rich values of Indian life. Stating that it was the purpose of Congress "to promote the study of Indian civilization," Title II directed the commissioner to use the staffs of existing boarding schools to prepare courses in Indian history, arts, and crafts, including the problems of Indian administration. It provided chartered communities with an annual $50,000 appropriation for training in their peculiar social and economic problems such as public health, management of forests, law enforcement, and the keeping of financial records. If Indian students lacked money for this special education, the government would pay all expenses, with half the tuition becoming a noninterest reimbursable debt to be repaid in installments, except during periods of unemployment. Indians of exceptional ability might also receive free tuition from a $15,000 annual scholarship fund.[31]

Title III, the most controversial part of the bill, proposed to establish an agricultural revolution on Indian land. Influenced by Mexico's *ejido* program, which restored land under communal title to Indian villages, Collier believed that the government could do little of lasting consequence to assist the Indians without basic "land reform."[32] Title III prohibited future land allotment, restored to tribal ownership existing surplus lands created by the Dawes Severalty Act, extended restrictions on the alienation of allotted land, and prevented the future sale of community property to non-Indians. In order to assist landless Indians, it authorized an annual appropriation of $2 million to purchase new land for existing reservations or to establish new colonies for scattered groups of Indians.[33]

The most radical sections of Title III concerned procedures to consolidate allotted and heirship lands into viable economic units for community use. Compulsory in nature, these sections directed the secretary of the interior to acquire restricted allotted land through "purchase, relinquishment, gift, exchange, or assignment," for the purpose of providing community land for landless Indians and for consolidating checkerboard reservations. In exchange, the allottee would receive a nontransferable, descendible certificate evidencing a proportionate interest in tribal lands of similar quality. Title III abolished inheritance among Indians, and directed that all restricted property return to tribal ownership after the death of the allottee. In return, the heirs would receive equivalent interest in tribal lands. To solve the problem of existing heirship lands, the bill authorized the secretary of the interior to sell this land to Indian communities who would pay the heirs money equal to the annual rental of the land or the equivalent right to use tribal property.[34]

Title IV, the last part of the Wheeler-Howard bill, established a Federal Court of Indian Affairs to provide a just, speedy, and inexpensive determination of legal controversies affecting chartered Indian communities. Consisting of a chief judge and six associate judges appointed by the president with the consent of the Senate, this court could exercise its authority either in full session or through one of its judges assigned to an Indian circuit court in a particular locality. The judges, who were to hold office for ten years, could be removed by the president "for any cause" with the approval of the Senate.[35]

The court's jurisdiction extended over all matters affecting Indian chartered communities such as the right of individual Indians to allotments and the question of heirship rights. The court also had authority over cases involving crimes committed on reservations and litigation where an Indian was at least one party. Local Indian courts had power to impose fines of up to $500 and jail sentences of six months, but most of their decisions could be appealed to the Federal Court of Indian Affairs. To assist the Indians in these legal matters, Title IV gave the secretary of the interior the power to appoint ten special attorneys to help interpret Indian law and take over the function of existing probate attorneys. All decisions of the Indian court could be challenged either in the Circuit Court of Appeals or eventually before the Supreme Court.[36]

Collier favored establishing this federal Indian court for several reasons. He pointed out that existing federal courts only had jurisdiction over a few major crimes such as murder, arson, rape, and incest. In other matters Congress had not created judicial machinery to handle the problem of law and order. Consequently, most legal problems on the reservations were settled in arbitrary administrative tribunals operated by the Indian Service. These tribunals did not provide attorneys or jury trials, instead the superintendent and his appointed Indian judges made decisions that could be appealed only to the secretary of the interior.[37] Collier also feared that if controversies involving chartered communities were litigated in existing federal courts, delays would put endless obstacles in the way of self-government and the return of land to communal ownership. Finally, he wanted an Indian court because the Indians used the services of the nearest district courts, often hundreds of miles away, only with great expense and difficulty. Collier believed that the state courts could not deal with these matters because the proposed chartered communities would exist as agencies of the federal government.[38]

When the Wheeler-Howard bill was considered in Congress during February 1934, it met resistance from members of the House and Senate Indian affairs committees who feared a policy of segregation and doubted the wisdom of communal ownership of property. Theodore Werner, a representative from South Dakota, told Collier that he disliked the measure because it would isolate the Indian "and make it impossible for him to ever become an assimilated part of the citizenship of the country."[39] The commissioner replied by citing the Mormons as an example of unique citizens who had the "advantages of cooperative living," but Werner still feared that the Indians would remain under the thumb of an unresponsive

The Wheeler-Howard Bill Controversy

federal bureaucracy.[40] He also opposed the bill because he believed that its sections depriving the Indians of their vested rights were unconstitutional.

In the Senate Indian Affairs Committee, Collier faced the hostility of Sen. Henry Ashurst, of Arizona, who thought that the Wheeler-Howard bill would give the secretary of the interior the power to extend the exterior boundary of the Papago Reservation. This proved a mistaken assumption, but Ashurst blocked further discussion of the legislation until he aired a problem that existed between the Papagos and whites in Arizona. The senator was particularly upset at a decision made by former Secretary of the Interior Ray Lyman Wilbur to temporarily withdraw certain Papago lands from mineral entry. Wilbur had taken this action on October 12, 1932, to prevent further harm to the Indian livestock industry and to give Congress a chance "to consider the claim of the Indians to the mineral rights within those lands."[41]

This executive order had proved controversial because most whites in Arizona insisted that the Papagos did not own the subsurface rights to their land. Ashurst pointed out that under the Gadsden Purchase Treaty of December 30, 1853, the Papagos did not have legal title to land in his state unless they had land grants recorded in the archives of Mexico. He also indicated that the whites had agreed to President Woodrow Wilson's executive order in 1917, adding over two million acres to existing Papago land, because it was expressly stipulated that subsurface mineral rights remain under government control and "subject to the existing mining laws of the United States." This had resulted in 122 claims for gold, copper, and silver mines covering approximately twenty-four hundred acres.[42]

These precedents, however, had been challenged by the "Hunter-Martin claims." In 1880 a number of Papago Indians had drawn up sixteen deeds to land in certain of their villages, one which included 16 million acres in the southwestern portion of Arizona. They gave one-half interest in these lands to Col. Robert F. Hunter, a Washington attorney, who worked to validate their title. For some unknown reason Hunter had not recorded these deeds, but in 1911 he entered into a contract with another attorney named Martin who attempted to establish Indian ownership in return for a three-fourths interest from Hunter. Three years later, Martin instituted a suit in the Supreme Court on one of the deeds covering the village of Santa Rosa in order to prove Papago title under Mexican land grants. The Interior Department had fought this case and the Court declared the deed void because it had not been executed as required by federal statutes. But the Court left the door open for further litigation by claiming that its decision should not prejudice the "bringing of any other suit" to recover Papago property.[43]

Ashurst told the Senate committee that this loophole had enabled Secretary Wilbur to hire the law firm of Graves, Slemp, and Calhoun on a 10 percent fee basis to determine the validity of the Hunter claims. The senator then asked Collier if he approved of this contract.[44] The commissioner, who had been a militant concerning Indian mineral rights during the twenties, gave a moderate reply. Worried about the passage of the Wheeler-Howard bill and convinced that the Papagos lacked evidence concerning Mexican grants, he indicated that they did not "own the minerals." But he refused to withdraw Wilbur's order preventing further mining because nobody could forbid these Indians "their day in court."[45] The hearings ended on this note with little progress made toward discussing the Wheeler-Howard proposal.

In response to the hostility he found in Congress and because of the opposition of several tribes to his earlier circular on Indian self-government, Collier took an unprecedented step. He decided to call a series of Indian congresses to discuss the controversial features of the Wheeler-Howard bill and gain Indian support before returning to Congress. The commissioner announced his decision in a press release where he cited a recent dispatch from the Umatilla Reservation at Pendleton, Oregon, as an example of misunderstanding concerning the bill. Victimized by white "leasing and land grabbing interests," these Indians had written him a letter of protest stating "thumbs down on Socialization and Communism."[46]

Collier hoped that the Indian congresses would dispel such unfounded anxiety. He believed that once the Indians understood that the government did not plan on depriving them of their "vested rights" to allotted and inherited land, they would support the administration. The commissioner also thought that he could convince the tribes that municipal home rule, cooperative merchandizing, cattle users associations, and corporations were not "socialistic devices, but commonplace necessities of modern life."[47]

Eventually ten congresses were held in various parts of the country and Collier personally attended most of these meetings. Opening the sessions with a general discussion concerning the evils of the Dawes Severalty Act, he then asked for written questions and comments concerning the Wheeler-Howard bill. Many natives supported the commissioner, but frequently he faced hostile Indians who believed the bill would destroy their heirship rights and confiscate their allotted land, giving it to poor Indians.[48]

When the Plains Indian Congress met at Rapid City, South Dakota, on March 2, 1934, for a four-day conference, Collier spoke before 200 delegates from forty tribes containing a population of 60,000. At this first meeting, the commissioner confronted "a horde of resentful redmen who glowered in the background," afraid that the bill was a "back to the blanket movement," and they immediately rejected his suggestion that an Indian preside over the meeting.[49] Realizing that he faced a hostile crowd, Collier asked the delegates to reject any fixed ideas about the legislation and "have open minds" because the proceedings of the conference would be sent back to Washington and read by members of the House and Senate committees on Indian affairs.[50]

In an attempt to allay the fears of many Indians, Collier indicated that the Wheeler-Howard bill could have been pushed "quickly and quietly" through Congress, but the government wanted their advice on this important matter. Once they understood the bill, the commissioner suggested that they would back him "practically one-hundred percent." He then proceeded to launch into a lengthy attack on the evils of the allotment system, using maps and charts of allotted reservations to clarify his arguments. According to Collier, this policy had resulted in the loss of 80 percent of their land. The Oklahoma Indians, for example, had 23 million acres before allotment, and all of this property had "melted away" except 3 million acres. The problem of heirship lands had also brought economic disaster because when the allottees died their estates were probated and passed into heirship status. It then became necessary under law to sell the land and divide the proceeds among the heirs or lease it and distribute the rental in a similar manner. Because of the large number of descendants, this had resulted in cases where individuals received as little as two and one-half cents a year for their interests in an allotment.[51]

Collier stressed that the Wheeler-Howard bill solved these problems by ending the allotment policy and returning heirship lands to communal ownership. More important, this legislation allowed Indians "to organize for mutual benefit, for local self-government and for doing business in the modern organized way." Tribes could use the bill's credit system to establish cattlemen's associations and cooperative societies such as creameries in order to "cut out the middleman's profits." Rejecting the notion that his plans were communistic, the commissioner stressed that both he and President Roosevelt wanted to help the "forgotten man." By allowing them to organize chartered communities and business corporations, the bill would help the Indians "who were staggering under the burden of the rich." They could use this legislation to get the "blind giant of big business off their backs."[52]

This rhetoric failed to satisfy many Indians, who were "boiling over with questions," so Collier opened the floor to discussion when the second session of the Rapid City Congress convened on March 3. Most of the questions concerned the section of the bill which gave the secretary of the interior the arbitrary power to transfer the title of allotted land to community ownership. Collier pointed out that Indian rights would be protected under this provision because they would receive a proportionate interest in tribal lands of similar quality. But he agreed to amend this "relatively unimportant point" and make all land exchange voluntary after most delegates indicated that they disliked this part of the bill. He also promised that they would retain all subsurface rights to oil and other minerals on their land, even if it was returned to community ownership.[53]

Several Sioux also objected to a provision of the Wheeler-Howard bill that gave the Indians a veto power over the expenditure of tribal money. They feared that some of their leaders might stop paying the tuition of children attending mission schools, which came from "treaty funds." Collier responded that this objection stemmed from a misunderstanding about the term "tribal funds." The government's appropriations in this matter stemmed from previous legislation that had expired. It was "practically certain that these particular funds from which tuitions were paid to church schools were not tribal funds and therefore they could not come under the control of chartered communities. But if a court in the future decreed that they were tribal trust funds, they would come under community control."[54]

This question had arisen because of Collier's testimony before the House Appropriations Committee during December 1933. Due to a previous arrangement between the Sioux and the United States, several Catholic educational institutions such as the Holy Rosary Mission in South Dakota had acquired an 80 percent monopoly of the total government grant for religious schools. Because this agreement had lapsed, Collier took the position at these hearings that the government should pay for only the physical maintenance at Catholic schools but not for the tuition of Indian students. He proposed to use the money saved to pay for the physical care of Indian children attending mission schools in all parts of the country, greatly aiding the Protestant establishments.[55]

Resentment by Roman Catholic Jesuits and their Indian parishioners in South Dakota over this testimony had turned into a defamatory campaign against Collier and the Wheeler-Howard bill, in the form of chain letters and attacks in the Catholic press. The *Catholic Daily Tribune* mistakenly warned its readers that the status of their schools was endangered by the bill and suggested that Collier did not "believe in religious influences." The *Little Bronzed Angel*, a Catholic periodical published by the Fathers at Marty, South Dakota, also carried this type of innuendo.[56]

Aware that many Sioux were hostile toward his program, Collier held a special meeting on the evening of March 3 with the delegations from Pine Ridge, Rosebud, Crow Creek, Brulé, Cheyenne River, Santee, and the Sioux of Fort Peck, Montana. George White Bull, from Standing Rock, spoke first and he indicated that many fullbloods were just "getting accustomed to the allotment system," and they did not trust the landless mixbloods who favored passage of the bill. He also disliked this legislation because no provision was made for Indian claims against the government. Collier replied that he planned to introduce a claims bill in Congress "to enable all Indian tribes to get their day in court without delay." But it was politically inexpedient to attach such a measure to the already expensive Wheeler-Howard bill. It would cost so much that Lewis Douglas, the director of the budget, "would faint."[57]

Another question that concerned many delegates was raised by Fire Thunder, from Pine Ridge. He wanted to know what would happen to the Sioux Benefits if the Wheeler-Howard bill passed. Under legislation passed in 1889 and successive congressional acts, certain Sioux had received cash payments when they acquired a land allotment. Fire Thunder and others were worried that this money would be lost when allotted land was restored to tribal ownership. Collier agreed that this question deserved consideration, and he believed that an amendment would be necessary to "protect these Sioux Benefits."[58]

During the last two days of the Rapid City Congress, representatives from each delegation rose to comment on the Wheeler-Howard bill. In a standing vote, thirteen delegations were for the proposal with amendments while four opposed it. Max Bigman, from the Crow Agency, spoke for many of the hostile Indians when he warned that it took "competition and big knocks to make a man" and criticized the bill because it promoted segregation "from my white friends." He received support from Joe Irving, from Crow Creek, who called Collier a "socialist" and indicated that he had little taste for community life. Jacob White Cow Killer, from Pine Ridge, also cautioned that the Republicans would oppose Collier and might modify the bill beyond recognition.[59]

Most delegations, however, swung from an earlier position of open defiance to support Collier's program. The Fort Belknap spokesman explained the success of their cattle association and urged all Indians to consolidate their grazing lands. George Yellow, from the Lower Brulé, also praised Collier's plans to end the allotment system, which had allowed white men to reach into his pockets and rob him "of everything except the soles of my shoes." This sentiment continued when Sam La Pointe, from Rosebud, suggested that the Indians call the commissioner "iron man" because he had "worn out every interpreter we have got." Finally, the Blackfeet demonstrated their support by adopting Collier into the tribe. They gave him the name "Spotted Eagle" because the Wheeler-Howard bill would rub off the checkerboarded spots on every Indian reservation.[60]

Collier had planned on addressing the Northwest Indian Congress held on March 8 and 9 at Chemawa, Oregon, but could not attend this meeting because he had lost his voice and suffered physical exhaustion after the lengthy discussions at Rapid City. Consequently, Asst. Commissioner William Zimmerman and other Indian Bureau officials explained the various sections of the Wheeler-Howard proposal, including the amendment that provided for the voluntary exchange of allotted land to tribal ownership. Zimmerman stressed that for two generations the Indians had steadily lost their property because of the "wicked and stupid" allotment laws. He pointed out that Collier's reform measure would change this evil system and help the Indians organize chartered communities to control their own destiny. But many of "the old timers" did not understand "what a community meant."[61]

Representatives from the Fort Hall, Flathead, and Sacramento agencies supported Zimmerman, but most of the delegates at Chemawa remained suspicious of any change in government policy. Chief Peter Mocktum, a Coeur d'Alene, stated that the whites had "broken all of the prosperity I ever had," but he wanted to keep his remaining allotments and heirship lands. Chief Ishadore, a Kutenai, affirmed this fear of change when he indicated that without a superintendent's guidance he "would feel like a child who would get lost when his guide left him." He was joined by Harry Shale, a Quinaielt, who indicated that his tribe was "getting along nicely" with their fishing and it did not need the bill, but they might accept some form of self-government if nearby Indians made a success of it.[62]

Several other delegations also offered objections to the Wheeler-Howard measure. John Wilson, a Nez Percé, claimed that his tribe opposed the bill because it might interfere with their $18 million claim against the state of Montana for ceded hunting grounds. The Umatillas, under the leadership of Jim Kanine, added to this protest by stressing that they were "happy and contented" and liked their superintendent. Kanine claimed that almost all of the Umatillas owned land, and the bill only caused unrest and made them fearful. Thomas Sam, a Yakima, supported this sentiment by suggesting that his tribe had "plenty of land" which they wanted to keep. If the government planned on purchasing property for landless Indians, it should be outside the reservation. Joe Buck, a Flathead, summed up the sentiment at Chemawa, when he pointed out that if you put "a bunch of twenty dollar bills on the table the Indian would be afraid to go and get them." He had learned to be "suspicious, but you can't blame him."[63]

On March 12, 1934, Collier met with a special session of the Navajo Tribal Council at Fort Defiance, Arizona. He explained that the Wheeler-Howard bill repealed the land allotment law of 1887 and warned that they should support his measure because some future administration might decide to divide their reservation, despite the Treaty of 1868. He pointed to the example of the Five Civilized Tribes who had treaties guaranteeing the ownership of the best farmland in Oklahoma. They felt secure, but the whites wanted the land for farming and tax revenue, so the allotment law was brought into action, which resulted in a loss of 13 million acres and 72,000 landless Indians. Several Navajo delegates responded to Collier's statement by asking whether the Wheeler-Howard bill would affect 6,000 allotments on the public domain. They were relieved of their anxiety when he said no; these Indians did not want to return their allotments to communal ownership or lose the right to pass it on to their heirs.[64]

Collier also discussed his unpopular stock reduction program at the Fort Defiance Tribal Meeting. In doing so, the commissioner made a strategic error, for many Indians confused this controversial issue with the Wheeler-Howard bill.[65] During the previous year, Collier had told the Navajos that to save their land from further erosion the tribe would have to kill 400,000 head of sheep, goats, and horses. By reducing the Navajo stock on a flat rather than graduated scale, his suggestion ignored the minimum number of animals the Indians needed for subsistence. While the wealthy Navajos culled their herds and eliminated worthless stock, many small owners found their livelihoods threatened. This conservation effort caused a great amount of friction in a tribe that measured social status in terms of domestic stock. When Collier called for a reduction of 150,000 goats at Fort Defiance, many Indians demonstrated their hostility by criticizing his proposal.[66]

Missionaries and traders attending the meeting at Fort Defiance added to this turmoil when they opposed the Wheeler-Howard bill. On March 13, 1934, a group of missionaries passed a series of resolutions warning that the Navajo "must be saved by a process of Christian assimilation of American life, not by carefully guarded and subsidized segregation." Fearing a "revival of tribalism," they believed that the bill "would put the clock of Indian progress back at least fifty years."[67] They received support from members of the United Traders Association who feared that Indian cooperatives might put them out of business.[68] Upset by this conflicting advice from local whites and government officials, the Navajos decided to postpone consideration of the bill until April 10, when the Tribal Council voted in favor of its passage.[69]

Leaving the confusion at Fort Defiance behind him, Collier looked forward to meeting with some of his old friends on the All Pueblo Council. On March 15, 1934, 117 delegates from nineteen pueblo tribes met at Santo Domingo to hear Collier explain why they should support the Wheeler-Howard measure. He warned that the status of their lands might be endangered by some future administration unless they endorsed his bill.[70] The Pueblos supported Collier because this reform did not threaten their traditional form of self-government, but after further consideration two pueblos offered objections. The governor of San Ildefonso opposed the section allowing a member of a chartered community to withdraw for a cash compensation, while Indians from Santa Clara suggested that they have the right to appeal from all decisions of local Indian courts. Split into factions, they feared that Indian judges selected by "majority groups" would try to ruin their political opponents "by fines and imprisonment."[71]

Unable to attend the next two Indian congresses, Collier departed for Washington, D.C., to prepare for congressional hearings on the Wheeler-Howard bill. When the Phoenix Congress met on March 15, 1934, A. C. Monahan, assistant to the commissioner, and Walter Woehlke, a bureau field representative, spoke for the government. They described the various sections of the bill and asked the Indians to submit written questions. The Papagos responded by doubting whether self-government would work on their reservation, which consisted of "independent ranching and farming communities, with no union between the villages." They did not want the government to abrogate their old laws regarding inheritance; more important, the government should protect their title to Mexican land grants before it tried new forms of land ownership.[72]

The Pimas and San Carlos Apaches also had qualms about the Wheeler-Howard proposal, but other tribes supported the measure. The Pimas indicated a desire to continue their restricted individual ownership of property, including mineral rights, without a "communistic land basis." Furthermore, they criticized the bill because it failed to guarantee Indian water rights. The San Carlos Apaches joined the Pimas because they falsely believed that the legislation would expropriate their cattle herd and put it under community control. But the Apache delegates from Fort McDowell favored the bill because it would protect the reservation that God had given them and it would end the government paternalism which "told us not to say anything and just put your head down." The Mojave and Colorado river delegates joined the Apaches and called for the passage of the bill.[73]

When the Indian Bureau officials convened the Indian Congress at Riverside on March 17, 1934, they discovered that the Indians of southern California, like those at Phoenix, had mixed feelings about the Wheeler-Howard proposal. Several mission Indians, led by Rupert Costo, agreed with an unsigned three-page circular that had been sent around the reservations which claimed that Collier's ideas were "communistic and socialistic." Concerned about "the pot at the end of the rainbow" or their claims for land ceded to whites, they believed the bill would reverse the policy of civilizing the Indian and force "him to revert to old conditions." Nevertheless, delegates from the Santa Rosa, Fort Yuma, and Pyramid Lake reservations supported the bill, but they believed that its section providing for a $2 million appropriation to acquire new land was inadequate—a mere "drop in the bucket."[74]

The final series of Indian congresses took place in Oklahoma, and Collier left Washington to attend these meetings. When the commissioner met with the Indians from western Oklahoma at Anadarko, on March 20, 1934, and with delegates from the Osage and Quapaw jurisdiction at Miami four days later, he faced open hostility. At Anadarko, Jasper Saunkeah expressed the opposition of the Kiowa Tribe, while James Otippoby, a Comanche, pointed out that "we love our allotments . . . and don't want to be segregated."[75] Representatives from the Arapaho and Cheyenne tribes supported him when they introduced a resolution rejecting "the plan of abolishing the allotment act."[76] At Miami, Ray McNaughton, a Peoria Indian, expressed the sentiment of many natives from Ottawa County when he warned that they had little interest in "returning to the hunting class." More opposition, however, focused around the fear of several Quapaws that the bill might destroy their rights to allotments containing lead and zinc mines.[77]

On March 22, 1934, the commissioner met with at least two thousand members of the Five Civilized Tribes at the city hall and federal courtroom in Muskogee, Oklahoma. The Congress opened on a positive note, with spokesmen for each of the Five Tribes welcoming Collier.[78] But an undercurrent of hostility remained because of the activities of Joseph Bruner, a Creek Indian and chief of the Indian National Confederacy, located at Sapulpa, Oklahoma. Bruner, who represented the assimilated members of the Five Tribes, led the opposition at Muskogee against Collier's efforts to return these Indians to a disintegrating tribal heritage. Bruner and his followers feared that the Wheeler-Howard bill would segregate them, eliminate the beneficial influence of missionaries, confiscate their oil and mineral rights, and take away their allotted land.[79] They received assistance from G. E. E. Linquist, a former member of the Board of Indian Commissioners, who asked his fellow missionaries and their Indian friends to oppose the bill because it would send the natives back to the blanket.[80]

Aware of this negative reaction to his program, Collier told the Five Civilized Tribes to disregard rumors that the bill was connected with "communism, socialism, and paganism." Contrary to many rumors, it did not destroy their property rights or compel them to organize into communities. Collier indicated that he realized the government had "crushed" their tribal organizations, but he warned that "organization in the modern world was the key to all power." In Oklahoma, the Indians could form colonies and use the concept of the business corporation, which came not "from Russia or Karl Marx," but was strictly an American product. If the Choctaw Tribe, for example, desired to become a chartered community, it could form a coal company to operate the mines, while other Indians could establish cattle cooperatives. Finally, Collier suggested that his legislation was "no more communism than the Empire State Building," which existed because "a great many people had pooled their investments."[81]

This rhetoric, however, failed to deter several delegates who asked Collier "a thousand and one questions," concerning segregation and possible loss of their property rights. His face turned "red," but one sympathetic observer believed that the commissioner answered all questions "to the satisfaction of practically all present," and his "steel blue eyes and winning smile captivated" the audience.[82] Impressed with Collier's obvious good faith, the eastern Emigrant and western Cherokees passed a resolution favoring the "immediate enactment of the Wheeler-Howard bill." The 6,000 fullblood Cherokees, who made up the Night Hawk Keetoowah Society, also "heartily approved the contents" of the bill. Joseph W. Hayes, the Chickasaw spokesman, added his endorsement because "every morning our children will be Indians." Hayes claimed his tribe favored the measure because they believed that Collier was "one white man with a red man's heart." The Creek and Choctaws did not officially act at Muskogee, but they endorsed the bill later at separate council meetings.[83]

Collier returned to Washington, D.C., on March 29, 1934, with his hopes high, but he discovered that the unity demonstrated by the Indian welfare assocations at the Cosmos Club in January had disintegrated because of the controvery concerning the Wheeler-Howard bill.[84] M. K. Sniffen, editor of the Indian Rights Association's journal, *Indian Truth*, opposed Collier's reform in an article entitled "Stop, Look, and Consider." Sniffen warned that the bill proposed "revolutionary departures" in Indian policy by perpetuating segregation under the guise of self-government and by "reversing the incentive which the authors of the allotment law had in mind for individual ownership of property leading toward citizenship."[85] Upset at this hostile attitude, Collier wrote the association's president, Jonathan Steere, that he was "momentarily bewildered" to find what amounted to "a denunciation of the bill they had agreed on only two and one-half months ago."[86]

Sniffen and Steere payed little attention to Collier's protest, instead they offered more extensive criticism of the bill in the May issue of *Indian Truth*. Referring to decisions made at a special meeting of the association's board of directors, Sniffen suggested that Collier rewrite or discard Titles I and IV of the bill which called for self-governing communities and a separate Indian court. He warned that these proposals were "artificial and impractical" for allotted reservations where Indians had amalgamated with the white race. Sniffen also rejected the idea of permanent Indian freedom from taxation, credit facilities that applied only to chartered communities, and the provision for taking Indian appointments out from under civil service requirements. Instead, he suggested that Congress draw up four or five separate bills in preference to the lengthy and imprecise Wheeler-Howard proposal.[87]

Collier responded to these criticisms and suggestions offered at the Indian congresses, including the favorable meeting held at Hayward, Wisconsin, on April 23–24, 1934, by preparing more than thirty amendments to the Wheeler-Howard bill.[88] The most important ones prevented the secretary of the interior from transferring the title of allotted land into communal ownership without the Indians' consent; continued the system of partitioning farmlands among heirs upon the death of the owner, as long as the land could be used as an economic unit; and prohibited individual title to minerals, such as gas and oil, from being transferred from individual to communal ownership. Other significant amendments protected the Sioux Benefits, stated that the claims of Indian tribes would not be affected by the bill, and gave every tribe the right to exclude itself from all provisions of the bill at a referendum held within four months after its passage.[89]

Much to Collier's dismay even this amended version met opposition during hearings before the Senate Indian Affairs Committee in April and May 1934. Burton K. Wheeler, chairman of the committee, admitted that the bill might work in the southwest but for the assimilated Montana Indians "it would be a step backward." Wheeler believed that instead of separating the Indians into self-governing communities, Congress should help them "as nearly as possible adopt the white man's ways and laws." As soon as they were capable of handling their own affairs, the government should end its supervision and give the Indians their property. Wheeler warned Collier that the Bureau of the Budget had not approved of this expensive bill and even if it did, Congress would never appropriate money and "turn it over to a tribe" for self-government. Finally, Wheeler expressed absolute opposition to a separate Indian court because it duplicated the jurisdiction of federal and state courts.[90]

Elmer Thomas, a Democrat from Oklahoma, joined Wheeler in opposing the amended Wheeler-Howard bill. He told Collier that the policy of assimilation had worked in his state, and he resisted any attempt to change that policy by putting the Indians back on reservations where they could "perpetuate their ancient tribal ways indefinitely." Thomas pointed out that for the Oklahoma Indians the bill would reverse the "trend of one-hundred years" and create an "Indian zoo." Like Wheeler, he also questioned whether Congress would indefinitely appropriate money for chartered Indian communities. Thomas believed that to assist the Oklahoma Indians the government needed only to start a land acquisition program for helpless natives, stop issuing fee patents, and extend the trust period on allotted land. He refused to allow Oklahoma to come under the bill until its provisions were worked out in "a more businesslike manner."[91]

Collier's amended bill faced even tougher opposition in hearings before the House Indian Affairs Committee. When the commissioner appeared before these hearings he pointed out that most Indians favored its passage. In votes taken during and after the Indian congress, fifty-four tribes, representing a population of 141,881, had expressed approval of the Wheeler-Howard bill while twelve tribes, with a population of 15,106, had voted against it.[92] In spite of these figures, Will Rogers, a representative from Oklahoma, doubted support for the measure. He stated that members of the House could not figure out what it was "going to do," thus how could the Indians understand the bill.[93] Representative Thomas O'Malley, from Wisconsin, also doubted whether this experiment in Soviet-type "collectivism" would prove successful.[94] Such skepticism caused many members of the committee to boycott the hearings during the first two weeks of May. Without their cooperation, the committee's chairman, Edgar Howard, could not formulate a compromise measure or obtain a quorum to report the bill to the floor of the House.[95]

Frustrated because Congress blocked his measure, Collier tried to insure its passage by impugning the motives of non-Indians who opposed it. In an article written for the *Washington Daily News*, he classified cattlemen, job seekers, real estate interests, attorneys, and missionaries as the major critics of his reform program. White cattle interests fought the bill, he argued, because they would gradually lose control of millions of acres of grazing lands rented to them by Indians. Several missionaries had embittered the Indians against the bill because they falsely believed that it would "return them to the blanket." The commissioner then accused a group of Oklahoma attorneys of discrediting the measure because they would lose Indians as clients in land litigation. Finally, he pointed out that many Indian Service employees had criticized the bill because they feared losing their positions once the Indians started the process of self-government.[96]

Secretary Ickes assisted Collier by attempting to stifle criticism of the bill within the Interior Department. On April 30, 1934, he sent a lengthy memo to "All Employees of the Indian Service," pointing out that it was not expected that personnel in the bureau would deliberately attempt to obstruct the new Indian program. Ickes ridiculed the "subtle, misleading propaganda against the new Indian program emanating from a minority of employees within the Indian Service." He warned the Indian Bureau staff that any person engaged "in this scheme to defeat our program" would be under "penalty of dismissal."[97] This action seemed reminiscent of the arbitrary decrees issued by the bureau during the twenties.

In order to weaken congressional opposition to his program, Collier also decided to ask for White House support. Earlier President Roosevelt had favored the bill, noting in a memo that "it was great stuff," but he had not put it on the administration's priority list.[98] Now, at Collier's instigation, both Secretary of the Interior Harold Ickes and Secretary of Agriculture Henry Wallace spoke to Roosevelt about this matter. After meeting with the chief executive, they assured Collier that the legislation would be given preferred status.[99]

On April 28, 1934, the president came to Collier's defense by endorsing the amended Wheeler-Howard bill in identical letters sent to Rep. Edgar Howard and Sen. Burton K. Wheeler. Roosevelt indicated that the land allotment system "must be terminated" because it had caused the Indians to lose more than two-thirds of their land. Calling the proposed legislation a measure of justice "long overdue," the president suggested that Congress "without further delay" should extend to the Indians the fundamental rights of political liberty and local self-government.[100]

Under pressure from the White House, both the Senate and House committees on Indian affairs reported bills which Congress passed. Signed by President Roosevelt on June 18, 1934, the Wheeler-Howard Act bore little resemblance to Collier's original proposal. Missing were Title I, which had established tribal communities with the powers of municipalities, and Title IV, providing for the creation of a special federal Indian court.[101] Furthermore, Sen. Henry Ashurst inserted in this revised legislation an unrelated section which revoked Ray Lyman Wilbur's previous order withdrawing Papago lands from mineral entry or claims under the public land mining laws.[102] Sen. Elmer Thomas also inserted an amendment excluding the Indians of his state from most of the act's provisions.[103]

This legislation, however, which became known as the Indian Reorganization Act, did establish a turning point in Indian history by abandoning future land allotment. The IRA also extended the trust period on restricted land, allowed for the voluntary exchange of allotments to consolidate checkerboard reservations, continued existing practices of inheritance, and restored to tribal ownership remaining surplus lands created by the Dawes Act. Empowering the secretary of the interior to initiate conservation measures on Indian land, the IRA authorized an annual appropriation of $2 million for acquisition of real estate at several reservations. Special civil service requirements allowed Indians to hold more positions in the Indian Service, while an annual appropriation of $250,000 provided tuition and scholarships for promising Indian students.[104]

Provision for the partial renewal of Indian political and social structures destroyed by the land allotment policy paralleled this restoration of land. The IRA authorized Congress to spend $250,000 annually for the expense of organizing chartered corporations. Operated by tribal councils that established a constitution and by-laws, these corporations could employ legal council, prevent the leasing or sale of land without tribal consent, and negotiate with federal or state governments for public services. Finally, chartered communities could borrow money from a $10 million revolving credit fund to promote tribal economic development.[105]

Commissioner Collier believed that the Indian Reorganization Act was merely an "emergency measure," but he hoped that the Indians would use it to establish modes of living different from the rest of American society.[106] In an address given at Haskill Institute, at Lawrence, Kansas, during November 1934, he warned young Indians to discard the "shallow and unsophisticated individualism" that was the life-limiting ambition "of the Babbitts of twenty-years ago." He indicated that they must avoid being indoctrinated with values that measured success in terms of profit, for they would not be "the views of the modern white world in the hundred years to come." Instead, they should work "for the tribe, the nation and the race, for their fulfillment would come by holding to ideas and passions that mattered."[107]

Collier's passion for preserving the beauty of Indian heritage had successfully altered the land allotment system and provided the Indians with the chance to insure their physical and spiritual survival. But his dreams for creating a Red Atlantis, where tribal communities offered an alternate way of living for white America, would remain unfulfilled.

NOTES

1. Because of his interest in the significance of tribal life for the modern world, Collier became a critic of the Indian Bureau, which had followed a policy of assimilating the Indian into white society. His career as an Indian reformer began in 1922 with the General Federation of Women's Clubs, where, as research agent for its Indian Welfare Committee, he helped the Pueblo Indians organize resistance to the Bursum bill which threatened their land grants. One year later, he became executive secretary of the American Indian Defense Association, a position he held for ten years. Under the influence of Collier, who worked as a lobbyist in Washington, D.C., the Defense Association made the 1920s a seedtime for Indian reform. Kenneth Philp, "John Collier and the American Indian, 1920–1945," *Essay on Radicalism in Contemporary America*, ed. Leon Blair (Austin: University of Texas Press, 1972), pp. 63–80.
2. John Collier, "The Red Atlantis," *Survey* 48 (October 1922): 16; idem, "The Pueblo's Last Stand," *Sunset* 50 (February 1923): 19; idem, "Plundering the Pueblo Indians," *Sunset* 50 (January 1923): 21.

3. Idem, "Our Indian Policy," *Sunset* 50 (March 1923): 13.
4. Idem, *From Every Zenith* (Denver: Sage Books, 1963), pp. 38–41; idem, *Indians of the Americas* (1947; abridged ed., New York: New American Library, 1947), pp. 20–24.
5. Idem, *Indians of the Americas*, pp. 7–16.
6. Idem, *From Every Zenith*, p. 93.
7. Vera Connolly, "End of a Long, Long Trail," *Good Housekeeping* 98 (April 1934): 249–50. Other welfare groups attending this conference included the American Civil Liberties Union, the National Council of American Indians, and the General Federation of Women's Clubs.
8. M. K. Sniffen, ed., "Washington Conference," *Indian Truth* 11 (February 1934): 3–4.
9. Collier to Prof. Forrest Clements, 20 November 1933, Records concerning the Wheeler-Howard Act, Part 10-A, Records of the Bureau of Indian Affairs, Record Group 75, National Archives Building. (Hereafter records of the National Archives Building are cited as RG—, NA.)
10. Ralph Linton to Collier (undated), ibid.
11. Oliver La Farge to Collier, 5 December 1933, ibid. For a sensitive portrayal of La Farge, consult D'Arcy McNickle, *Indian Man: A Life of Oliver La Farge* (Bloomington: Indiana University Press, 1971).
12. Ibid.
13. Collier to "Superintendents, Tribal Councils and Individual Indians, Indian Self-Government," 20 January 1934, Kiowa Agency, Box 361697, RG 75, Federal Records Center, Fort Worth, Tex.
14. Ibid.
15. Ibid.
16. W. O. Roberts to Collier, 31 January 1934, Records concerning the Wheeler-Howard Act, RG 75, NA.
17. O. H. Lipps to Collier, 25 January 1934, ibid.
18. P. W. Danielson to Collier, 15 February 1934, ibid.
19. Carpio Martinez to Collier, 10 February 1934, ibid.
20. Resolution of the Eastern Band of Cherokees in North Carolina to Collier, 14 February 1934, ibid.
21. Ibid.
22. Henry Lee Tyler to the Honorable Commissioner of Indian Affairs, 20 February 1934, ibid.
23. Ray Clamore, chairman of the Cheyenne-Arapaho Tribal Council, to Collier, 15 February 1934, ibid.
24. John Buckman, president of the Fort Belknap Tribal Council, to Collier, 7 February 1934, ibid.
25. See the following letters: Forrest Stone, superintendent of the Blackfeet Agency, to Collier, 8 February 1934; John Snake and other Shawnees to Collier, 10 February 1934; Edwin Cloud, Ute chief, to Collier, 12 February 1934; and Barney Rickard, secretary of the Colville Indian Association, to Collier, 27 February 1934, ibid.
26. Collier, *Indians at Work* 1 (15 September 1933): 1–5.
27. Idem, "The Purposes and Operations of the Wheeler-Howard Indian Rights

Bill," 29 February 1934, Bronson Cutting Papers, box 30, Library of Congress, Washington, D.C. Nathan Margold, solicitor for the Interior Department, and his assistants, Felix Cohen and Charles Fahy, helped formulate the Wheeler-Howard bill.
28. Collier was also influenced by the writing of Sir Henry Maine, a British author, who wrote about village life in India, and Lester F. Ward, the American sociologist. John Collier, "Sir Henry Maine and the Primitive Communities of British India and the Suggestion for American Indian Policy," Series 1, Item 43, RG 200, NA.
29. H.R. 7902, a bill to grant Indians living under federal tutelage the freedom to organize for purposes of local self-government and economic enterprise; to provide for the necessary training of Indians in administrative and economic affairs; to conserve and develop Indian lands; and to promote more effective justice in matters affecting Indian tribes and communities by establishing a Federal Court of Indian Affairs, 12 February 1934, Records concerning the Wheeler-Howard Act, RG 75, NA.
30. Collier, "The Purpose and Operation of the Wheeler-Howard Indian Rights Bill," 19 February 1934, Bronson Cutting Papers.
31. H.R. 7902, 12 February 1934, Records concerning the Wheeler-Howard Act, RG 75, NA.
32. Collier, *Indians of the Americas*, pp. 89-98; and Vera Connolly, "End of a Long, Long Trail," *Good Housekeeping* 98 (April 1934): 251-52.
33. H.R. 7902, 12 February 1934, Records concerning the Wheeler-Howard Act, RG 75, NA.
34. Ibid. If a fee patent had been issued, the Indians could either keep their land or voluntarily return it for equal rights in community property.
35. Ibid.
36. Ibid. The Wheeler-Howard bill exempted the Indians of New York from all of its provisions except Title II concerning education. It also did not prevent the removal of restrictions on taxable lands of members of the Five Civilized Tribes or change the present laws relating to the guardianship of minor and incompetent members of the Osage or Five Civilized Tribes.
37. U.S., Congress, House, Committee on Indian Affairs, *Hearings on H.R. 7902, Readjustment of Indian Affairs*, 73d Cong., 2d sess., 1934, pp. 315-17.
38. Collier, "The Purpose and Operation of the Wheeler-Howard Indian Rights Bill," 19 February 1934, Bronson Cutting Papers.
39. U.S., Congress, House, Committee on Indian Affairs, *Hearings on H.R. 7902, Readjustment of Indian Affairs*, 73d Cong., 2d sess., 1934, pp. 33-36, 64.
40. Ibid., pp. 64-65.
41. Ibid., Senate, Committee on Indian Affairs, *Hearings on S. 2755, to Grant Indians the Freedom to Organize*, 73d Cong., 2d sess., 1934, pp. 33-49.
42. Ibid.
43. Ibid.
44. Ibid., p. 35.
45. Ibid.
46. Collier, "For the Press, Meeting at the Secretary's Office," 16 February 1934,

The Wheeler-Howard Bill Controversy 197

Records concerning the Wheeler-Howard Act, Envelope 3, RG 75, NA.
47. Ibid.
48. Indian congresses were held at Rapid City, S. Dak., March 2-5, 1934; Chemawa, Oreg., March 8-9; Fort Defiance, Ariz., March 12-13; Santo Domingo, N. Mex., March 15; Phoenix, Ariz., March 16; Riverside, Calif., March 17-18; Anadarko, Okla., March 20; Muskogee, Okla., March 22-23; Miami, Okla., March 24; and Hayward, Wisc., April 23-24.
49. Newspaper clipping, "Collier Goes Slowly on His Indian Plan," 3 March 1934, Records concerning the Wheeler-Howard Act, Part 9, RG 75, NA; Newspaper clipping, "200 Indians Gather for Big Parley," ibid.; and Minutes of the Indian Congress, Rapid City, S. Dak., 2 March 1934, ibid., p. 3.
50. Ibid., p. 4.
51. Ibid., pp. 5-14, 23.
52. Ibid., pp. 15-18. Dr. Henry Roe Cloud, a Winnebago educator, spoke at this and other Indian congresses in support of the Wheeler-Howard bill.
53. Ibid., pp. 47-54, and 3 March 1934, pp. 22-25, 40-41.
54. Ibid., 3 March 1934, pp. 29-30.
55. Collier, Memorandum for Secretary Ickes, 18 April 1934, ibid.
56. Collier to Editor of the *Catholic Daily Tribune*, 18 April 1934, Part 6-BB, ibid.; idem, Memorandum for Secretary Ickes, 18 April 1934, Collier Papers, Yale University Library, New Haven, Conn.
57. Minutes of the Indian Congress, Rapid City, S. Dak., Special Evening Session, 3 March 1934, RG 75, NA, pp. 1-7.
58. Ibid., pp. 20-23.
59. Ibid., 4 March 1934, pp. 12-13, 18-19, 27-28.
60. Ibid., pp. 4-7, 29, 31; and 5 March 1934, Afternoon Session, ibid., pp. 1-2.
61. Proceedings of the Conference at Chemawa, Oreg., 8 March 1934, RG 75, NA, pp. 10-14, 28-29. After the Chemawa Congress, E. A. Towner, an Indian attorney from Portland who spoke for the Umatillas, wrote Collier that his people disliked the bill because it was "too communistic and would not develop initiative and independence." Towner claimed that the northwest Indians did not want to be experimented with like "a medical guinea pig" and suggested that the plan be "tried on the whites first." If it killed them, the Indians would be "at least safe for a time." E. A. Towner to Collier, 14 March 1934, Records concerning the Wheeler-Howard Act, Part 10-A, RG 75, NA.
62. Proceedings of the Conference at Chemawa, Oreg., 9 March 1934, RG 75, NA, pp. 54, 56-57.
63. Ibid., pp. 43, 63, 65, 70.
64. Minutes of the Special Session of the Navajo Tribal Council, Fort Defiance, Ariz., 12-13 March 1934, Records concerning the Wheeler-Howard Act, Part 2-A, RG 75, NA.
65. Many of the Navajos disliked Section 15 of Title II, which authorized the secretary of the interior to restrict the number of livestock grazed on Indian land to prevent soil erosion.
66. Collier, "Indians at Work," *Survey Graphic* 23 (June 1934): 260-65; and Alden Stevens, "Once They Were Nomads," *Survey Graphic* 30 (February 1941): 64-67.

67. "The Missionaries' View on the Wheeler-Howard Bill," resolutions adopted by a group of missionaries at Fort Defiance, Ariz., 15 March 1934, Records concerning the Wheeler-Howard Act, Part 6-BB, RG 75, NA. The greatest opposition stemmed from the Christian Reformed Church, Presbyterians, Baptists, and an independent Hopi mission.
68. Berton Staples, president, United Traders Association, to Collier, 3 April 1934, ibid.
69. U.S., Congress, House, *Hearings on H.R. 7902, Readjustment of Indian Affairs*, 73d Cong., 2d sess., 1934, p. 384.
70. Minutes of the All Pueblo Council at Santo Domingo, N. Mex., 15 March 1934, Records concerning the Wheeler-Howard Act, Part 2-A, RG 75, NA. Collier argued that unless the Pueblos supported the Wheeler-Howard bill, some government official in the future might try to apply land allotment against the executive order part of their reservations. He also indicated that the bill would protect their ancient land grants, which might eventually face allotment because the status of the grants had not been decided by the Supreme Court.
71. U.S., Congress, House, *Hearings on H.R. 7902, Readjustment of Indian Affairs*, 73d Cong., 2d sess., 1934 pp. 380–82.
72. Minutes of the Indian Congress, Phoenix, Ariz., 15 March 1934, RG 75, NA, pp. 1–23, 32.
73. Ibid., pp. 25, 27, 35, 45–46, 66, 70–75.
74. Proceedings of the Conference for the Indians of Southern California, 17–18 March 1934, Riverside, Calif., RG 75, NA, pp. 34–37, 40, 47–48, 54, 65–66, 113.
75. Minutes of the Meeting at Anadarko, Okla., 20 March 1934, Kiowa Agency, Box 361697, RG 75, Federal Records Center, Fort Worth, Tex.
76. Ibid. The tribal business committees representing the Pawnee, Ponca, Kaw, Oto, and Tonkawa tribes also introduced a resolution opposing the Wheeler-Howard bill.
77. Minutes of the Meeting Held at Miami, Okla., 24 March 1934, Records concerning the Wheeler-Howard Act, Part 2-A, RG 75, NA.
78. Proceedings of the Conference for the Indians of the Five Civilized Tribes of Oklahoma, 22 March 1934, Muskogee, Okla., RG 75, NA, pp. 1–4.
79. Newspaper clipping, "Collier Attack Made by Bruner," *Tulsa Daily World*, 3 May 1934, Records concerning the Wheeler-Howard Act, Part 5-B, RG 75, NA; and Joseph Bruner to John Collier, 28 May 1934, ibid.
80. Proceedings of the Conference for the Indians of the Five Civilized Tribes of Oklahoma, 22 March 1934, Muskogee, Okla., RG 75, NA, p. 67.
81. Ibid., pp. 7–8, 13–18, 22.
82. Newspaper clipping, "Collier Would Revise Bill for Five Civilized Tribes," *Bartlesville Morning Examiner*, Oklahoma, Records concerning the Wheeler-Howard Act, Part 5-A, RG 75, NA.
83. Proceedings of the Conference for the Indians of the Five Civilized Tribes of Oklahoma, 22 March 1934, Muskogee, Okla., RG 75, NA, pp. 42–43, 60–61, 67–68; and Collier to Jenkin Lloyd Jones, associate editor, *Tusla Tribune*, 7 May 1934, Collier Papers.
84. The National Association on Indian Affairs, under the leadership of Oliver La

The Wheeler-Howard Bill Controversy

Farge, and the American Indian Defense Association, directed by Allan Harper, favored the principles embodied in the Wheeler-Howard bill with only minor reservations. Consult U.S., Congress, Senate, Committee on Indian Affairs, *Hearings on S. 2755, to Grant Indians the Freedom to Organize,* 73d Cong., 2d sess., 1934, pp. 325–28.

85. M. K. Sniffen, ed., "Stop, Look and Consider," *Indian Truth* 11 (March 1934): 1–3. The New Mexico Association on Indian Affairs, under the influence of Herbert Hagerman, a former governor of New Mexico and special commissioner to the Navajos during the Hoover administration, joined the Indian Rights Association. Herbert Hagerman to Charles Rhoads, 22 March 1934, Series 1, Item 49, RG 200, NA.
86. Collier to Jonathan Steere, 30 March 1934, Records concerning the Wheeler-Howard Act, Part 6-BB, RG 75, NA.
87. M. K. Sniffen, ed., "The Future of the Indians," *Indian Truth* 11 (May 1934): 1–7.
88. At the Hayward Congress, the delegates from the Bad River and Lac du Flambeau reservations feared that the bill might destroy their hunting and fishing rights. But the overwhelming majority of tribes supported the measure. They included the Chippewas from Grand Portage, Red Lake, White Earth, Red Cliff, and L'Anse. The Wisconsin Menominees, Winnebago, and Oneidas also favored the bill, as well as the Mount Pleasant Potawatomies from Michigan. Consult, "Testimony Taken at Hayward, Wisc.," 23–24 April 1934, RG 75, NA, pp. 1–74.
89. U.S., Department of the Interior, Memorandum for the Press, 15 April 1934, Collier Papers.
90. U.S., Congress, Senate, *Hearings on S. 2755, to Grant Indians the Freedom to Organize,* 73d Cong., 2d sess., 1934, pp. 66–69, 96, 101, 146, 151, 177.
91. Ibid., pp. 52, 97–98, 156, 239.
92. U.S., Congress, House, *Hearings on H.R. 7902, Readjustment of Indian Affairs,* 73d Cong., 2d sess., 1934, pp. 422–25. Tribes voting against the bill as of 7 May 1934 included those on the Rincon Reservation in California, the Crow of Montana, the Yankton Sioux of South Dakota, the Klamath of Oregon, the Colville, Spokan, and Snoqualmie of Washington, and the Arapaho and Shoshone of Wyoming.
93. Ibid., p. 310.
94. Ibid., p. 311.
95. Newspaper clipping, "Indian Group Attacks Werner's Activities," Records concerning the Wheeler-Howard Act, RG 75, NA; and Harold Ickes, Memo for Colonel McIntyre, 4 May 1934, Franklin Delano Roosevelt Library, Hyde Park, N.Y. (hereafter cited as FDRL), File No. 6-C.
96. Newspaper clipping, "Selfish Groups Block Indian Aid, Collier Claims," *Washington Daily News,* 20 April 1934, Records concerning the Wheeler-Howard Act, Part 6-B, RG 75, NA. Collier had already abolished more than six hundred jobs held by whites. Connolly, "End of a Long, Long Trail," p. 249. The commissioner followed this assault with two feature articles, on 6 May 1934 in the *Washington Post* and *New York Times,* demonstrating the evils of the allotment system and explaining the reform proposed by the New Deal.

97. Harold Ickes, Memorandum to All Employees of the Indian Service, 30 April 1934, Records concerning the Wheeler-Howard Act, Part 7, RG 75, NA.
98. John Collier, Memorandum for Secretary Ickes, 21 February 1934, FDRL, File No. 6-C.
99. Henry A. Wallace to Collier, 20 April 1934, Records of the Office of the Secretary of Agriculture, RG 16, NA.
100. Franklin Roosevelt to Edgar Howard and Burton K. Wheeler, 28 April 1934, FDRL, File No. 6-C.
101. U.S., *Statutes at Large* 48:984–88.
102. Ibid. At the insistence of Collier and Sen. Burton K. Wheeler, who opposed Henry Ashurst on the floor of the Senate, the Indian Reorganization Act did protect the Papagos's surface rights. Whites had to pay the Papago Tribe damages for loss of improvement on their land opened to mining. An inadequate yearly rental not exceeding five cents an acre also had to be paid to these Indians for the loss of land withdrawn for mining operations. Finally, any party desiring a mining patent had to pay the Papagos a one dollar per year fee in lieu of annual rental. See Collier, "The Papago Mineral Question in Relation to the Wheeler-Howard Indian Bill," 31 May 1934, RG 75, NA; and U.S., Congress, Senate, *Congressional Record*, 73d Cong., 2d sess., 12 June 1934, 78, pt. 10: 11122–37.
103. Ibid. The Klamath Indians of Oregon were exempt from Section 4 which prevented the sale of restricted land to whites.
104. Ibid.
105. Ibid.
106. Newspaper clipping, "Collier to Drop Part of the Bill," 9 May 1934, Series 1, Item 49, File on the Wheeler-Howard Bill, RG 200, NA.
107. Collier, "Address Given at the 50th Anniversary Ceremonies of the Haskell Institute, November 11–12, 1934," *Indians At Work* 2 (1 December 1934): 36–45.

Facing page: *Detail of President Ulysses S. Grant's executive order of April 9, 1874, creating the Hot Springs Indian Reservation in New Mexico Territory intended for the Chiricahua Apache. Reservations were established by three methods: treaty stipulation, executive order, and act of Congress. The practice of creating executive order reservations began as early as 1855, but its legality was questionable until the General Allotment Act of 1887 recognized the validity of these reservations. Reservations created by executive order, however, also could be abolished by executive order. When the Chiricahua declined to remove to Hot Springs, Grant reduced the size of the reservation in 1875; two years later President Rutherford B. Hayes issued an executive order restoring all the lands to the public domain. (RG 75)*

Executive Mansion.
April 9th 1874.

It is hereby ordered that the following described tract of Country in the Territory of New Mexico, be, and the same is hereby withdrawn from sale and reserved for the use and occupation of such Indians as the Secretary of the Interior may see fit to locate thereon, as indicated in this diagram, viz:

Beginning at the mouth of an ancient Pueblo in the valley of the Cañada Alamosa river, about seven miles above the present town of Cañada Alamosa, and running thence due East ten (10) miles; thence due South twenty-five (25) miles; thence due West thirty (30) miles; thence due North twenty-five (25) miles; thence due East twenty (20) miles to the point of beginning.

U. S. Grant

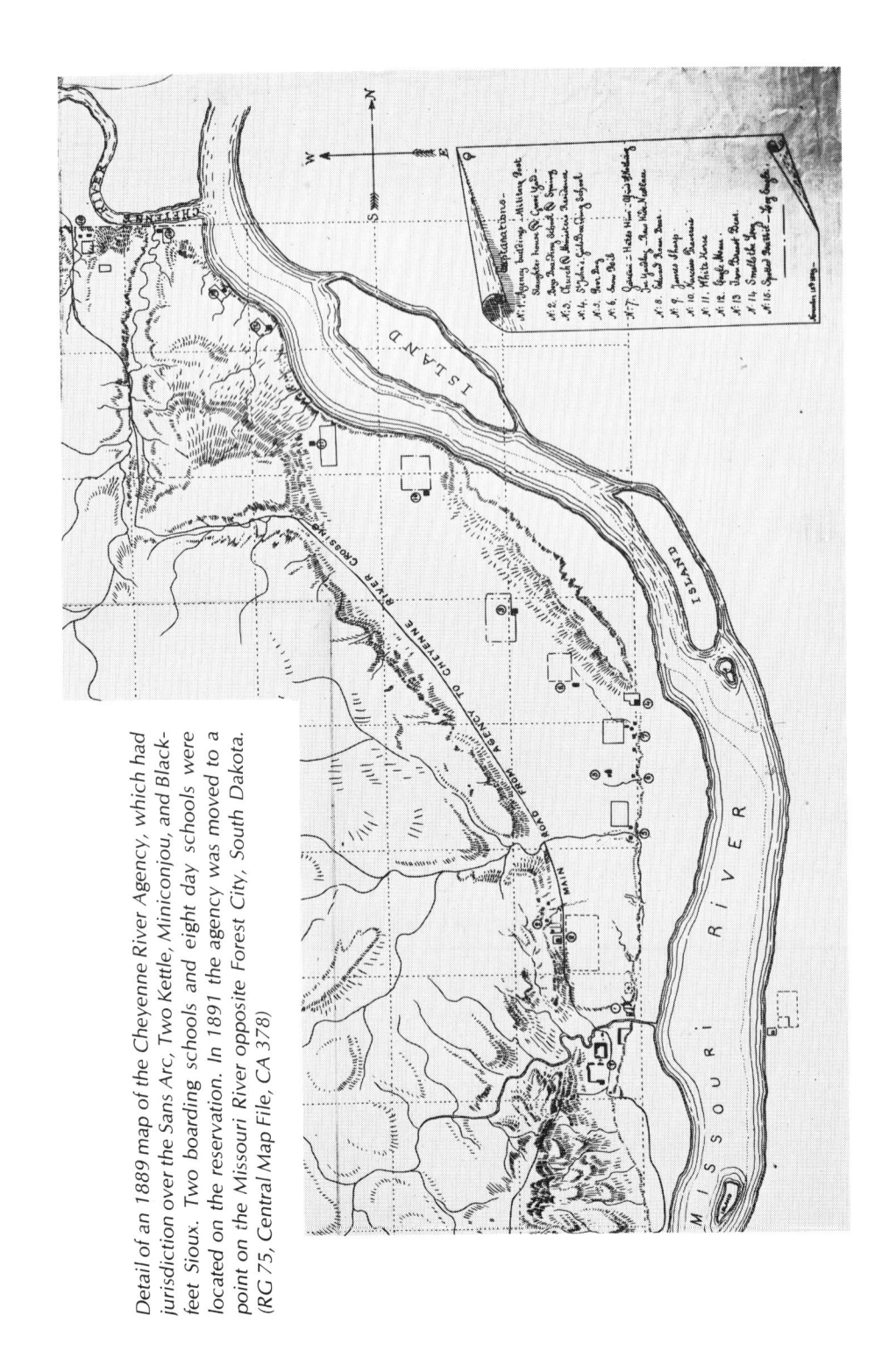

Detail of an 1889 map of the Cheyenne River Agency, which had jurisdiction over the Sans Arc, Two Kettle, Miniconjou, and Blackfeet Sioux. Two boarding schools and eight day schools were located on the reservation. In 1891 the agency was moved to a point on the Missouri River opposite Forest City, South Dakota. (RG 75, Central Map File, CA 378)

An undated view of the Crow Creek Agency in what is now South Dakota. (RG 75, No. 75-IP-2-72)

A view of the Nez Percé Agency, Idaho Territory, in 1879. (RG 75, No. 75-IP-1-43)

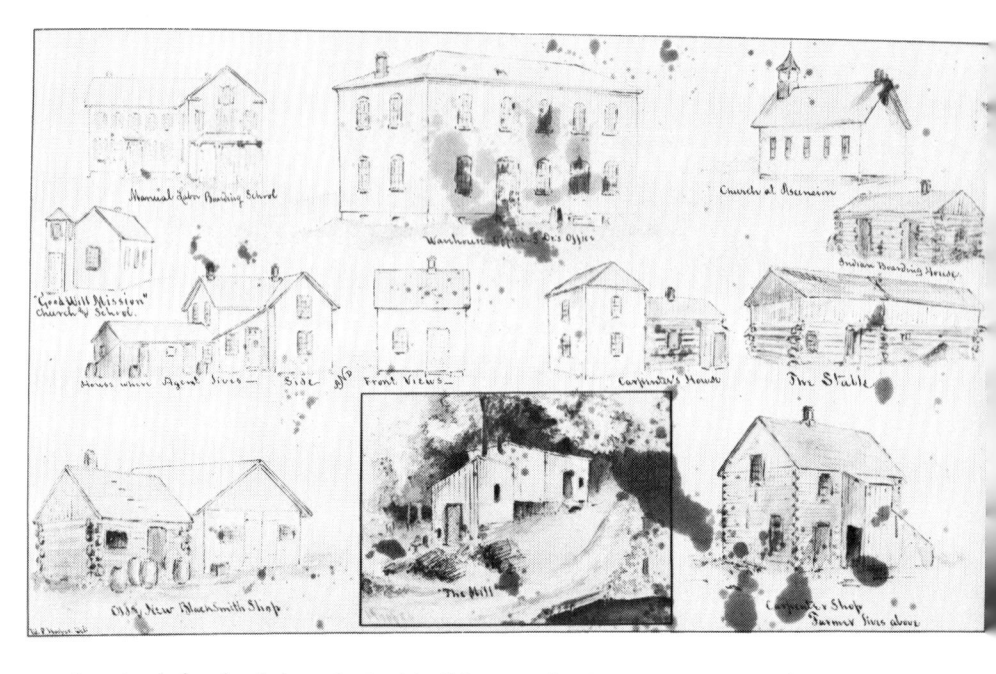

A stained sketch of the principal buildings at the Sisseton Agency, Lake Traverse Reservation, Dakota Territory, ca. 1875. Top row, left to right: the Manual Labor Boarding School, the warehouse including offices for the agent and physician, and the church at Ascension. Second row, left to right: the "Good Will Mission" church and school, side and front views of the agent's home, the carpenter's home, and the stable. Bottom row, left to right: the old and new blacksmith shop, the mill, and the carpenter shop with lodgings on the upper floor for the agency farmer. (RG 75)

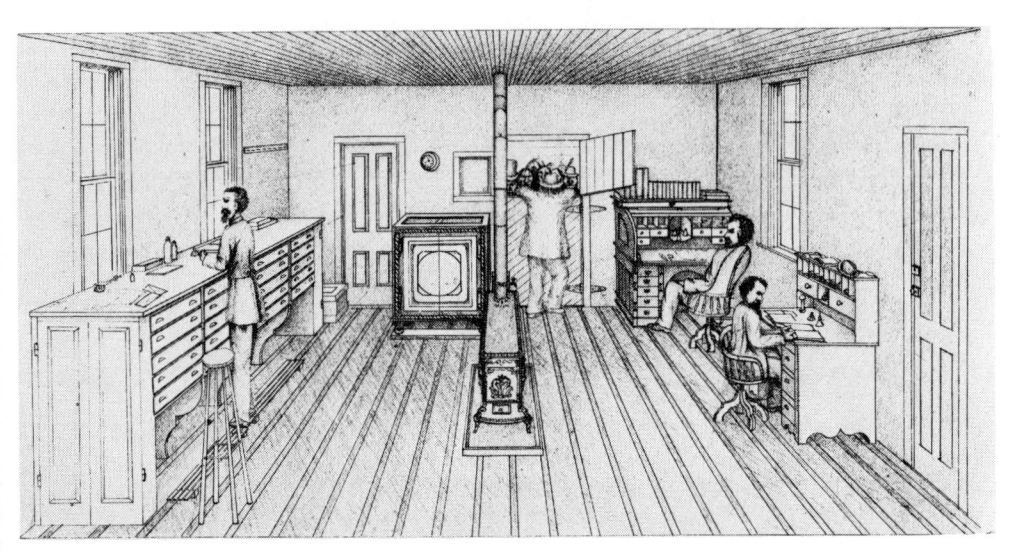

The interior of the office at the Rosebud Agency, South Dakota, in 1879 as drawn by James McCoy, one of the agency's carpenters. The clerk's desk is next to the outside entrance on the right and the agent's desk is in the corner. The agency's interpreter is shown talking to some of the Indians at a door leading to the Indians' councilroom. The office safe sits between the councilroom door and a door leading to the clerk's dormitory. The large desk on the left stored blank forms and stationery. The agency had jurisdiction over Spotted Tail's Band of Brulé Sioux and other bands of Sans Arcs, Oglala, Hunkpapa, and Miniconjou Sioux. (RG 75, Central Map File, 989)

The blending of two cultures is illustrated by this home of a fullblood Potawatomi located on an allotment in Kansas (1922). Here a wickiup-type dwelling stands in the front yard of a substantial frame farmhouse. (RG 75, Industrial Survey)

COMMENTARY

Roy W. Meyer

I find myself in disagreement with Dr. Hagan in only one minor particular, which I will address first in this commentary. The title of his paper is "The Reservation Policy: Too Little and Too Late." I would suggest that, in the light of the evidence he presented, the paper might well have been titled "The Reservation Policy: Too Much and Too Soon." For the architects of the reservation policy expected the Indian to undergo in a single generation a cultural transformation that our European ancestors took centuries to accomplish. That Secretary Harlan and his fellows saw this transformation primarily in terms of the replacement of hunting by agriculture and stockraising merely illustrates their perhaps unavoidable myopia. They seem to have had no conception of the profound changes it would necessitate in value systems, in the respective roles of the sexes, and in the whole cultural inheritance of the American Indian.

If only the material culture of the Indian had needed to be changed, one might suppose that, when applied to tribes with an agricultural tradition and longer exposure to European influences, the reservation system would have achieved its stated objectives more quickly than when applied to the nomadic tribes. In the long run it did, but in terms of the immediate goals of the system the effect of reservation life on these tribes was much the same as on those nomadic tribes that form the subject of Dr. Hagan's paper. Assuming the validity of his conclusions about the failure of the reservation system as applied to the nomadic peoples, a useful follow-up to his investigations would be a comparison between the effects of the system on these tribes and on Indian groups presumably better prepared for the transformation sought by Secretary Harlan, by the successive commissioners of Indian Affairs, and by the members of Congress.

For example, how well did the reservation policy work, in terms of its stated purposes, with such groups as the Mandan, Hidatsa, and Arikara Indians of the Fort Berthold Reservation, who had an agricultural tradition extending back several centuries? And how well did it work with the Santee Sioux of Nebraska, who had come strongly under white influence and had begun farming on a significant scale before their expulsion from Minnesota in 1863? Besides being in some degree agricultural, the Fort Berthold tribes were not compelled to leave their homes; their reservation included the village in which all three tribes were then living. Surely, then, if the reservation system had a chance for success anywhere, here would be the place. What in fact happened?

Contrary to what one might expect, during most of the period treated by Hagan the Fort Berthold people were, if anything, more dependent upon government-supplied rations than the Teton Dakotas. The Santee Sioux, though less heavily dependent, were nevertheless regular recipients of rations and would have suffered severe hardship without them. If we look at the present conditon of these tribes and confine our attention to the reservation populations, we will not find that the descendants of the semi-agricultural groups are noticeably better off economically than the Pine Ridge Sioux or the western Oklahoma tribes—the Kiowas, Comanches, and Cheyennes, among others.

Why did the reservation policy fail (if it did) just as badly in the case of tribes with an agricultural tradition as it did in the case of the nomadic bison hunters of the High Plains? In part, of course, the failure may be attributed to the general incompetence and inefficiency of government operations, which Hagan justly characterizes as "too little and too late." The Fort Berthold Indians and the Santee Sioux were often the victims of niggardly appropriations by Congress, of late-arriving supplies, of inferior goods, and of incompetent or dishonest agents. Like the other tribes, they were repeatedly threatened with removal to some new location. Efforts were made in the 1870s to persuade the Fort Berthold people to accept a new home in Oklahoma, and the Santee Sioux were subjected to pressures to join their Teton relatives on the Great Sioux Reservation.

But more serious than these obstacles to assimilation was the fact that these tribes, no less than the nomads, were expected to undergo a cultural transformation that involved far more than the way they made their living. Although the Fort Berthold people, at the time the reservation was established in 1870, had been practicing agriculture in the Missouri valley for a long time, they derived only a part of their subsistence from this source. White observers disagree widely on the relative importance of agriculture, hunting, and food gathering to these tribes, but it is unlikely that their limited hoe culture accounted for more than half the food they consumed in the mid-nineteenth century. As with many other Indian groups, the work was principally the responsibility of the women and girls. Prestige and honor for men were obtained from the performance of acts of courage in warfare and by successful hunting. By the late 1860s and the 1870s, the three tribes were so severely reduced in numbers by disease that they could no longer compete with the Sioux, and they were penned up in their village, scarcely daring to venture forth to hunt. And by the time the menace of the Sioux was removed, the bison were also gone.

So the reservation policy, as it manifested itself in the generation after the Civil War, affected the Fort Berthold tribes in much the same way as it did the nomadic peoples. They too were subjected to intense pressure for swift cultural change, both through the deliberate efforts of government officials and missionaries and through the force of circumstances indirectly resulting from white occupation of the continent. The Santee Sioux were in a somewhat different situation. Unlike the Fort Berthold people, they had been exiled to an unfamiliar environment, where what they had learned about farming in Minnesota was not wholly applicable. Their culture had been disrupted but not destroyed, and there were sharp intragroup conflicts between people with differing degrees of acculturation. Factionalism, we have been told, was at once partly a product of the reservation system and a contributory cause of its failure. Despite routinely cheerful announcements of progress in the agents' annual reports, the evidence is conclusive that the reservation system was not working as well as its promoters had expected.

Yet, as Dr. Hagan says of the reservation policy as applied to the nomadic tribes, it could have been worse. And it was less of a failure in the case of the semiagricultural tribes than it was elsewhere. Once the threat of Sioux attack was a thing of the past, the Fort Berthold people were persuaded to leave Like-a-Fishhook village and scatter out over the reservation on individual farms. It was high time. The Mandans and Hidatsas had lived there for forty years, longer than they had customarily remained at one site, and both the soil fertility and the timber supply had been seriously depleted. Although many of them drifted back to new communities over the next half century, others remained on their farms and achieved a measure of economic well-being superior to that of most Plains tribes.

Likewise, the Santee Sioux accepted allotment several years before the Dawes Act and became at least moderately successful farmers, so much so that by 1917 it was deemed expedient to discontinue the Santee Agency. It was thought then that only a few elderly or handicapped people would need to continue receiving services from the government. This supposition proved overoptimistic, as the 1930s demonstrated, but it was not Indians alone who needed help during the depression period. The Fort Berthold people survived the depression in better shape than their

Plains neighbors, but the loss of their best land—the heart of their reservation—upon the construction of the Garrison Dam threw many of them back into a state of dependency on government aid and unearned income.

Looking at the Fort Berthold and Santee reservations today, one sees little to suggest that the outcome of the reservation policy was significantly different for them than, for example, the Pine Ridge or Cheyenne-Arapaho reservations. But perhaps it is unfair to look only at the reservation populations. Hagan spoke of the "ultimate objective" of the reservation policy as the "absorption of the Indian population on the basis of complete equality." If this was in fact its objective, then the proportion of a tribe that left the reservation and entered what in the 1950s was called the mainstream of American life is surely a legitimate measure of the policy's success or failure in terms of its own stated goals.

Much further research is needed before definitive answers can be found. Individual case studies would have to be made of the people whose names appear on the tribal rolls drawn up in connection with the recent claims award to the Santee Sioux to find out where they have gone and how successful they have been in the white society. Certainly the two or three hundred people who still linger on the Santee Reservation represent but a small proportion of the total number of descendants of those who lived there in the late nineteenth century, and it is unlikely that they constitute a fair cross section of those descendants.[1] Since the building of the Garrison Dam there has been a considerable exodus from the Fort Berthold Reservation. We need to know what has become of those who have left. In the absence of such evidence as detailed research would provide, however, I would guess that a far higher proportion of the Fort Berthold and Santee people have "made it" in the off-reservation community than would be true of, for example, Pine Ridge. Although many Pine Ridge people have in recent years migrated to Rapid City, they have tended to gather in Indian communities and to retain close ties with the reservation.

Finally, therefore, I would like to submit, not as a conclusion but as a tentative working hypothesis, to be confirmed or refuted by future research, that the reservation policy in the late nineteenth century, as it affected these Indian groups and probably others, had two seemingly contradictory results. On the one hand, it had a leveling effect, which tended to reduce the tribes subjected to it to a more or less uniform plane of dependency, poverty, and apathy. But on the other hand, some tribes, perhaps because they had an agricultural tradition, a greater sense of community identity, or a more sophisticated political system, emerged in the twentieth century economically better off than others. Whether this was because they were more successful at exploiting such opportunities

Commentary

as the reservation system offered or whether they simply resisted its pressures more effectively remains for future research to discover.

NOTE

1. This statement might require modification in the light of recent developments on the Santee Reservation. A massive housing program on the site of the old agency, which had been largely abandoned for many years, is having social consequences that as yet cannot be measured. There may be occurring a movement back to the reservation and a revival of a sense of group identity.

COMMENTARY

Mary E. Young

I found the papers of William Hagan and Kenneth Philp to be very interesting, but not particularly surprising. Professor Hagan has outlined very neatly the circumstances in which the reservation system developed and how these circumstances contributed to its failure during the first generation on the reservation. That this policy was too little and too late, or too much and too soon—whichever way you want to put it—is a rather familiar conclusion. Nor should we be surprised that when John Collier decided to reverse the assimilationist trend in Indian policy, return to a kind of utopian pluralism, and let the Indians do our social experimenting for us, many tribes assumed on the basis of their past experience that the government must surely be trying to take something away from them.

Less superficially, there is a puzzle. If the reservation system was as great a failure as some of its critics imply and if assimilation was as unacceptable to many Indian groups as they imply, why did an attempt at reversing the assimilation policy meet with such widespread criticism on the part of Indians? In answering that question, I would like to try to put the Indian reservation system in a context of the development of American social institutions generally. The reservation is in some respects a unique institution, but it is by no means isolated from the mainstream of social development.

It is a commonplace that over the past two centuries there has been a lot of migration going on—a westward movement in the United States, a northward and southward movement in Africa, an eastward movement in Russia—in addition to urbanization, bringing together people of diverse cultures and diverse attitudes about how people ought to behave. One of the standard ways of accommodating to the discomfort involved in this kind of contact is to establish systems of segregation. The white middle class suburb is one kind of example of this, as are the ethnic or racial ghetto and the Indian reservation.

There is a second kind of segregation which is also important to our understanding of the way Indian reservations operated. It involves the isolation of people in separate institutions on the basis of their special needs and on the basis of their current unassimilability into the mainstream of the working public. The public school for children is one example of such an institution; prisons and mental hospitals are others. You can attribute the establishment of such institutions to industrialization, urbanization, specialization, or the irresistible impulse of the WASP majority to impose its norms on other people, but the alleged function of all these institutions—including the Indian reservation—is therapeutic. They are supposed to process people so that they can enter or re-enter the mainstream population.

Social critics have observed that the impact of many of these isolated institutions is otherwise than it is supposed to be. For one thing, they are public institutions, and as Hagan's paper abundantly demonstrates, public institutions tend to be supported as little as possible with the resources required to do their tasks. In fact, they are supported less than is possible consistent with the avoidance of scandal. This is true of the public school, the private city of Philadelphia, the prisons of Ohio, mental hospitals that become snakepits, or the Navajo Reservation.

The second part of the problem has to do with the development of specialized subcultures within the institutions. Those who run the institutions often develop a vested interest in keeping their clients dependent and submissive because it is easier for them to run the establishment that way. This is an aim which is inconsistent with the development of the independence and initiative the inmates are supposed to be learning in order to enter the mainstream. A friend of mine, for example, told me that his daughter in elementary school learned more about close-order drill in her first weeks in school than he learned in his first weeks in the army. Similarly, on an Indian reservation, though the agent might have suffered as he watched his charges standing in line for rations, he obviously suffered a great deal more when, on their own initiative, they took to their ponies to chase their own cattle—to say nothing of when they decided to go out and chase the settlers' cattle. Independence was simply inconsistent with the pattern of peaceable and orderly behavior that was to be imposed.

On the other hand, such institutions develop a subculture among their clients. One of the principal aims of such subcultures, whether it is students cheating in school (which one critic of the educational system says is the most creative thing children do in school) or prisoners teaching criminal techniques to each other, is to resist change. The subculture enables the objects of reform to resist the kind of authoritarian pressure they are under to change their behavior. In this respect also, the Indian reservation is not unique.

You might then suppose that the idea of a Red Atlantis would meet with a great deal of enthusiasm among Indians who wanted to run their own institutions in their own communities. Why did this not happen? A cynic might say that there is almost no institution so defective that its clients do not develop vested interests in it. Public schools have their "A" students, prisons their trustees, and reservations their Uncle Tomahawks. To be less cynical, we need to recognize that as well as working badly, these institutions often do function as they are supposed to function for some people at some times. The interesting problem is, for which people, at what time, where, and why? Historians might profitably follow the example of anthropologists in paying a good deal more attention to this problem. Some of us (and I include myself) remind me of James Thurber's statement about the wife in *Let Your Mind Alone*. He said she was better acquainted with the latent content of her husband's mind than she was with its manifest content. I think a lot of us are a good deal better acquainted with the latently dysfunctional aspects of reservations as institutions than we are with those people in those situations in which the aim of assimilation—whether you like it or not—was in part achieved.

A very good example of such a situation might be the off-reservation boarding school, which has been and still is very severely criticized. Some of its severest critics are its graduates, who have gone on not to become alcoholic or insane but rather to become leaders in their tribes or organizers of Pan-Indian movements—in other words, to lead very useful and constructive lives.

In conclusion, perhaps it would help us to understand the reservation system better if we looked at its "successes" as carefully as we have looked at its failures. If this were done, we might give much more credit to the Indian people who were on the reservations. Rather than viewing Indians as passive, pathetic victims of policy, we might see them as people who in fact showed a great deal of durability, adaptability, and creativity in making a variety of responses to what was often a tragic situation. In the course of such research we might find information that would be not only interesting but possibly even surprising.

COMMENTARY
W. David Baird

Though the two papers in this section address themselves to different eras of American history, there is a single theme common to both. Each discusses directly and indirectly the reservation—defined as a delimited tract of land—as an instrument of Indian policy. One paper demonstrates how nineteenth-century America depended upon the reservation to destroy aboriginal culture, while the other recounts a twentieth-century effort to use the reservation as a basis for a Red Atlantis. Professor Hagan has superbly assessed the post-Civil War reservation system. Drawing primarily upon materials in the National Archives, he has presented an insightful, thought-provoking analysis of a policy that succeeded primarily in its negative goals—dispossession of the Indian's "surplus" lands. The positive objective of aboriginal assimilation remained unfulfilled, at least in the nineteenth century, because Congress failed to provide rations, farm equipment, and educational opportunities. It was a matter, Hagan suggests, of it always being "too little . . . too late." The implication, of course, is that if there had been *more, earlier* reservation policy might have brought the desired absorption of the Indian population. Though I question the efficacy of money in solving problems of social dimensions, Professor Hagan's conclusions nonetheless are balanced and judicious.

My principal concern here, however, is to comment upon, more precisely to elaborate upon, Dr. Philp's account of John Collier's quest for a reservation-based Red Atlantis. Professor Philp has presented an equally interesting and well-researched paper. Depending primarily upon records relating to the Wheeler-Howard Act in the Archives, he has also drawn upon materials in the Federal Records Center at Forth Worth, manuscript collections at Yale and the Library of Congress, printed congressional hearings, Collier's published works, and pertinent contemporary publications. Altogether his research is impressive and more than adequately substantiates his study.

With clarity of style, Philp has recounted John Collier's fight for a Red Atlantis that would instruct white America in the advantages of the common life. Frequently labeled the Indian New Deal, the initial Wheeler-Howard bill would have ended allotment of Indian land, returned to tribal control those acres not only unallotted but also those already allotted, gathered landless Indians on consolidated reserves, established a viable tribal government with corporate privileges beyond the control of the local states, instilled appreciation for aboriginal culture, and created a tribunal to deal specifically with Indian legal affairs. Most critical to the commissioner's Red Atlantis, however, was the reservation, upon which the American Indians could return to their traditional common life, find inner strength in their contact with Mother Earth, and sustain themselves economically. Since preservation of the people and ancient tribal values was Collier's objective, the Wheeler-Howard bill, like so much of the New Deal, was more conservative than radical. Also, the measure had a white-liberal orientation that reflected more of what the reformers thought desirable than that actually demanded by the Indians.

But what Collier wanted was not what Collier got. As Philp has indicated, despite the commissioner's elaborate propaganda campaign, the legislation as initially drafted had little or no resemblence to the measure passed. To be sure, the Indian Reorganization Act terminated the allotment procedure and extended restrictions indefinitely, but it did not provide for the mandatory return of previously allotted lands or the establishment of new reservations. The commissioner rationalized the final act as an "emergency measure" and as a "first step," but the fact remains that relative to his original proposal it was no step at all.

Why did Collier, an earnest friend of the Indian, fail to reinstitute the common life among the American aboriginals? It is to this question that I will address the remainder of my commentary, which is intended to be more of an extension of Professor Philp's paper rather than a criticism of it. My view is that nothing short of a careful examination of the general *Indian* reaction to the Wheeler-Howard bill can fully explain the commissioner's failure. In other words, something more than the activity of whites accounts for Collier's lack of success. To recount the total Indian response is beyond the capability of this short paper, yet an examination of the Oklahoma Indian reaction can give insight into the total aboriginal response. As a case in point, let us consider the Quapaw tribe.

Initially an Arkansas people, the Quapaws were assigned a reservation of 150 sections in northeastern Indian Territory in 1833. Exempt from the General Allotment Act, they unilaterally allotted their domain in March 1893, the only tribe to do so, and then two years after the fact won congressional approval. Each allottee received a 240-acre tract restricted against alienation for twenty-five years. In the early decades of the twentieth century valuable lead and zinc deposits were discovered on some of the allotments, which by 1934 had paid nearly $11 million in royalties to the few fortunate allottees. Those Quapaws not so lucky—and they represented the vast majority of the tribe—largely disposed of their inheritance at the conclusion of the restricted period. Accordingly, by 1934, of the 191,000 acres initially allotted only 35,000 primarily mineral-rich acres remained under Quapaw control. With the majority of their people landless, the tribe matched the profile of those Indians Collier hoped to assist.[1]

But from the beginning, the Quapaws aligned themselves with the opposition to the proposed legislation. Indeed, on March 10, 1934, the tribal council, led by Chief Victor Griffin, formally rejected the bill and directed its attorney, Vern E. Thompson of Joplin, Missouri, to appear before Congress and make known tribal objections.[2] Two days later, the Quapaws endorsed a resolution of the Association of Indian Tribes based at Miami, Oklahoma, that labeled the measure "as a flagrant slap at Indian intelligence."[3] And on March 14, at a Muskogee, Oklahoma, meeting of the Indian National Confederacy, they joined in the general condemnation of the Red Man's New Deal.[4] The latter group was led by Joseph Bruner, a fullblood Creek, whose opposition to Collier's program prompted the commissioner to label him as a "sociological curiosity."

In the meantime, Vern Thompson specified the Quapaw objections before the House Committee on Indian Affairs. Labeling the Wheeler-Howard bill as unconstitutional because it would infringe upon fee simple titles, he protested the loss of heirship rights and the return of previously allotted land to common ownership. It was inconceivable to him that provident Indians should be forced to share their inheritance with the improvident. "The good Lord has given them something that Congress or no one else intended that they have," he said, "and now that they have it they are being asked to give it back." Also, he questioned the creation of Indian communities that would exist beyond the authority of state control, a process that the *Muskogee Daily Phoenix* had seen as driving "the red man from the channels of commerce and sending him scurrying back to his tepee" on "communized, thoroughly 'Russianized' reservations."[5] Thompson asserted also that such a procedure would force the Indians to virtually withdraw from the citizenship body of which they had been a part for more than one hundred years. Finally, Thompson noted that the legislation would deprive the wealthy fullbloods of their mining royalties and distribute them instead to prodigal and profligate mixed bloods. Obviously, the Quapaws were more concerned about the personal sacrifices demanded by the measure than they were about the communal advantages.[6]

The tribe, therefore, was openly hostile when John Collier arrived at

Miami on March 24 to preside over the ninth of his celebrated "Congresses." According to the *Miami Daily News-Record*, he had come to northeastern Oklahoma in a "hostile frame of mind" because of erroneous assessments of his proposal circulating throughout the West and the reception he had received at Muskogee two days earlier. Nevertheless, the commissioner patiently explained the provisions of the Wheeler-Howard bill to the 550 gathered in the auditorium of the local junior college.[7] Emphasizing the dramatic loss of Indian lands since the General Allotment Act, he also hammered home the optional features of the measure and the advantages to be derived from reestablished reservations. As was his custom, he followed his remarks with a question and answer period, in the course of which the Quapaw's reiterated their opposition.[8]

Vern Thompson, just home from Washington, spoke for the tribal council. He queried the commissioner as to how the bill would affect heirship rights, vested interests in lead and zinc deposits, and state citizenship—issues to which he had just directed the attention of Congress. Other inquiries, though not inspired specifically by the Quapaws but that reflected their views, related to the very purpose of the bill. "If the Indian is not considered by you as inferior," one asked, "why do you seek to place him in a community by himself?" Another inquired: "Indians and whites have been citizens of Oklahoma for twenty-seven years. . . . Why do you propose a change? Who is the bad apple in the barrel?"[9]

Collier responded to these questions for the most part with patience and good humor. Yes, the measure with some exceptions called for the return of allotted lands to the tribe upon the death of the allottee; no, tribal communities on reservations would not lose state citizenship rights; no, he did not think the Indian inferior; no, his proposal was no more communistic than General Motors Corporation, and so on. Yet on occasion his comments and attitude doubtlessly offended his hearers. By emphasizing the erosion of the Indian land base, he left the unmistakable impression that Indians had proved incapable of managing their own affairs. His explanation as to what would happen if the Wheeler-Howard bill were rejected sounded more like a threat than a warning. And his earnestness in advocating a white-liberal reform program suggested that skeptical, conservative Indians did not always know what was best for themselves. On the whole, however, the commissioner favorably impressed his Miami audience. Additionally, he quieted many of their fears. The mineral rich Quapaws, for example, learned with relief that their vested interests in zinc and lead deposits would not be disturbed.[10]

Yet Collier's congress at Miami, as well as at Muskogee and Anadarko, failed to produce any ground swell of support for a Red Atlantis.

Opposition, if somewhat less hysterical, continued unabated. To be sure, as Professor Philp has indicated, the Keetoowah Cherokees and some tribal leaderships did endorse the Wheeler-Howard bill, but the Quapaws and most Oklahoma Indians remained unalterably opposed. Indeed, three days after Collier's visit to the Quapaws, the tribal council resolved to continue its resistance to the legislation despite the commissioner's explanations. And on April 9, Vern Thompson presented the council's formal resolution of opposition to the House Committee on Indian Affairs, at which time he revealed another dimension of Quapaw skepticism: any community that the tribe formed under the provisions of the bill would necessarily include those that had previously sold their allotments. As the landless Quapaws made up a majority of the tribe, those whose inheritance provided the basis for a new reservation would have little say in the administration of *their* lands. Obviously, the individual sacrifices demanded by Collier's reform proposal were much too high.[11]

But the basis of opposition was not always economic. The Oklahoma Indians believed that the passage of the Wheeler-Howard bill would force them to "retreat" from civilization. They had come to accept the federal government's traditional dictum that "civilization" meant individual ownership of land. To return to the common life as advocated by Collier would, therefore, place the aboriginals outside the pale of "civilization," bestow upon them second-class citizenship, and return them to "supervised barbarism." Rather than conserve the best of the present, Collier's program appeared to call for a gigantic leap backward.[12]

Once transmitted to Washington, these views of the Indians had a telling effect upon Congress. Even with the modifications proposed by Collier, the Wheeler-Howard bill languished in committee. Only after President Roosevelt took a personal interest in late April did an informal subcommittee of both Senate and House members produce a measure acceptable to Congress. Reducing the bill from forty-eight to eight pages, the subcommittee scuttled Collier's Red Atlantis by deleting sections that would have returned previously allotted lands to tribal ownership and consolidated fractionalized reservations. And if that were not enough, in mid-June Sen. Elmer Thomas of Oklahoma secured the exclusion of all Oklahoma Indians from most of the provisions of the rewritten bill. As a consequence the Indian Reorganization Act, a shadow of the original Wheeler-Howard bill, did not apply to 30 percent of the Indian population.

Two years later, though, Congress reexamined its action and extended the major benefits of the IRA to those Oklahoma Indians previously excluded. One might suppose that the passage of the Oklahoma Indian Welfare Act constituted belated local support for Collier's Indian New

Deal. It did not. The Quapaws completely ignored the measure and have refused to this day to organize under its provisions, even though their heirship rights and civilized status would remain unaffected. And they were not alone. Of the 103,000 eligible for the Oklahoma Indian Welfare Act, some 90,000 spurned its benefits. These, along with 86,000 Indians outside of Oklahoma who between 1934 and 1936 specifically rejected the IRA, meant that a majority of all American Indians repudiated even adulterated forms of Collier's program.[13]

And the commissioner's opponents did not just stop with a refusal to cooperate with the New Deal. Immediately after the adoption of the IRA, they launched a program designed to dismantle and discredit it. Organized into the American Indian Federation and led by Oklahoma-based Indians, they credited the initial Wheeler-Howard bill to the "subversive" influence of the American Civil Liberties Union, accused the commissioner of atheism, and labeled the Red Atlantis as an un-American, communist "Jew Deal." When the Senate Indian Affairs Committee in 1939 adopted a measure that would have repealed the IRA in five states, Collier attributed the report to the influence of the American Indian Federation. Moreover, in hearings before the House Committee on Indian Affairs, he impugned the motives of his antagonists and intemperately accused the federation of being a "fifth column" Nazi conspiracy that plotted to overthrow the national government. Why else, he asked, did Hitler declare the Indians to be Aryans?[14]

Though the commissioner successfully prevented the dismantling of the IRA, in Oklahoma at least he failed to secure widespread support for even the minimal goals of the Indian New Deal. The rejection was not so much of Collier as it was of his hopes for the Indian. Frankly, in the 1930s the Quapaws and other Oklahoma Indians by-and-large sought assimilation into the dominant white society. To be sure, they valued the memory of Heckaton, Dragging Canoe, and Pushmataha, but as contemporary examples, they looked to Robert L. Owens, Charles Curtis, W. W. Hastings, and Will Rogers.[15] For them, a revived race settled communally on reservations was a retreat from "civilization," a view that signaled the triumph, however belatedly, of the nineteenth-century policy described by Professor Hagan. And because that policy succeeded in Oklahoma, John Collier's attempt to create a Red Atlantis, as recounted by Professor Philp, necessarily failed.

NOTES

1. No satisfactory study of Quapaw tribal history exists.
2. U.S., Congress, House, Committee on Indian Affairs, *Hearings on H.R. 7902*, 73d Cong., 2d sess., 1934, pt. 5:157.

Commentary

3. *Muskogee Daily Phoenix*, 18 March 1934.
4. Ibid., 15 March 1934.
5. Ibid., 8 March 1934.
6. For Thompson's testimony, see U.S., Congress, House, Committee on Indian Affairs, *Hearings on H.R. 7902*, 73d Cong., 2d sess., 1934, pt. 5:165.
7. *Miami Daily News-Record*, 25 March 1934.
8. Minutes of Meeting Held at Miami, Oklahoma, 24 March 1934, Quapaw Agency, Records of the Bureau of Indian Affairs, Record Group 75, Federal Records Center, Fort Worth, Tex.
9. Ibid.
10. Ibid.
11. For Thompson's 9 April 1934 testimony, see U.S., Congress, House, Committee on Indian Affairs, *Hearings on H.R. 7902*, 73d Cong., 2d sess., 1934, pt. 5:167–72.
12. *Tulsa Tribune*, 3 March 1934 and 27 March 1934. See also *Muskogee Daily Phoenix*, 25 March 1934.
13. U.S., Congress, House, Committee on Indian Affairs, *Hearings on S. 2103*, 76th Cong., 3d sess., 1940, pp. 390–98.
14. Ibid., pp. 32, 68–118.
15. See Minutes of Meeting Held at Miami, Oklahoma, 24 March 1934, Quapaw Agency, Records of the Bureau of Indian Affairs, Record Group 75, Federal Records Center, Fort Worth, Tex.

DISCUSSION NOTE

Henry Fritz opened the discussion by questioning Hagan's suggestion that the objectives of the Dawes Act of 1887 would have been achieved even if the act itself had not been passed. He pointed out that the act was intended to secure Indian title to specific lands and to assimilate the Native Americans by eliminating the reservation system as quickly as possible. Were these objectives aided by the Dawes Act or could similar goals have been achieved without the law? Hagan agreed that the Dawes Act probably expedited the achievement of its objectives but noted that prior to its passage Congress enacted legislation opening several reservations and passed similar legislation after the Dawes Act became law. Dawes himself sponsored a special act to open the Dakota Reservation after 1887. Although the Dawes Act of 1887 reduced the amount of legislation necessary to open the reservations, they would have been opened even if it had not been passed.

Theodore W. Taylor of the Bureau of Indian Affairs was curious about the influence of the depression on the Wheeler-Howard Act. He recalled reading that Collier favored the movement back to the land because he believed the Indians would have difficulty competing in the industrial scene during the depression. Both Philp and Baird agreed that the favorable legislative climate during Roosevelt's first term facilitated passage of the Wheeler-Howard Act. The act, however, was a culmination of reform efforts originating in the 1920s.

Senapaw of the Creek Nation asked Philp several questions about the nature of the failure of Collier's concept of a Red Atlantis. Philp replied that Collier's plan to preserve and revitalize tribal cultures failed because he was unable to establish the politically and economically strong tribal communities necessary for its success. Philp agreed with Senapaw that even today it is unlikely that the Indian reservations can be made economically viable communities.

Michael T. Smith of the Bureau of Indian Affairs remarked that the speakers tended to overlook what he thought was a most important aspect of Collier's policy. Collier helped the Indians overcome their psychological depression by showing them that they did not have to become white to be acceptable. This point was enlarged upon by D'Arcy McNickle who stated that the Indians found it difficult to vote on Collier's proposals. For generations they had been treated as inferiors, and it was hard for them to see themselves objectively. Only now, years later, are Indians beginning to take pride in being Indian, a self-awareness that Collier was trying to promote.

Ralph W. Goodwin of East Texas State University asked the speakers to comment on the Indian assimilationists who opposed Collier. Baird replied that Collier was disturbed by the size of the American Indian Federation's constituency. When he attempted to discredit its leader, Joseph Bruner, a thoroughly assimilated Indian, by referring to him as a sociological curiosity who did not really represent the people he presumed to speak for, Will Rogers came to Bruner's defense. In reality, a host of Oklahoma Indians were associated with the federation. Philp added that the size of the federation's Oklahoma following was due in a large part to the federation's sponsorship of a bill calling for a cash settlement for many Indians. Consequently, they supported Bruner in his opposition to Collier.

Bruce Davies of the American Indian Press Association commented that many traditionalist Indians opposed Collier because they saw him as just another alien who was trying to impose his ideology upon them.

Frederick D. Kershner of Teachers College, Columbia University, was interested in knowing how influential anthropologists had been in formulating policy, particularly in the post-Civil War period. Hagan said he could find no evidence of their influence. He believed Indian policy was designed to open Indian lands to white exploitation. Anything else was a secondary consideration. Kershner amplified his question by citing a dissertation by one of his students showing that American history and geography textbooks persistently portrayed the development of the West as a clash between civilization and barbarism. Hagan replied that he found that interpretation to be merely a rationalization for what was essentially a policy of exploitation. Philp pointed out that a formal group of anthropologists replaced the Board of Indian Commissioners under Franklin Roosevelt's administration. They were an important influence in his administration and to some extent were responsible for the development of stereotyped views of Indians.

Fritz asked McNickle to comment on the idea that the Indian response to the Wheeler-Howard Act reflected the destruction of Indian culture accomplished by the implementation of the Dawes Land-in-Severalty Act of 1887. McNickle replied that Indian opposition to turning their lands back into a general pool indicated the effectiveness of the Dawes Act, which fostered private ownership of property. Some tribes such as the

Jicarilla Apache, however, were fairly traditional and they did turn back their allotments. There is no doubt that the Dawes Act severely damaged the underlying social fabric of the reservations, but it did not destroy it. McNickle concluded that the Indian communities now are more viable places to live in than they were in the 1930s.

VI

Some Aspects of Twentieth-Century Federal Indian Policy

INTRODUCTION
Alvin M. Josephy, Jr.

The papers so far have dealt with the evolution of federal Indian policy. Lawrence Kelly's essay will bring us up to the present, and then the commissioner of the Bureau of Indian Affairs will discuss current problems and concerns. Kelly's paper is an assessment of John Collier and the New Deal. Kelly was born in Oklahoma City, went to Marquette University, and received his M.A. and Ph.D. from the University of New Mexico. He has published two books on the Navajo.

As a historian, myself, I have viewed the underlying strain running throughout the history of relations between whites and Indians as the recognition that before the arrival of whites in the New World the Indians were free peoples—free societies—who managed and controlled their own affairs to their own satisfaction. When we came over here, we put them on the defensive, fighting for their continued existence and for their freedom. They have been engaged in that fight ever since. Once the military conflict ended, the Indians for a time had no opportunity to continue their fight for freedom. Gradually, however, that fight began again among all the different Indian societies. It has accelerated so that today it is probably the main theme of relations between Indians and whites in our society. This really is the subject we are dealing with here—the Indians' fight for self-determination, for the right to manage and control their own affairs, the right to be as free as the rest of us, not free from their reservations or property but free in their tribal organizations and groups.

The preceding papers are what I might call the white society's interest in and relations with the American Indians. The last two papers will be the voice of the American Indian—the Honorable Louis R. Bruce, commissioner of Indian Affairs, and D'Arcy McNickle. Commissioner Bruce was born on the Onondaga Indian Reservation near Syracuse, New York, and was raised on the Saint Regis Reservation in northern New York. His father was a Mohawk Indian, and his mother was an Oglala Sioux from South Dakota, a descendent of Sitting Bull. He is an enrolled member at Pine Ridge, South Dakota, where he has a 160-acre allotment. He attended and graduated from Syracuse University where he majored in psychology and business administration. He has had a varied career, has held many honorary positions both in Indian and non-Indian organizations, and has received numerous awards. I think that there will be echoes of Professor Kelly's paper in his presentation. Forty years ago Collier's proposals did not work. Today the same ideas are being advocated and the question is, will they work now.

D'Arcy McNickle, a participant in John Collier's administration, is, so to speak, living history. He was born at Saint Ignatius, Montana, on the Flathead Indian Reservation and is a member of the confederated Salish and Kutenai tribes. He entered government service in 1935 and in the following year joined the staff of Commissioner of Indian Affairs John Collier. He has been active in Indian affairs ever since, and I think his comments are most significant.

John Collier and the Indian New Deal: An Assessment

Lawrence C. Kelly

When John Collier became commissioner of the Bureau of Indian Affairs in the spring of 1933 he brought to that office a depth of experience in Indian matters unsurpassed by any of his predecessors. He also brought a sympathy for the Indian way of life which was considerably in advance of that of most of his contemporaries. From the time of his first appearance on the Indian scene in 1921, Collier was a vigorous and unrelenting critic of the land allotment provisions of the Dawes Act, the administration of Indian policy by the Bureau of Indians Affairs, and the prevailing belief that Indians should be assimilated into the superior white society.

By temperament Collier was a reformer. His entire career, including the years prior to his entrance into the field of Indian affairs, was devoted to remaking American society. Not unlike other intellectuals of his generation, Collier came to question and then to reject many of the values of Western, capitalistic civilization. From 1907 to 1919, as a staff member of the People's Institute in New York City, he labored to transform the city's immigrant poor into a politically and economically viable community where cooperation would replace competition, community action would supplant individualism, aesthetic values would become more highly esteemed than material ones, and grassroots democracy would replace the unresponsive and autocratic rule of city hall.

During these New York years, Collier sought to change the system by working within it, convinced, as he later wrote, that unless "the Occidental ethos and genius" were made to work, they would eventually become the source of the "world's doom." The shattering impact of World War I upon all forms of domestic reform embittered him. The People's Institute experiment collapsed in 1919 and with it went all his hopes and dreams for a better world. "The year 1919," he later wrote, "saw the fading away of practically all that I, we, all of us, had put all of our being into. My own disillusionment toward the 'occidental ethos and genius' as being the hope of the world was complete." At age thirty-seven, his faith in Western civilization destroyed, Collier abandoned New York and began a search for a new career in the West. Within two years he had discovered the American Indian and a new way of life.[1]

Collier's initial contact with Indians came at Taos, New Mexico, in the winter of 1920–21, although almost two years were to pass before he could free himself from other commitments in order to champion their cause. "The Taos experience," he wrote, "changed my life plan." It was for him an almost religious experience, a mystical revelation of a way of life which he had only just concluded was doomed. There entered into him, he wrote, " a new direction of life—a new, even wildly new, hope for the Race of Man." At Taos he discovered, functioning and intact, the communal society which he had labored in vain to create in New York City. Here were men and women who possessed and used "the fundamental secret of human life—the secret of building great personality through the instrumentality of [their] social institutions." He vowed on the spot that "this effort toward community must not fail, there can be no excuse or pardon if it fails."[2]

Several things are important to note about Collier's discovery of the American Indians and his simultaneous decision to undertake their defense. First, it came at a time when he had just rejected his own cultural heritage, and, as his vow quoted above indicates, he embraced the Indian cause with the dedication and the zeal of the newly converted. Second, his contact with Indian culture was with one of the most sophisticated and most highly integrated Indian cultures, one which had been unusually successful in resisting the inroads of American society, the New Mexico Pueblos. Third, in addition to believing that the Indian way of life was worth preserving for the Indians' sake, Collier also attached additional significance to its preservation; namely, that only through adopting the Indian value system could the larger white society save itself from eventual self-destruction. Collier's crusading zeal in behalf of the Indians, his tendency to view all Indians as though they were Pueblos, and his insistence that the preservation of Indian culture was essential to the survival of Western civilization were to constitute both the strength and the weakness of his administration.

At the time of Collier's entrance into the field of Indian affairs, most Americans assumed that the days of the Indians as a separate cultural entity in American society were numbered. The Dawes Act, passed in 1887, envisioned the "assimilation" of most Indians into the dominant society within a generation after its passage. Accordingly, it abolished

Indian tribal life and ordered the dissolution of the communally owned reservations into individual allotments. At the end of a twenty-five-year guardianship period, the act provided that the holder of an allotment would be made a citizen of the United States, be issued a fee-patent title to his land, and then be severed from further federal responsibility. In 1906 the withdrawal of federal responsibility was quickened through an amendment to the Dawes Act which authorized the secretary of the interior to discharge "competent" Indians from federal control prior to the expiration of the twenty-five-year guardianship period. Between 1917–21 Commissioner of Indian Affairs Cato Sells, acting on the advice of a specially created competency commission, terminated federal responsibility over thousands of Indians despite their protests of incompetency. As a result of these actions, all hastening the day when the federal government would withdraw completely from the Indian field, sentiment grew in the Congress for the abolishment of the Bureau of Indian Affairs and for an end to federal responsibility for the Indians.

Following an extensive investigation of Indian affairs in 1919–20, numerous bills were introduced in the Congress in the early 1920s to abolish the Bureau of Indian Affairs and to allot the remaining reservations. Commissioner of Indian Affairs Charles Burke and Secretary of the Interior Albert B. Fall, both of whom were sympathetic to ending federal responsibility, lent their support to many of these measures. Indeed, Fall, who since 1912 had been seeking unsuccessfully to allot the Indian reservations in New Mexico, added fuel to the fire through his support of a bill designed to settle land and water rights along the Rio Grande claimed by both whites and Pueblo Indians. According to its terms the whites would be favored in the determination of titles, a solution which Fall and his constituents found eminently reasonable. The bill would probably have passed in 1922 had it not been for a loud protest which arose from the artist communities in Taos and Santa Fe. During the struggle over this so-called Bursum Bill, Collier was but one of many who denounced Fall, but by the time the bill had been defeated, he had translated the issue into an all-out defense of Indian rights against rapacious and arrogant bureaucrats in the Indian Office. In 1922–23, with the backing of the newly formed American Indian Defense Association, Collier helped defeat another bill sponsored by Fall that would have created a National Park adjacent to his Three Rivers ranch from land belonging to the Mescalero Apache Indians. He also led the assault on a third bill favored by Fall which would have removed the last vestiges of federal responsibility over thousands of Indians through the dissolution of their tribal treasuries. In 1923 Fall resigned from office, and Collier, now authorized by the American Indian Defense Association to conduct a full scale investigation of Indian affairs, turned his guns on Commissioner Burke.[3]

As a result of his successful attack on Albert Fall, John Collier became a national figure. The relentless and oftentimes merciless assault he mounted against the Indian Bureau and Commissioner Burke from 1923 to 1929 further enhanced his reputation as the Indians' chief defender. And yet, despite the fact that his goal from the very beginning was a basic change in federal policy, away from the traditional goal of assimilation toward the preservation and conservation of Indian cultures and societies, Collier rarely made this point clear during the 1920s. In general, he avoided a direct confrontation with Congress over changes in federal Indian law, which would be necessary to obtain his desired goal. Instead, he was content to follow the path that had brought him to a position of leadership: continued exposure of the extralegal and arrogant way in which the Indian Bureau often discharged federal responsibilities for the Indians.

During the 1920s, Collier repeatedly charged that the Indian Bureau had callously presided over one of the largest land grabs in history—the reduction of the Indian landed estate from 139 million acres in 1887 to 47 million acres during Burke's administration. Burke and Fall, he maintained, had further conspired to void Indian titles to an additional 16 million acres of land claimed by the Indians but not protected by treaty arrangements. The Indian Bureau, he alleged, willfully assisted missionary societies in their attempts to subvert the native religions and cheerfully expended tribal trust monies to support schools run by the missionaries. It deliberately acted to weaken the authority of native leaders and arrogantly assumed to itself and its agents autocractic powers, which were used to destroy the fabric of Indian culture. The bureau also connived with western interests to levy debts against tribal funds for projects of value mainly to whites. Its execution of guardianship over tribal funds generally was a sorry record of mal-, if not corrupt, administration.[4] By the end of the decade, as a result of this steady barrage of charges against the Bureau of Indian Affairs, Collier had attracted much favorable publicity to the plight of the American Indian. Congressional demands for abolishment of the Indian Bureau on the ground that it was no longer needed to protect the Indians, so prevalent at the beginning of the 1920s, had now been translated into a demand for drastically curtailing its functions on the ground that Indians needed protection from the bureau itself.

In 1926, largely as a result of these charges of Indian Bureau ineptitude, mismanagement, and indifference to the well-being of its wards, Secretary of the Interior Hubert Work invited an investigation of the bureau by the Institute for Government Research. A task force of experts, directed by Lewis M. Meriam, studied the bureau and Indian affairs generally for eighteen months. In its report issued in February 1928, the investigating

The Indian New Deal

team concluded that reforms were indeed needed in the Indian field. But while it was often critical of the bureau's leadership, the Meriam Report concluded that the basic difficulty lay not in the work of the Indian Bureau or the personality of its leaders but, rather, in the goals of federal Indian policy. Sharply critical of the assimilationist philosophy, the land allotment provisions of the Dawes Act, and the boarding school system of Indian education, the Meriam Report urged the federal government to adopt a policy of cultural pluralism with respect to the American Indian by recognizing the fact that some Indians preferred to remain Indians:

> The position taken, therefore, is that the work with and for the Indians must give consideration to the desires of individual Indians. He who wishes to merge into the social and economic life of the prevailing civilization of this country should be given all practicable aid and advice in making the necessary adjustments. He who wants to remain an Indian and live according to his old culture should be aided in doing so.[5]

Specifically, the report called for the repeal of the land allotment provisions of the Dawes Act, an end to assimilation as the only goal of federal policy, the encouragement of corporate land ownership, the abandonment of boarding schools and other measures which tended to weaken cultural and tribal ties, and greatly increased congressional appropriations in the fields of health, education, and administrative assistance.

Following the publication of the Meriam Report, Collier, who had followed its progress with some degree of suspicion,[6] found himself in a difficult position. The Meriam Report had, after all, embraced most of the reforms which he had been advocating since 1922. It did not, however, advocate restoration of Indian societies and cultures, only a removal of restrictions on their activities. Nor did it lessen the powers of the Indian Bureau. Indeed, the Meriam Report advocated greatly increasing the supervisory powers of the Indian Bureau in order to implement its recommendations. For Collier, these differences were crucial. Convinced that the Meriam Report had not gone far enough and possibly irked that it had taken the initiative of reform away from him, Collier persuaded his supporters in the Senate to conduct their own investigation of Indian affairs. Following Collier's leadership, a special Senate subcommittee on Indian affairs was created one week after the submission of the Meriam Report. Although Collier envisioned the subcommittee as a means for expounding his own ideas for reform, he was to find, after he became commissioner of Indian Affairs in 1933, that it had developed a mind of its own, one which was not always in sympathy with his.

From 1928 to 1933 Collier led the senators on a strenuous tour of Indian reservations, in the course of which he exposed additional weaknesses in the Indian Bureau. Indian schools were seen to be almost universally poor, understaffed, and overcrowded, and their curriculums removed from the realities of Indian life. Sanitation and housing were subnormal in most instances, and medical facilities were woefully inadequate and in all too many cases nonexistent. The allotment system was a failure, and landless Indians everywhere were being systematically victimized by the white society which surrounded them. The Indian trust estates were being depleted at an alarming rate, too often on projects of doubtful utility to the Indians. With every new investigation and revelation, the indignation of the senators grew. Burton K. Wheeler, the old progressive who hounded Attorney General Harry Daugherty from office in the early 1920s, and who had lacked a cause since, emerged as the dominant figure on the subcommittee. Always delighted by the opportunity to badger a witness, Wheeler specialized in attacking spokesmen of the Indian Bureau whom Collier served up at regular intervals. He was never happier than in 1929 when he forced Commissioner Burke into retirement. The subcommittee's investigation of the bureau subsided temporarily in 1929 when Charles Rhoads, a Quaker philanthropist sympathetic to the recommendations of the Meriam report, succeeded Burke. But when Rhoads failed in his bid to have the Meriam recommendations enacted into law, Collier and Wheeler returned to the assault, attacking Rhoads and his principal subordinates in a manner reminiscent of the earlier attacks on Fall and Burke.[7]

For Collier, though, there was an essential irony in this work. Although he had succeeded in making the point that reform was necessary, he had done so by playing upon the traditional hostility of the Congress to the Bureau of Indian Affairs. As a result, it was he more than anyone else who was responsible for the general impression in Congress that it was the bureau, not the Congress, which was to blame for most of the evils that existed in the field of Indian affairs. Collier's own position on reform, beyond limiting the powers of the Indian Bureau, extending basic civil rights to Indians, and halting the land allotment policy, had not yet been revealed, even to those members of the Senate subcommittee who were his major supporters. Thus it was that the very tactic which Collier used to dramatize the need for reform—his attack on the Indian Bureau—also served to obscure rather than to clarify the basic issue: the necessity for Congress to abandon the historic goal of assimilation.

The shift in national leadership following the 1932 elections resulted in Collier's appointment as commissioner of Indian Affairs in April 1933. Harold Ickes, the new secretary of the interior, was one of the original members of the American Indian Defense Association; he turned instinctively to Collier after his own appointment had been confirmed.

The Indian New Deal

Collier's candidacy, however, was not uncontested. Ickes received many letters opposing Collier's nomination on the ground that his critical and uncompromising temperament was unsuitable to a sensitive administrative position requiring tact and patience. In reply to one of these letters, Ickes wrote that while he had had "serious differences of opinion with John Collier" in the past, his choice was based on the fact that "no one exceeds him in knowledge of Indian matters or his sympathy with the point of view of the Indians themselves." Ickes then went on to state his belief that Collier would rise above the partisan squabbles of the past:

> While conceding that there may be faults of temperament in Collier I am persuaded that these have been over-emphasized. He has been an advocate. He has had to fight hard to convince people that the Indians are entitled to consideration. [But] you know as well as I that many a hard-hitting lawyer, when he goes on the bench as a judge, looks at things from an entirely different point of view. I believe John Collier will do the same thing. At any rate the experiment is worth trying.[8]

At first, Ickes seemed to be right. Immediately upon his confirmation Collier set about demonstrating that a sympathetic commissioner could right many wrongs. He proclaimed the principle of religious freedom for native religions, and he issued new regulations forbidding the forced attendance of boarding school pupils at Christian religious services. He halted the sale of allotted Indian lands and canceled debts against tribal treasuries which had been incurred without Indian approval. He persuaded President Roosevelt to abolish the ineffectual Board of Indian Commissioners, which he had long accused of dragging its feet on necessary reforms and of encouraging assimilationist policies. He successfully steered through Congress a bill for the settlement of Pueblo claims against the federal government, which had been pending since the mid-1920s. He also received authority in the Johnson-O'Malley Act to contract for state and local services to Indians in the areas of education, medical care, and relief, and he secured the repeal of twelve objectionable "espionage" laws passed in the nineteenth century which limited the Indians in their exercise of basic civil liberties. These actions were generally applauded by Collier's congressional supporters, but when in 1934 he unveiled his plans for a radical alteration of federal Indian policy, much of this support rapidly dwindled.[9]

The Indian Reorganization Act was to be the crowning achievement of Collier's twelve-year fight to free the American Indian from arbitrary federal controls and slow destruction through the policy of assimilation. The lengthy forty-eight-page document which Collier and a battery of lawyers drafted "as a successor to the greater part of several thousand pages of Indian" law contained four major provisions, each designed to pave the way for a restoration of Indian autonomy.

First, there was a provision to grant all Indians the right "to organize for purposes of local self-government and economic enterprise to the end that civil liberty, political responsibility, and economic independence shall be achieved. . . ." Indians who chose to exercise these rights would be granted a charter of government specifying their rights and responsibilities by the secretary of the interior. Once such a charter was granted the secretary would begin to relinquish to the newly chartered community those powers of government and those controls over Indian funds and assets that had previously been invested in him by federal law. To achieve the goal of economic independence, the Congress was asked to create a revolving credit fund for development loans to Indian communities which agreed to assume responsibility for their own affairs.

Second, the Congress was asked to declare as "its purpose and policy" the promotion of "the study of Indian civilization, including Indian arts, crafts, skills, and traditions" and to fund this policy through an annual appropriation over and above the usual educational appropriations.

Third, the Congress was asked to pledge its support for "a constructive program of Indian land use, in order to establish a permanent basis of self-support for Indians living under federal tutelage." To this end it was asked to abolish the allotment system, compel the transfer of allotments previously made back to the newly chartered communities, appropriate $2 million annually for the purchase of new lands, and inaugurate a federal program to restore the fertility of depleted lands.

Fourth, Congress was asked to create a special court of Indian affairs, whose procedures and rules would be consonant with Indian traditions and customs, to serve as "a court of original jurisdiction" for all cases involving the self-governing Indian communities or any of their members.[10]

In essence, the Congress was being asked to grant Indians the right to control their own affairs. Once the Indian Reorganization Act went into effect, Indian communities which voted to accept responsibility for themselves would be freed of administrative supervision by the federal government and would be dependent upon it only in the sense that they would look to Congress for financial support.

For Collier there was apparently no doubt but that all Indians would agree to the provisions of the IRA. His personal experience, primarily with the Indians of the southwest whose lands, customs, and systems of local government remained essentially intact, led him to conclude that Indians everywhere would wish to return to tribal, communal life, if given the opportunity. For this reason, the Indians were not consulted while the

The Indian New Deal

bill was being drafted and for this reason also, the original draft contained many mandatory provisions relating to the transfer of privately owned lands back to tribal control. Moreover, the original bill was drafted in such a way that unless the Indians agreed to the reimposition of tribal controls, they could not participate in the credit or education loan programs.

From the very beginning, there was evidence that not all Indians shared Collier's enthusiasm for the restoration of tribal life and communal ownership of land. In Oklahoma, particularly, and among the Plains Indians, where individual land ownership was the rule rather than the exception and where some degree of intermarriage and assimilation had already weakened tribal cohesion, there were many Indians who opposed the Indian Reorganization Act.

It was also evident that Congress was opposed to the aim of restoring Indian culture and to the provisions for Indian political autonomy. Both Indian committees deleted the broad statements of new policy in the bill's preamble and the section promoting the preservation and enhancement of Indian civilization and culture. Senator Wheeler was adamantly opposed to any extension of self-government and economic aid to Indians who were no longer members of a recognized tribe, and he was likewise opposed to relinquishing the authority of the secretary of the interior to chartered Indian communities. As a result, the self-governing powers of the Indians were severely curtailed, and the provisions for economic aid were restricted to tribes, not to individual Indians whose tribal ties had been dissolved. Sen. Elmer Thomas of Oklahoma, another member of the Senate subcommittee, was suspicious of the impact which land acquisition and tribal self-government might have in Oklahoma, and he succeeded in excluding the Indians of his state and those of Alaska from most of the act's provisions. A clause which would have made all persons of one-fourth Indian blood eligible for benefits under the IRA and the section on the court of Indian affairs were quashed in committee. At the insistence of Congressman Edgar Howard of Nebraska, the chairman of the House Indian Affairs Committee and a cosponsor with Wheeler of the bill, the tribes were given the right to reject the act.[11]

As the Indian Reorganization Act emerged from Congress, it represented a compromise between Collier's dream of a new federal policy designed to encourage the growth of Indian society and culture and the traditional forces of assimilation. A dramatic break with the past had been achieved through the abolishment of the allotment system and through the authorization for land purchases. These provisions insured the preservation of a land base from which those tribes whose lands and tribal cohesion were still intact might work out their future as a people. The provision for access to credit further strengthened this possibility. Had

FIFTY YEARS AGO THE GOVERNMENT THOUGHT TEPEES AND
HEADDRESSES HAD SERVED THEIR DAY. IT WANTED NO MORE
IT WANTED THE INDIANS MADE OVER INTO WHITE MEN. BUT
YEARS THE INDIAN AND HIS PECULIAR CEREMONIES AND WAYS
STILL FLOURISH. HIS IS THE FASTEST GROWING POPULATION
THE COUNTRY. EVEN THE FULL BLOODS ARE INCREASING.
LAST THAT THE INDIAN SHOULD BE GIVEN A CHANCE TO
UPPER LEFT HAND CORNER: BLACKFEET TEPEES ON SUMMIT OF LOGAN PASS, GLACIER NATIONAL PARK.
HEADS - LEFT TO RIGHT:
LOWER LEFT HAND CORNER: SANTA CLARA PUEBLO INDIAN WOMEN MAKING POTTERY.
CENTER: THE PIPE CEREMONY, BLACKFEET TRIBE, MONTANA.

A poster explaining the main points of the Indian Reorganization Act for viewers of the 1941 exhibit of Native American art at New York City's Museum of Modern Art. The portraits are of representatives of the Blackfeet, Creek, Gros Ventre, and Navajo tribes. Also shown in the circular insets are John Collier, left, and William Zimmerman, his assistant commissioner of Indian Affairs. (RG 435)

Collier accepted the compromise nature of the final bill, it is conceivable that his administration and the Congress might have worked together during the next eleven years to achieve the limited reforms which the IRA permitted. But as it was, Collier steadfastly refused to accept the compromise. Instead, he insisted upon achieving the rejected goals of the original bill by executive action, a maneuver which proved successful until 1941. His open defiance of congressional intent, however, aroused and strengthened the forces of assimilation, which had been partially neutralized by the passage of the IRA.

Collier's success in circumventing the limitations on Indian self-government and the revitalization of Indian cultural life stemmed largely from his ability to obtain funds from a host of New Deal relief and recovery agencies. When the House Appropriations Committee, for instance, refused to appropriate the full amounts authorized in the IRA for land purchases and rehabilitation, Collier turned to the Civilian Conservation Corps and the Public Works Administration for soil conservation, irrigation, and road building funds that eventually totaled more than $100 million. From the Resettlement Administration and the Farm Security Administration, he obtained over a million acres of submarginal lands for Indian use. Through the Federal Emergency Relief Administration, the Civil Works Administration, and especially the Works Progress Administration, he obtained relief funds which kept Indians on the reservations and stimulated their involvement in industries devoted to traditional arts and crafts. Throughout the Indian country he employed men and materials authorized by these and other New Deal agencies in the construction of community centers and tribal headquarters in an effort to strengthen, and in some cases to create, tribal political activity. On his own initiative, he introduced new courses in the Indian schools devoted to the teaching of Indian languages, Indian history and culture, and Indian religious beliefs. All of these actions produced growing hostility in the House Appropriations Committee which, after 1938, severely curtailed all appropriations authorized by the IRA. When the war came in 1941, the emergency appropriations ended and the New Deal agencies that he had relied upon for support were disbanded. His vulnerability to congressional controls then became painfully evident and the Indian New Deal essentially came to an end.[12]

In the long run, however, it was the hostility which Collier aroused in the Senate that proved most damaging to his plans for the restoration of Indian civilization. By the time the IRA worked its way through Congress and into law in 1934, Senator Wheeler and his colleagues on the Senate Indian Subcommittee had come to distrust Collier's leadership. During the late 1920s and early 1930s, they had come gradually to recognize the necessity for some reform in federal policy, but the kind of reform that they envisioned was narrowly limited to the areas of administration and economics. They favored halting the forced alienation of Indian lands; the improvement of Indian living standards, schools, and health services; and, especially, the removal of arbitrary controls over the Indians by the Indian Bureau. They were, moreover, willing to make some amends for past injustices by subscribing to the land purchase and the credit program, but beyond this point they were unwilling to go. Collier's original proposals for strong, virtually autonomous tribal governments and for the restoration of Indian culture were unacceptable to the senators because they believed these measures would set the Indians permanently apart and encourage them to remain separate from the rest of American life.

Collier's resort to executive action to achieve the rejected goals of the original IRA bill provoked the revival of all the old charges of Indian Bureau intransigence and arrogance, which he himself had popularized in the previous decade. With the consent of Wheeler and Thomas, the Senate subcommittee once again became a sounding board for complaints against the Bureau of Indian Affairs. A small but highly vocal band of dissident Indians, calling themselves the American Indian Federation, were given frequent opportunities to assail Collier's program on the ground that it was restricting the religious, political, and economic freedom of Indians who opposed the restoration of tribal controls. Charges that Collier was wielding his control over federal jobs to punish Indians who resisted his programs were eagerly entertained and Collier was given little opportunity to defend himself effectively.

The most telling point which the committee made was Collier's reluctance to implement his own earlier recommendation that the Indian Bureau's technical functions be turned over to other state and federal agencies, which could do the job more efficiently. Instead of transferring the Indian forestry division to the United States Forest Service or the irrigation division to the Reclamation Service, Collier strengthened and enlarged both these divisions with the aid of CCC and PWA contracts. Similar charges were leveled against the bureau's health and education divisions. Collier's attempts to rebut these charges by arguing that huge emergency appropriations had swamped these agencies with work fell on deaf ears. Having learned all too well under Collier's own direction how to harass the bureau, the subcommittee steadily built up charges of coercion, dictation, and bureaucratic meddling, until by 1938 Collier was spending much of his time appearing before congressional committees to answer charges initiated by the Senate subcommittee.

In 1939 the subcommittee reported a bill recommending the repeal of the IRA. In 1943 it followed with another bill which would have stripped the bureau of all its essential functions. Both of these measures failed to be adopted, but it was evident that the wheel had come full circle. Angered by Collier's unwillingness to accept the compromise nature of the IRA and frustrated by his ability to pursue an independent course with the aid of the New Deal alphabet agencies, the Senate had revived the demand for abolishing the Indian Bureau and for terminating federal responsibility over the Indians.[13]

In the relatively sparse literature on the Indian New Deal, most of it sympathetic to Collier and his goals, the impression has been created that in the IRA Congress broke with the traditional philosophy of assimilation and adopted instead a policy encouraging Indian cultural, political, and economic autonomy. This paper suggests that this interpretation is in need of reevaluation. Despite John Collier's frequent assertions to the contrary, the IRA did not represent a departure from the assimilationist tradition, although it did mark a break with the idea that individual land holdings were an essential part of the assimilation process. Like most of the other programs of the first New Deal—Agricultural Adjustment Administration, National Industrial Recovery Administration, and Taylor Grazing Act—the IRA was an essentially conservative response to a problem of long duration, a response which sought not so much to reform the system as to freeze it where it was, a response that sought solutions in the maintenance of the status quo.

In his efforts to preserve and nurture the cultural heritage of all Indians and to stimulate the rebirth of political vitality among those whose tribal ties had been weakened or dissolved, John Collier challenged the Congress much as he had earlier challenged the Indian Bureau. The crusading tactics which had served him well in the 1920s, however, were not appropriate to the new struggle with the Congress, and eventually they shattered the fragile compromise with the forces of assimilation which the IRA represented. It is not too much to say that the seeds of the termination movement which surfaced in the early 1950s were planted in the latter years of the Collier administration.

NOTES

1. The quotations are found in John Collier, *From Every Zenith* (Denver: Sage Books, 1963), pp. 68, 115.
2. Ibid., pp. 123–26; John Collier, *The Indians of the Americas*, rev. ed. (New York: Mentor, 1961), pp. 7–11.
3. Kenneth Philp, "Albert B. Fall and the Protest from the Pueblos, 1921–23," *Arizona and the West* 12 (Autumn 1970): 237–54.
4. Collier, *From Every Zenith*, pp. 136–44. For a contemporary account, see Collier's numerous articles in *Sunset* and *Survey* magazines during the years 1922–28.
5. Lewis Meriam, ed., *The Problem of Indian Administration* (Baltimore: John Hopkins University Press, 1928), p. 88.

The Indian New Deal

6. Alida C. Bowler/John Collier correspondence in California League of American Indian Papers, Carton 6, Bancroft Library, University of California, Berkeley, Calif. See also Collier to Sen. Lynn Frazier, 23 May 1928, Collier Papers, Paige Box 5, Yale University Library, New Haven, Conn.
7. U.S., Congress, Senate, Committee on Indian Affairs, *Hearings, Survey of Conditions of Indians of the United States, 1928–43*, 43 vols. (Washington, D.C.: Government Printing Office, 1928–44).
8. Ickes to Francis Wilson, 11 April 1933, File 5-1-Pueblo-Pueblo Lands Board, Part 4, Records of the Office of the Secretary of the Interior, Record Group 48, National Archives Building. Years later, when it had become apparent that Collier's aggressive tactics had alienated the Congress, Ickes described the appointment in different terms. He had chosen Collier, he said, because he wanted "a two-fisted, fighting man, a Commissioner who would commit mayhem if necessary to protect his Indians wards." See FDR Official File 6, 1936, Franklin D. Roosevelt Library, Hyde Park, N.Y.
9. Kenneth R. Philp, "John Collier and the American Indian, 1920–1945" (Ph.D. diss., Michigan State University, 1968), pp. 132–41; John L. Freeman, Jr., "The New Deal for Indians" (Ph.D. diss., Princeton University, 1952), pp. 112–14.
10. U.S., Congress, House, Committee on Indian Affairs, *Hearings on H.R. 7902*, 73d Cong., 2d sess., 1934; ibid., Senate, *Hearings on S. 2755*, 73d Cong., 2d sess., 1934.
11. Ibid.; see also ibid., House, *Report 1804*, 73d Cong., 2d sess., 1934; ibid., Senate, *Report 1080*, 73d Cong., 2d sess., 1934; and U.S., *Statutes at Large*, vol. 48, pp. 984–88. In 1936 the Indians of Oklahoma and Alaska were admitted to the land purchase and credit programs authorized in the IRA.
12. Collier, *From Every Zenith*, pp. 185–214; Philp, "John Collier and the American Indian," pp. 186–224; Freeman, "The New Deal for Indians," pp. 358–435; Donald L. Parman, "The Indian and the Civilian Conservation Corps," *Pacific Historical Review* 40 (February 1971), pp. 39–56.
13. U.S., Congress, Senate, Committee on Indian Affairs, *Hearings, Survey of Conditions of Indians of the United States,"* 76th Cong., 1st sess., 1939, pt. 37; ibid., Appropriations Committee, *Hearings, Interior Department Appropriations Bill, Fiscal 1938*, 75th Cong., 1st sess., 1937 ibid., *Report 1047*, 76th Cong., 1st sess., 1939; ibid., *Report 310*, 78th Cong., 1st sess., 1943.

The Bureau of Indian Affairs, 1972

Louis R. Bruce

When President Nixon appointed me commissioner of the Bureau of Indian Affairs in August 1969, I immediately set about the monumental task of acquainting myself with as much as possible of the written material about American Indians that is available in the libraries and archives of Washington, D.C., and New York. I confess I did not even finish all of the annual reports of my predecessors in the Office of the Commissioner of Indian Affairs. Nor was I able to get through so much as a small percentage of the massive collection of historical and social documents that make up the extant body of American Indian history.

I did, however, take note of the fact that most of what I read and reviewed had not been written by Indians. I realized that the very complex circumstances that would have made it possible for any estimable part of this history to have been written by Indians themselves did not exist when the largest part of it was written. From this experience I concluded: The day will come soon when American Indians will write and judge their own history as it relates to the overall history of this continent. I think I can now say that it is no longer an impossibility for Indian scholars and writers to take charge of this academic territory.

Since I came to Washington in 1969, the face of Indian America has undergone some dramatic and far-reaching changes. Not in this century has there been such a volume of creative turbulence in Indian country. The will for self-determination has become a vital component of the thinking of Indian leadership and the grassroots Indian on every reservation and in every city. It is an irreversible trend, a tide in the destiny of American Indians that will eventually compel all of America once and for all to recognize the dignity and human rights of Indian people.

The Bureau of Indian Affairs

For the past three years, I have been at the vortex of this surge toward true and lasting self-determination. The Bureau of Indian Affairs has been undergoing an unprecedented metamorphosis due to this activity.

Soon after I assumed the position of commissioner, I announced, with President Nixon's approval, a realignment of the top positions in the BIA central office and appointed a new executive staff composed of fifteen Indians and Alaskan natives. This marked a milestone in BIA history. Today more Indians than ever before are holding key BIA management positions and working to implement the self-determination policy of this administration. Indian direction of Indian Affairs has become the cornerstone for policy making in the Nixon administration.

In his July 1970 special message to the Congress on Indian Affairs, President Nixon set forth future federal Indian policy directions. He called for a "new era in which the Indian future is determined by Indian acts and Indian decisions." The president urged the Congress "to renounce, repudiate and repeal" the policy of terminating federal aid to Indian reservations expressed in 1953 in House Concurrent Resolution 108. Last December, the Senate acted on this recommendation to repeal the termination policy toward Indians and replace it with a new policy that would make self-determination a major goal. The switch was embodied in a "Sense of Congress" resolution that was adopted by voice vote without dissent. The resolution is now awaiting action in the House of Representatives.

In his Indian message, President Nixon announced proposals for Indian control of Indian education, Indian direction of federally funded programs, an Indian trust counsel authority, an Indian credit program, an assistant secretary for Indian and territorial affairs in the Interior Department, and restoration of Blue Lake to the Taos Indians of New Mexico. The first of the president's proposals to be enacted was legislation returning Blue Lake and the surrounding land to the Indians of Taos Pueblo.

In keeping with the president's legislative proposals just mentioned, my staff and I began working to restructure the bureau at all levels so that its policies and programs would reflect more closely the thinking and feelings of Indian people. Five policy goals were announced in November 1970 to guide the bureau in its new administration of Indian affairs:

(1) transformation of the BIA from a management to a service organization;
(2) reaffirmation of the trust status of Indian land;
(3) making the BIA area offices fully responsive to the Indian people they serve;
(4) providing tribes with the option of taking over any or all BIA

program functions, with the understanding that the bureau will provide assistance or reassume control if requested to do so; and

(5) working with Indian organizations to become a strong advocate of off-reservation Indian interests.

The idea of self-determination—the right of Indians to make their own choices and decisions—is, as I indicated earlier, becoming a reality as Indian people begin to assume the authority to manage their own affairs. In his message, President Nixon proposed legislation which would empower tribes, groups of tribes, or any other Indian community to assume the control or operation of federally funded and administered programs. As the BIA is gradually being converted from a management organization to an agency of service, counsel, and technical assistance, we are encouraging and assisting tribes in their assumption of program operations. We cannot and do not intend to force this policy on the Indian people. We are allowing them to decide whether they want to take over programs and, if so, how much responsibility they are willing to assume.

The Zuni Tribe of New Mexico accepted the responsibility for directing BIA activities at the pueblo in May 1970. Almost a year later, the BIA signed a contract with the Miccosukee Tribe of Florida enabling them to administer BIA programs on the reservations.

The response to this takeover policy has been a somewhat cautious one. Many tribes have waited to see how others responded and how the few tribes that have assumed control fare under the federal-tribal relationship. Indian people still remember the disastrous results of the termination policy of the 1950s.

A legal vehicle for tribal takeovers of BIA program activities has been the Buy Indian Act of 1910. Buy Indian contracting within the bureau has evolved from procurement of needed supplies into a method for the training and employment of Indians and, finally, into an instrument for greater Indian involvement in the conduct of their own affairs. In fiscal year 1972, dollar value of Buy Indian contracts between Indian tribes and the BIA may reach an estimated $42.5 million. In 1969, only $3.8 million in contracts were negotiated between Indian groups and the bureau.

We in the bureau have been keenly aware of the recent emergence of a strong and positive attitude on the part of Indian people that they want and will have better lives. Indians of all ages, representing all tribes, are undertaking unprecedented efforts to overcome the problems confronting them. Evidence of this new attitude is apparent in the establishment of the National Tribal Chairmen's Association (NTCA), a new organization of elected tribal chairmen. Created in April 1971, NTCA has advised the bureau on numerous matters relating to policies, budgets, and programs affecting reservation Indians. As chairmen, they are men who know firsthand what problems are facing their people and what solutions are needed to solve these problems. Through this group and the National Congress of American Indians, the National Council on Indian Opportunity, and other groups, reservation Indians have presented a single, united voice in shaping the future of Indian affairs.

During the past few years we have also witnessed Indian organizations, such as the American Indian Movement, working to bring recognition to the problems of Indians in off-reservation communities. Since World War II, when thousands of Indians left the reservations for military service or for wartime jobs, a steady off-reservation movement has been taking place. This was given an additional boost in the early 1950s with the initiation of the BIA Employment Assistance Program, which assisted Indians in locating permanent employment in nonreservation areas. The urban Indian movement of the last two decades has resulted in more than three hundred fifty thousand Indians living off the reservations today.

Under its current policy, the bureau limits BIA services to reservation Indians with some exceptions. There are, however, many people both in the bureau and outside who believe that the federal trust responsibility extends to tribal Indians wherever they are. The government's trust responsibility is to people, not land, and any attempts to deprive Indians of their treaty and constitutional rights is a subversion of sovereignty and the trust responsibility.

In January 1972, the Bureau of Indian Affairs announced plans for a redirection of the BIA's programs for the future. We presented a five-point program designed to assist Indians toward self-determination through economic, educational, and social development on the reservations.

Today we believe that all people should have the right to determine their own destinies. Unlike past programs, which have all been designed to lead to Indian assimilation, the new BIA program directions deal with developing natural and human resources on the reservations, not off. All programs and policies are aimed at establishing viable economies for the growth of self-sustaining Indian communities.

The number one priority in 1972 is a reservation-by-reservation development program. There is a great need on reservations for an overall developmental plan which integrates all of the tribe's natural and human resources. In the past, program areas have often been in conflict with one another because of the lack of such a plan. The bureau is now assisting twenty-eight tribes who were selected to participate in the bureau's Reservation Acceleration Program, better known as RAP. Still other tribes, from Oklahoma and California, are being selected for the BIA's Tribal Acceleration Program, TAP. The tribes involved are negotiating changes in existing local BIA program budgets to insure that these programs *support tribal priorities.*

In 1972 an intense collective tribal consultation on the BIA budget was considered and is being meshed with the fiscal 1974 BIA budget process. We now feel that we are on the brink of making self-determination and consultation an operational reality.

A new thrust is being provided to the Indian forestry program on those reservations that have significant areas of commercial forest lands. Until now, a large part of the federal government's costs for administering the reservation forestry programs has been reimbursed by deducting administrative fees from the stumpage prices paid by purchasers of Indian timber. Effective July 1, 1972, the tribal owners of such forest lands will be given the opportunity to invest those fees in the intensified development of their tribally owned forests, rather than to have it credited to federal accounts in the United States Treasury. The total amount of the fees that will thus be diverted into intensified forest management is expected to average approximately $3 million per year. This will not only contribute to a stronger economic base for the local Indian communities but will substantially increase the contribution made by Indian forest lands to the nation's requirements of lumber and other forest products.

To assist with development on the reservation, we are redirecting our BIA Employment Assistance Program to develop job skills on the reservations. As was mentioned previously, the Employment Assistance Program was an outgrowth of the termination policy of the 1950s, designed to relocate Indians in urban areas where jobs were thought to be more plentiful. For some, the relocation strategy worked, but for many it has meant removal to an urban ghetto. At the same time, it has meant a draining from the Indian communities of those who could best become leaders at home. Now, the relocation strategy has been reversed and employment assistance resources are being directed into the reservation economies instead of dissipating in the non-Indian communities. Indian men and women are being trained for work not in the cities but in their own home areas.

One of the most exciting methods of implementing this program is the Indian Action Team. The Indian Action Team is a self-help program in which the tribes identify their needs and problems and train their tribal members through specific work projects on the reservations.

Legal issues with regard to water in the western United States arise only when the resource becomes scarce. The competition for the water becomes intensive because in the arid West, water is money. At this date, there is an increasing demand for water to support the economic growth of the American West. However, there is a limited supply. As a result, Indian peoples' reserved right to water is not very popular with other interests. Secretary of the Interior Rogers Morton established an Indian Water Rights Office to protect Indian water resources. This office is undertaking inventories of the water resources available and is carrying out studies for establishing and confirming the water rights of Indians. We will establish firmly tribal rights to water, thereby protecting them so that the tribes may be assured that they have the water they need in the development of their reservations. The Office of Indian Water Rights reports directly to me, and I in turn report directly to the secretary of the interior on water rights issues. This procedure was designed to avoid the conflicting interests of other Interior Department agencies. We are now considering further proposals which will assure us of eliminating any conflicts.

Roads are the basic physical infrastructure upon which all social and economic systems develop. The treaty relationships established the obligation of the federal government to build an Indian road system. One of the most shocking statistics of American history is that not one linear foot of roads was constructed from 1900 to 1935, the period when mainstream America built its basic road system.

As of now, of the bureau's 21,665 miles of Indian roads, only 1,000 miles are paved. We will upgrade this to a 10,000-mile paved system by 1978. This has meant increasing our road budget from $20 million a year to $106 million a year and will ultimately require over $800 million over a seven-year period.

The final, but very vital, part of our five-point plan calls for more tribal control of education programs. In accordance with the policy enabling tribes to assume control of federally funded programs, the BIA believes that any Indian community wishing to do so should be able to assume control of its own schools. We recognize that in order for Indian educational programs to become truly responsive to the needs of Indian children and parents, it is imperative that the control of those programs be in the hands of Indian communities. In 1972 we had fifteen federal schools controlled by Indian corporations, four statewide Johnson-O'Malley programs operated by tribes, seventy-five other educational programs operated by tribal groups, and three reservation junior colleges controlled by Indians. We hope to have at least half of all BIA schools under Indian direction by 1976.

Local Indian communities not ready to undertake actual responsibilities toward the schooling of their children have, in increasing numbers, formed advisory boards of education. Today, all of the BIA's 200 elementary and secondary schools have Indian advisory school boards, which are assuming greater management of the schools' curriculums, staffing, construction, and educational objectives.

Our education staff is now working on establishing goals in education by which we can measure our own progress over the four-year period 1972–76. We are planning to establish a management information system which will monitor our program's successes and failures. We are also making plans to establish a student bill of rights that will be in effect by the opening of the 1972 fall term.

Since my appointment I have repeatedly emphasized that we are advocating self-determination and repudiating the paternalism and termination of past national Indian policies. We must and we will continue to oppose any doctrine of termination under whatever name and in whatever form. The Menominee Restoration Act is presently before the Congress. I personally have been working closely with both the tribe and concerned federal officials to improve the conditions of the tribe. A lengthy bureau economic evaluation actually documents the catastrophic effects which termination has had on this group. We are working to have the full range of bureau services once again made available to the Menominees. In addition, the trust status of Menominee County should be reinstated so that the dissipation of their land ceases.

We are committed to a policy of tribal involvement in Indian programs and in the operation of activities providing services to Indian people. The purpose of this policy is to cause the bureau administration to be more responsive to the views of Indian people and to give Indians the opportunities to gain experience in the administration of activities affecting their own people. Two important parts of this policy are consultation in the selection of bureau employees for certain positions and consultation on general personnel programs.

Section 12 of the Indian Reorganization Act contains a statute which relates to Indian preference in employment within the Bureau of Indian Affairs. The interpretation of this act has been the source of considerable interest in recent years. The Indian preference law, if not understood in its economic and historical context, may very well be misunderstood. We feel that this is not a racial matter, but merely an attempt by the framers of an enlightened law to give the Indian people the right to control the programs which relate to their own domestic dependent nations. Recognition of this fact is even contained in the Civil Rights Act of 1964. The authors of the act avoided impairing the relationship between Indian tribes and the United States government. As a matter of fact, it exempted enterprises and businesses on or near Indian reservations from the prohibitions of the act. This has had the effect of extending the preference act by creating a private employment preference right to Indians, so that tribes may hire Indians 100 percent in private businesses or enterprises on the reservations.

Indian attorney Browning Pipestem most appropriately titled his position paper on this subject, "Indian Preference—A Preference to Conduct Self-Government." Until now, preference has only been applied to initial appointment. Our proposal to the secretary of the interior contains a request to extend Indian preference to promotions. We expect an affirmative answer to that request.

A most essential part of the self-determination policy is financial independence. Because of a lack of understanding of Indian matters, the private banking industry of the United States has not been adequately serving Indian financial requirements. The placement of industries on the reservations and the development of Indian natural resources have brought to our attention the need of a financial service to Indian individuals and Indian tribes. The American Indian National Bank was established to help fulfill this need. This bank is not competitive with the private banking industry, but is an adjunct and an educational procedure to teach banks that banking with Indian people is not an unachievable objective. The American Indian National Bank will have its headquarters in Washington, D.C., with services extended to reservations that can justify the establishment of such a facility. Stock in the bank will be owned by Indians.

We have recognized for some time a very important area in our relationship with tribes, especially the small tribes and poor large tribes, that has been not only overlooked, but avoided. Simply stated, many tribes do not have the money to carry on their most basic governmental functions —this being the case in spite of the fact that over the years we have pushed on the tribes elaborate governmental plans and structures supposedly to illustrate self-government. Couple this with the very real fact that the BIA has never had enough money or staff to supply services to many of the smaller Indian tribes. In order for the small tribes to get "a piece of the action," we hope to fund a new program of aid to tribal governments, which, for the first time, should provide money for these fiscally poor tribes to use to conduct their own tribal governments efficiently and adequately.

I think that all of this—aid to tribal governments, an aggressive National Tribal Chairmen's Association, an Indian bank, the Indian action teams, tribal control of Indian education and a strong bill of rights for BIA boarding school students, roads on the reservations, establishment of viable Indian economies, and Indian preference and consultation—spells self-determination as we have been trying to identify it in our efforts during the present administration. This we are doing in a time when American Indians have more direct involvement with the federal government than ever before in determining the shape and direction of the policies and programs that vitally affect their lives.

I think that all of this, once finally achieved and implemented, and many other self-determination programs now in the planning stage, will be the subject matter of American Indian history for the 1970s that will reflect an era—the long-awaited era—when Indian people achieve full recovery from the unjust past, achieve equality and justice in this society, and respond to the challenge of making an outstanding contribution to the advancement of all things human in this land.

To conclude this on a practical and realistic note and, lest I seem too euphoric, I have only to read my daily mail to know that no matter how hard we try or how sincere our efforts are, it is never fast enough and there is never money enough. We are fortunate if we accomplish just a little and please a few. We will keep trying as best we can for more. That is our assigned task, our solemn responsibility. Indian self-determination is going to be a complete reality not too far ahead of today, and when it is, one of the incomplete chapters of American history will then have been completed.

COMMENTARY

D'Arcy McNickle

Two papers have been presented dealing with John Collier and the New Deal. I expected to learn from these assessments or evaluations just what John Collier had accomplished. To my disappointment, however, the presentations were not what I had hoped for.

Commissioner Bruce mentioned matters that were of concern during the Collier regime, for example, the budget process. One of the provisions of the Indian Reorganization Act that managed to survive in the final draft was a requirement that Indians be consulted in the preparation of budgets. The provision was never honored in practice, due largely to lack of interest among field officers.

Another subject mentioned by Commissioner Bruce was Indian preference in employment. Although this too was in the Indian Reorganization Act, it was largely disregarded. Indians were employed but in the lower echelons. I believe the present commissioner is attempting a reversal of this trend.

Also unanswered in these papers was what impact John Collier's concern had on the Indians. When I taught in Canada from 1966 to 1971, one of the things that struck me immediately was the number of Indian and non-Indian students who asked about John Collier. They asked for his books. It is fairly well known in Indian country now, but the New Deal period was an exciting time. It is true that Indians were distrustful when the draft of what became the Indian Reorganization Act was taken out to the field for discussion. Someone mentioned in an earlier comment that Indians did not know who the white man was who came out to talk with them. They were afraid of what he might have in mind, of what might result if they went along with him.

One Crow Indian who was at the Billings Conference put it very succinctly. He said that before the white man came the Indians had the buffalo and the buffalo gave them everything they needed—food, shelter, clothing. The white man came and took the buffalo away. But he gave them the government and now they want to hold onto the government. That is their buffalo.

The Indians were afraid this white man might have some scheme to do away with their new buffalo. It was a distrustful period and yet things happened, as they are happening now. New ideas were being tried out, new people were being brought in. Professor Kelly referred to the fact that Collier tried to outwit Congress by going to other agencies of government to get financial support. But this was the spirit of the New Deal. Anyone who lived in Washington through that time will remember how these things happened. The New Deal agencies had money to spend and they grabbed at the chance of including Indians in their plans and programs. Indians in most instances were in greater need of assistance than any other group.

One thing especially that should have been noted in the course of evaluating these New Deal days was Collier's interest in and attempt to apply social science methods to administration. He was in a sense fathering what later came to be called applied or action anthropology. He set up an anthropological unit in the bureau, but I am not sure it did much good at the time. The men who were recruited wrote an academese jargon that the field people could not understand even if they tried. The anthropologists of the period were interested primarily in what was later called salvage ethnology. They were still under the impression that Indians were going to die out and they wanted to learn all they could before their subjects passed out of the picture.

It was that kind of background they brought to the bureau, rather than ideas for working with people. Nevertheless, it was a breakthrough that later on led to technical assistance programs all over the world. Here at least was a beginning.

Collier wanted to find out what the bureau's schools were doing. He authorized a study of Indian high school graduates—what happened to them and whether they were being trained for the kinds of careers they eventually went into. The study revealed that about 90 percent came back to the reservation, although the schools were presumably training them to leave the reservation. Willard Beatty, who was director of education at that time, decided that since the students were returning to the reservations, they should learn how to run a ranch and how to use modern equipment in the house. Later on, the bureau was criticized for this. The critics wanted Indian young people transformed into standard white Americans through standardized education.

Collier was interested in reducing Indian languages to written form. Accordingly, he called upon Father Berard Haile, the Franciscan, and John Harrington, of the Smithsonian Institution, among others, to assist in developing this program. As a result, bilingual texts were printed in

Navajo and Sioux. Later, I learned that some school officials did not approve the use of these texts and simply dumped them. I found quantities of them gathering dust in a government warehouse on the Navajo Reservation.

In cooperation with the Committee on Human Development of the University of Chicago, Collier undertook a study of personality development in Indian communities to determine what processes make one infant—one new arrival—French or Sioux or Navajo. More specifically, he wanted to discover, if he could, how the child was affected by the kinds of schooling provided by the bureau. In what way could knowledge of the human development process be used to advantage in developing schools?

With Collier's encouragement, Alexander Leighton made one of the first studies of Navajo curing ceremonies. Leighton, who was trained as an M.D. and as a pyschiatrist, discovered that native medicine made a lot of sense. It cured people!

The Indian Bureau operated one of the war relocation centers for the internment of Japanese who were moved away from the Pacific Coast. Collier established a social science observation post at this center to observe what was happening, particularly to determine which administrative devices were successful and which ones did not work. Again, he sought to introduce a more intelligent approach to the administrative function.

None of these activities made him very popular with Congress, which had the idea one did not need to know anything in order to run Indian affairs and, indeed, the less one knew the better. The Appropriations Committee kept cutting off money for one program or another. The anthropological unit was abolished, and Collier had to appoint its staff members under other titles. Gordon MacGregor, one of his anthropologists, under the guise of an educational specialist, made the study of high school graduates mentioned earlier.

These are some of the things I was hoping would be discussed. I will not go into them here but they do deserve examination at some length.

Collier did not ask Congress to promote the study of Indian civilization and Indian culture in isolation, as Dr. Kelly states. He wanted Indians to take control of their affairs and manage their reservations, and he realized they needed training to assume this responsibility. Title II was proposed primarily as a training program for Indians. If they were to run their own affairs, they had better know something about themselves, their history, and how they got to be where they were. So part of the Title II program was to be devoted to a study of Indian history—the very thing that is being promoted now in Indian studies programs all across the country. This was Collier's interest.

Dr. Kelly also stated that Indians were not consulted in the drafting of the Wheeler-Howard Act. But in fact regional conferences were conducted for that purpose. The draft, which was prepared by the lawyers in Washington and carried out to the nine or ten regional meetings, was heavily criticized. The changes made in that final draft came not just from Congress, but from these regional meetings as well. The astonishing thing, not mentioned by Dr. Kelly, is that this was the first time anything of this sort ever happened. No commissioner had ever taken a piece of legislation out to the field and asked the Indians to give him their opinion of it.

What bothers me most about these papers is the discussion about assimilation. It was said in several passages that Collier was opposed to the philosophy of assimilation, the tradition of assimilation in Congress. Congress had no such philosophy. I will explain in a moment what I think was actually happening, but assimilation is a slippery term to deal with.

Actually, two themes have persisted from the very first Indian-white contact, two quite opposite views about the Indians. During certain periods of history, one of these views was in the ascendency, and at other times the opposite view prevailed. One is the humanist view that goes way back in history. Soon after the Spanish came to the New World, a great debate arose as to whether the New World inhabitants were humans or beasts of the forest. The Pope had to issue a Papal Bull, an opinion or declaration, to the effect that Indians were truly human. Having established that, it was possible to argue that as humans they were entitled to certain rights.

The Spaniard, Vitorio, spelled out what those rights were. They were entitled to the land they occupied, which could not be taken from them except in a "just" war or for compensation. This idea was echoed later in the Royal Proclamation of 1763 when the British government declared that the lands occupied by Indians were not to be taken except in proper negotiation, with the British Crown participating to ensure that the Indians received fair treatment. Otherwise, Indians were not to be molested in the lands they were then occupying.

After establishment of the United States, some of the first officials who were concerned with establishing policy were members of this humanist group. Henry Knox, for example, first secretary of war and thus the first federal official in charge of Indian affairs, argued that the Indians were "possessors of the soil" they occupied. Some people suggested that the question of land title could be settled most effectively by exterminating the Indians. A debate was in process at the time as to whether Indians should not be exterminated and get the thing over with, but Knox argued that this solution would not only be dishonorable but it would be expensive. Thomas Jefferson was in the same tradition. He said, let our settlements and theirs meet and blend together.

I am calling this a humanist view, but it was assimilation in the correct sense—the idea of people of different cultures coming together and adapting to each other, without coercion on either side. Jefferson assumed this would happen if the Indians and whites lived side by side, and that eventually they would exchange ideas, take something from each other, and find an accommodation.

The other view has been that Indians have a lesser claim on the natural world because they are heathen—one could say, non-European. The New England divines were very much of the opinion that the Indians were disciples of Satan—all the bad things that Christians of that period abhorred. They were inferior, largely because their technology was inferior to that of the incoming Europeans. As nomadic hunters roaming over the land, they had less right to the land than hard-working farmers. John Quincy Adams was very eloquent on this point. Indians were standing in the way of progress and civilization. It was intolerable that roaming hunters should hold back a great nation from development.

As late as 1871, one senator, during a Senate debate on whether to discontinue making treaties with Indians, argued that the Indians were incapable of civilization and must be treated as savages. I suspect others since then have shared the senator's view. Quite a few people until recently had the notion that the Indian race was going to die out, presumably because of a genetic inferiority. What disease did not take, alcohol would, and the Indians would physically disappear.

These ideas were all a part of this second tradition, which justified the preemption of Indian lands and the assumption of authoritarian control over the lives of these people, usurping their right to self-determination.

John Collier's dilemma was contending with the second view. He was saying that Indians are people, as good as any other people. They have their own values, and they should be allowed to work out their own destinies without being beaten down by superior power. That really is what the argument was all about.

Collier was not antiassimilationist. He was not what a social scientist would call a theoretician. He was a man of feeling, a man of intuition. He was really a poet, not an administrator, although he did fairly well considering that he took over an organization that had been for so long under the control of persons influenced by the idea of Indian inferiority. We hear now about deadwood in the bureau. In the thirties it really was dead, wormwood dead. That is the organization Collier had to try to administer. He was a man of sentiment, a man of feeling. He knew what ought to happen. He was not antiassimilationist, if you employ the term in the sense I was first using it—people accommodating to each other. This is now called acculturation rather than assimilation. Assimilation means blotting out one culture, one way of life. Collier did not favor that.

Collier himself said, after the Indian Reorganization Act was adopted, it "not only ends the long, painful, futile effort to speed up the normal rate of Indian assimilation by individualizing tribal land and other capital assets, but it also endeavors to provide the means, statutory and financial, to repair as far as possible, the incalculable damage done by the allotment policy and its corollaries."[1]

In 1938 he said, "We . . . define our Indian policy somewhat as follows: So productively to use the monies appropriated by the Congress for Indians as to enable them . . . to earn decent livelihoods and lead self-respecting organized lives in harmony with their own aims and ideals, as an integral part of American life."[2] In other words, as a people who have adapted to a changed environment, to a new system surrounding them.

What Collier encountered was the opposition of men who were frustrated by the actions he and Secretary Ickes were taking, by clamping down on further allotments and the granting of fee patents. It is interesting that shortly after Collier resigned in 1945, the flood gates were opened. It started with the case of Molly Leaves Her Behind. The newspapers thought that was a very funny name. She wanted a fee patent and having been turned down by Collier and Ickes, she went to Congress. I believe Congressman D'Ewart of Montana championed her cause by introducing a private bill. After meeting some resistance when it was first introduced, the bill eventually did pass Congress. Then a whole series of similar bills was introduced by congressmen who were angry at Ickes and Collier for their policy on Indian lands.

The resulting situation became so serious that, as recently as 1958, Senator Murray of Montana expressed shock when he discovered what was happening. In a ten-year period 2.5 million acres of Indian land had passed out of trust protection, largely through these devices. That was the tidal wave Collier was trying to prevent, of lifting restrictions and letting Indians' lands go on the market. Even worse, Indians who held key tracts that might control water in a grazing area were allowed to break up that economic unit by selling their land to outsiders rather than to the tribe.

The controversy over recognizing land rights in Alaska can be traced to this same frustration. There are people who do not like to see Indians get rich or even get a fair break, and Alaska land represents minerals, timber, and very profitable fisheries. Allowing Indians to claim what they were entitled to as a result of the treaty with Russia meant that some natives in Alaska might get rich.

I think these papers have not paid enough attention to the role Congress plays in Indian affairs. The bureau has taken the brunt of criticism, but it is Congress that writes the policy and votes the money, and Congress can freeze out the bureau at any time. Although I said Congress, policy is developed by committees and often by a single person in a committee, the staff person, who more or less tells the congressmen what stands they should take. Congressmen do not have time to read all these bills, which sometimes are very complicated and lengthy, and so they depend upon a staff person. Consequently, these staff assistants can become extremely powerful. John Collier was whipped in this area because one man in the Senate committee, the staff clerk, was bitterly opposed to him. Collier had refused to name this man as chief counsel of the bureau at the beginning of his administration. Collier was never forgiven.

The Indians did not always realize immediately the impact of Collier's policies. Often when he spoke to them at meetings they were rather stunned by what he told them. They listened to him in silence, but later they would discuss what he said. They were not used to hearing a government man speak with such sympathy for their beliefs. Before Collier became commissioner, the entire Taos Council was rounded up by Indian police and put in jail in Santa Fe for practicing their religion. Although the council members were disobeying regulations in effect at that time, Collier encouraged them to go to jail rather than submit to the regulations. Indians were not used to being told by a white man to defy white man's authority. And at the time that the Navajos were very upset about the stock reduction program, Collier was acquiring, through trades with the Santa Fe Railroad and other means, quite a bit of land to be turned back to the Navajos. The Navajos did not know this was being done while they were fighting stock reduction, and they realized it only when the lands were added to the reservation. In about 1960 I took a Navajo man and his wife to visit Collier, who was then about eighty years old and living outside of Taos. I was amazed when this Navajo man put his arm around John Collier, who was very frail at this point, and thanked him for all he had done.

NOTES

1. U.S., Department of the Interior, *Annual Report of the Secretary of the Interior, 1934* (Washington, D.C.: Government Printing Office, 1934), p. 79.
2. U.S., Department of the Interior, *Annual Report of the Secretary of the Interior, 1938* (Washington, D.C.: Government Printing Office, 1938), p. 210.

DISCUSSION NOTE

Alvin Josephy opened the discussion by observing that sufficient time has elapsed since the establishment of Collier's system of tribal government to permit a judgment of the effectiveness of the tribal councils. He noted that some of the tribal councils appear to be emerging almost as tools of the federal government. Their cooperation with business and industry seeking entry to the reservations marks the beginning of a brand new assault on the reservations.

Commissioner Bruce stated that as the Indians have become more vocal and aggressive on their own behalf, Congress has become more cooperative and more generous with appropriations for Indian affairs. His administration has had a good working relationship with Congress. In an acknowledgment of Collier's contributions, the commissioner noted that even today some of Collier's ideas are considered too progressive for implementation. At this point D'Arcy McNickle was asked to comment on Collier's impact on the Indian spirit. McNickle said that he supposed the Indians appreciated Collier more in retrospect as they realized what he had done for them. He added that they found it difficult to adjust to a government official who was so sympathetic to their beliefs.

A question concerning a current problem involving Indian students at the University of Oklahoma led to a discussion of the bureau's plan to revise the budget system. Ernie Stevens, the director of Economic Development for the Bureau of Indian Affairs, said that under the new system funds would be distributed more effectively to the lower administrative levels, preventing the delays in distribution that often occur at intermediate levels.

Richard LaCourse, a member of the Yakima tribe and an employee of the American Indian Press Association, remarked that as he saw it the development of some of Collier's policies, which are being revised and expanded by the Nixon administration, would result in fully functioning separatist Indian societies by the end of this century. He asked Kelly to comment on white America's view of such a cultural, social, and economic revival and also requested Ernie Stevens to give his opinion of the idea. Kelly agreed that separate Indian societies were the ultimate goal of both Collier and the present administration. In his opinion white America would be more receptive today to such a development than it was in the 1930s.

Ernie Stevens compared the Indian reservations to some of the island possessions of the United States that are now seeking self-determination. Ideally, the reservations would have permanent status with fixed exterior boundaries, and all whites would be removed from the interior. The reservations would then be economically viable units surrounded by a sea of land. In his view, the best possible kind of assimilation will be achieved when the Indians can join the mainstream of society and deal with the whites as economic equals.

BIOGRAPHICAL SKETCHES

ROBERT G. ATHEARN. Native of Montana, educated at University of Minnesota (Ph.D., 1947) . . . member of history faculty of University of Colorado (1947 to present) . . . Ford Foundation fellow (1954–55) . . . Fulbright fellow, University College of North Wales (1960–61) . . . author of *Westward the Briton; William Tecumseh Sherman and the Settlement of the West; High Country Empire; Rebel of the Rockies: The Denver and Rio Grande, Western Railroad; Forts of the Upper Missouri;* and *Union Pacific Country* . . . coauthor of *The American Heritage New Illustrated History of the United States,* American Heritage, volumes 1–16, and *America Moves West* (4th edition, 1964).

ROBERT H. BAHMER. Native of North Dakota, educated at North Dakota State Teachers College and the Universities of Colorado and Minnesota (Ph.D., 1941) . . . member of faculty of Ironwood Junior College (1932–34) . . . secretary to Congressman Frank Hook (1935–36) . . . archivist, National Archives (1936–42) . . . deputy archivist, National Archives and Records Service (1948–66), archivist of the United States (1966–68), retired . . . secretary general, International Council on Archives (1956) . . . fellow and past president, Society of American Archivists.

W. DAVID BAIRD. Native of Oklahoma, educated at Central State University (Oklahoma) and University of Oklahoma (Ph.D., 1969) . . . member of history faculty of University of Arkansas (1968 to present) . . . author of *Peter Pitchlynn: Chief of the Choctaws* and of articles published in *Chronicles of Oklahoma, Maryland Historical Magazine,* and *Arkansas Historical Quarterly.*

ROBERT F. BERKHOFER, JR. Native of New York, educated at New York State College for Teachers and Cornell University (Ph.D., 1960) . . . member of history faculties of Ohio State University, University of

Biographical Sketches 261

Minnesota, University of Wisconsin at Madison (1969–73), and University of Michigan (from 1973) . . . author of books and articles, including *Salvation and the Savage: An Analysis of Protestant Missions and American Indian Response, 1787–1862*, and *A Behavioral Approach to Historical Analysis*.

DONALD J. BERTHRONG. Native of Wisconsin, educated at University of Wisconsin (Ph.D., 1952) . . . member of history faculties of Universities of Kansas City, Oklahoma, and Purdue (since 1970) . . . Fulbright Lecturer, University of Hong Kong (1965–66) . . . Award of Merit, American Association of State and Local History (1964) . . . editor, *Joseph Reddeford Walker and the Arizona Adventure* . . . author of *The Southern Cheyennes* and articles published in *Wisconsin Magazine of History, Ethnohistory,* and *Arizona and the West*.

LOUIS R. BRUCE. Native of New York, educated at Cazenovia Seminary and Syracuse University . . . special assistant to commissioner for Cooperative Housing, Federal Housing Administration (1959–61) . . . executive director of the Zeta Psi Educational Foundation and Fraternity (1966–69) . . . commissioner, Bureau of Indian Affairs (1969–73) . . . executive and legislative director, National Congress of American Indians . . . awards include the American Indian Achievement Award and the Freedoms Foundation Award presented by President Eisenhower for "outstanding contributions in promoting the American way of life."

C. GREGORY CRAMPTON. Native of Illinois, educated at the University of California (Ph.D., 1941) . . . member of history faculty of University of Utah (1945–) . . . Rockefeller Foundation traveling fellow, Latin-America (1941–42), and postwar fellow (1948–49) . . . United States Department of State Exchange Professor, University of Panama (1955) . . . member of board, American West Publishing Company (1966–) . . . editor, historical archaeologist, oral historian, and author of books and articles, including *Standing Up Country: The Canyon Lands of Utah and Arizona* and *Land of Living Rock: The Grand Canyon and the High Plateaus—Arizona, Utah, Nevada*.

ANGIE DEBO. Native of Kansas, educated at the University of Chicago and University of Oklahoma (Ph.D., 1933) . . . member of history faculties of colleges in Texas and Oklahoma . . . author of many books, articles, and reviews about Indian and western history, including *The Rise and Fall of the Choctaw Republic* (awarded John H. Dunning Prize of the American Historical Association, 1935); *And Still the Waters Run; The*

Road to Disappearance: A History of the Creek Indians; The Five Civilized Tribes of Oklahoma: Report on Social and Economic Conditions; and *A History of the Indians of the United States.*

RICHARD N. ELLIS. Native of New York, educated at University of Colorado (Ph.D., 1967) . . . member of history faculties of Murray State University (1967–68) and University of New Mexico (since 1968) . . . author of books and articles, including *General Pope and U.S. Indian Policy* . . . editor, *New Mexico, Past and Present: A Historical Reader* and *The Western American Indian: Case Studies in Tribal History.*

JOHN C. EWERS. Native of Ohio, educated at Dartmouth University and Yale University . . . curator, Museum of the Plains Indian (1941–44); associate curator of ethnology, United States National Museum, Smithsonian Institution (1946–56); planning officer (1956–59), assistant director (1959–64), and director (1964–65), Museum of History and Technology, Smithsonian Institution; senior ethnologist, Department of Anthropology, Smithsonian Institution (since 1965) . . . recipient, first Exceptional Service Award, Smithsonian Institution (1965) . . . fellow, American Anthropological Association . . . specialist in history and ethnology of the Plains Indians—combining fieldwork with Indian informants and library, archival, and museum resources . . . member, editorial board, *The American West* . . . author of many books and articles including *Plains Indian Painting, The Horse in Blackfoot Indian Culture, The Blackfeet: Raiders on the Northwestern Plains,* and *Artists of the Old West* . . . editor, *Adventures of Zenas Leonard, Fur Trader; Crow Indian Medicine Bundles; Five Indian Tribes of the Upper Missouri;* and *O-Kee-Pa, a Religious Ceremony and Other Customs of the Mandans* (George Catlin).

HENRY E. FRITZ. Native of Kansas, educated at Bradley University and University of Minnesota (Ph.D., 1957) . . . member of history faculties of University of Wisconsin, Milwaukee, and Saint Olaf College (1958 to present) . . . initiated and directed the American Minorities Program at Saint Olaf College under a grant from the National Endowment for the Humanities (1970) . . . faculty fellow of the Newberry Library Seminar in the Humanities, sponsored by the Associated Colleges of the Midwest (1968–69) . . . author of *The Movement for Indian Assimilation* and numerous journal articles.

WILLIAM T. HAGAN. Native of West Virginia, educated at Marshall University and University of Wisconsin (Ph.D., 1950) . . . member of history faculties of North Texas State University (1950–65) and State University of New York College at Fredonia (1965 to present) . . . author of *The Sac and Fox Indians*, *American Indians*, *Indian Police and Judges*, and various articles.

OLIVER W. HOLMES. Native of Minnesota, educated at Carleton College and Columbia University (Ph.D., 1956) . . . staff assistant, Public Library, New York, New York (1926–28); editorial assistant, Encyclopedia Britannica (1928–29) and Columbia University Press (1929–34) . . . associate archivist, National Archives (1936–38); chief, Division of Interior Department Archives (1938–41); director, Research and Records Description (1942–45); program advisor (1945–48); chief archivist, Natural Resources Records Branch (1948–61); executive director, National Historical Publications Commission (1961–72) . . . professorial lecturer, History and Administration of Archives, The American University (1957–64) . . . fellow and past president, Society of American Archivists . . . author of articles in professional historical journals and in the *American Archivist*.

ALVIN M. JOSEPHY, JR. Native of New York, educated at Harvard University . . . associate editor, *Time Magazine* (1951–60); writer and editor, *American Heritage* (1960—); presently a vice president and senior editor of American Heritage Publishing Company . . . recipient of Eagle Feather Award, National Congress of American Indians (1964) . . . editor and author of many articles and books, including *The Patriot Chiefs*, *The Nez Percé Indians and the Opening of the Northwest*, *The Indian Heritage of America*, and *Red Power*.

LAWRENCE C. KELLY. Native of Oklahoma, educated at Marquette University and University of New Mexico (Ph.D., 1961) . . . member of history faculties of Lewis College, Indiana University, Fort Wayne, and North Texas State University (1968 to present) . . . American Philosophical Society summer resident grant (1964) . . . Harry S. Truman Library grant-in-aid (summer 1965) . . . National Endowment for the Humanities fellow (1970–71) . . . author of *Navajo Roundup* and *The Navaho Indians and Federal Indian Policy, 1900–1935*.

D'ARCY MCNICKLE. Native of Montana, educated at University of Montana, Oxford University, and University of Grenoble . . . executive director, American Indian Development, Inc. (1952–66) . . . professor of anthropology, University of Saskatchewan, Regina (1966–71) . . . program director, Center for the History of the American Indian, Newberry Library (1972 to present) . . . cofounder, National Congress of American Indians . . . fellow, American Anthropological Association, Society for Applied Anthropology . . . awarded Guggenheim Fellowship (1963–64) . . . author of books and articles, including *The Surrounded*,

They Came Here First, Runner in the Sun, Indians and Other Americans, coauthored with Harold E. Fey, and *Native American Tribalism: Indian Survivals and Renewals* (revised edition, 1973).

ROY W. MEYER. Native of Minnesota, educated at Saint Olaf College and University of Iowa (Ph.D. in English-American Civilization, 1957) . . . member of English faculties of State Teachers College, Valley City, North Dakota (1950–54, 1955–57) and Mankato State University (1957 to present) . . . held Fulbright lectureship at the Flinders University of South Australia (1969) . . . author of *The Middle Western Farm Novel in the Twentieth Century, History of the Santee Sioux,* and articles published in *Minnesota History, Kansas Historical Quarterly, Western American Literature, Midcontinent American Studies Journal,* and elsewhere.

KENNETH R. PHILP. Native of Michigan, educated at University of Michigan and Michigan State University (Ph.D., 1968) . . . member of history faculty of University of Texas at Arlington (1968 to present) . . . author of reviews and articles published in *Arizona and the West, Rocky Mountain Social Science Journal,* and elsewhere.

LORING B. PRIEST. Native of New Jersey, educated at Rutgers University and Harvard University (Ph.D., 1937) . . . member of history faculties of New Jersey College for Women, Rutgers University, Biarritz American University, Gannon College, and Lycoming College (1949 to present) . . . author of *Uncle Sam's Stepchildren* and various reviews and articles.

FRANCIS PAUL PRUCHA, S.J. Native of Wisconsin, educated at Wisconsin State College at River Falls, University of Minnesota, and Harvard University (Ph.D., 1950) . . . member of history faculty of Marquette University (since 1960) . . . engaged in study of American Indian policy as a Guggenheim Fellow (1967–68) and as a senior fellow of the National Endowment for the Humanities (1970) . . . author of books and articles, including *Broadax and Bayonet, American Indian Policy in the Formative Years, Sword of the Republic,* and *Indian Peace Medals in American History.*

CARMELITA S. RYAN. Native of Massachusetts, educated at Emmanuel College, Boston University, and Georgetown University (Ph.D., 1962) . . . archivist, National Archives and Records Service, (1951—); Educational Programs Division (1951–54); Social and Economic Division (1954–63); Civil Projects Division (1963–66); Records Appraisal Division (1966–73); Records Disposition Division, Office of Federal Records Centers, (1973—) . . . author of articles in professional journals.

Biographical Sketches

ROBERT M. UTLEY. Native of Arkansas, educated at Purdue University and Indiana University (M.A. 1952) . . . historian, Joint Chiefs of Staff, United States Department of Defense (1954–57) . . . regional historian, southwest region (1957–64); chief historian (1964–72); director, Office of Archaeology and Historic Preservation, National Park Service (1972 to present) . . . a founder and past president, Western History Association . . . member of the editorial board of the *American West Magazine*, the *Western Historical Quarterly*, *Arizona and the West*, and the Yale University Press Western American Series . . . editor of *Battlefield and Classroom: Four Decades with the American Indian* . . . author of books and articles, including *Custer and the Great Controversy; The Last Days of the Sioux Nation; Frontiersmen in Blue: The United States Army and the Indians, 1848–1865*; and *Frontier Regulars: The United States Army and the Indians, 1866–1891*.

HERMAN J. VIOLA. Native of Illinois, educated at Marquette University and Indiana University (Ph.D., 1970) . . . assistant editor, *Indiana Magazine of History* (1966–67) . . . archivist, National Archives and Records Service (1967–72); National Historical Publications Commission (1968); editor of *Prologue: The Journal of the National Archives* (1968–72) . . . director, National Anthropological Archives, Department of Anthropology, Smithsonian Institution (1972 to present) . . . recipient of American Philosophical Society Research Grant and Leland Award, Society of American Archivists (1971) . . . author of *Thomas L. McKenney, Architect of America's Early Indian Policy: 1816–1830*, and articles in various journals.

THURMAN WILKINS. Native of Missouri, educated at University of California, Los Angeles; University of California, Berkeley; and Columbia University (Ph.D., 1957) . . . member of English faculties of Columbia University (1951–64) and Queens College (1964 to present) . . . awards include Guggenheim Fellowship (1960) and Certificate of Commendation, American Association of State and Local History (1971) . . . author of articles in various journals, biographical dictionaries, and encyclopedias and of several books, including *Clarence King: A Biography*, *Thomas Moran: Artist of the Mountains*, and *Cherokee Tragedy: The Story of the Ridge Family and the Decimation of a People*.

MARY E. YOUNG. Native of New York, educated at Oberlin College and Cornell University (Ph.D., 1955) . . . member of history faculties of Ohio State University and University of Rochester (since 1973) . . . recipient of Robert Schalkenbach Foundation grant (1952–53); Social Science Research Council faculty research grant (1969); and Louis Pelzer Award,

Mississippi Valley Historical Association (1955) . . . associate editor, *The Frontier in American Development: Essays in Honor of Paul Wallace Gates* . . . author of *Redskins, Ruffleshirts and Rednecks: Indian Land Allotments in Alabama and Mississippi, 1830–1860,* and articles in various journals.

Appendix
NATIONAL ARCHIVES RESOURCE PAPERS

The following resource papers were distributed at the National Archives Conference on Research in the History of Indian-White Relations:

"Guide to Records in the Military Archives Division Pertaining to Indian-White Relations"
>   Marie Bouknight, Robert Gruber, Maida Loescher, Richard Myers, and Geraldine Phillips

"Guide to Records in the Civil Archives Division Pertaining to American Indians"
>   Richard C. Crawford and Charles South

"Records in the General Archives Division Relating to American Indians"
>   Edward E. Hill

"Guide to Records of the Bureau of Indian Affairs in the Archives Branches of the Federal Records Centers"
>   Staffs of the Archives Branches

"Audiovisual Records Relating to Indians of the United States"
>   Joe Thomas

"Indian-Related Materials in Records of the Continental and Confederation Congresses and the Constitutional Convention: A Preliminary Guide"
>   Howard H. Wehmann

Index

Abbott, Lyman, 68, 71
Acoma pueblo, 127
Adams, John Quincy, 255
African View (Huxley), 178
Agents, selection of, 21, 59–61, 66–67, 96, 152
Agriculture, as means of assimilation, 47, 49, 158, 162, 164; at Fort Berthold, 207–11
Alaskans, 22, 243, 256
Aleuts, 127
Allison bill, 65
Allotment, 156, 256; among Five Civilized Tribes, 186–87; among Apaches, 224; among Omahas, 69, 72; among Puyallups, 69; among Quapaws, 216–17; among Sioux, 65, 69, 165, 185, 209; effects of, 120, 175, 183, 186, 187, 193, 232; opposition to repeal, 175, 177, 182–87, 189, 190, 192, 217–19; pressure to enact, 61–72, 79, 80, 82–83, 147, 149, 164–65, 229; pressure to repeal, 173–74, 177, 179, 180, 193–94, 216, 227, 231, 234, 235. *See also* Dawes Act
American Board of Commissioners for Foreign Missions, 47, 48, 49, 65, 66
American Civil Liberties Union, 220
American Indian Culture and Research Journal, xviii
American Indian Defense Association, 173, 229, 232
American Indian Federation, 220, 223, 239
American Indian Historical Society, xvii

American Indian Movement, 245
American Indian National Bank, 249
American Indian Quarterly, xviii
Annals of the American Academy, 91
Annuities, 103
Anthropologists, in BIA administration, 223, 252, 253
Apaches, 115, 127, 128; and Wheeler-Howard bill, 188, 224; as seen by army, 138, 140; Mescalero lands, 229; reservation maps, 135, 200–201
Appraisal of Modern Public Records (Schellenberg), 34
Arapahos, 59, 63, 89, 127, 159, 210; and guns, 105; and Wheeler-Howard bill, 177, 189
Arikaras, 127; on reservation, 207–11
Armstrong, Samuel C., 68
Army, on frontier, 131–43, 146–50, 152, 158–59, 160
Art, Indians in, 108–10
Arthur, Chester A., 59, 67
Artifacts, in Indian history, 101–8
Ashurst, Henry, 181–82, 193
Assimilation, as goal of army, 140, 147–48; as goal of Indians, 220, 223; as goal of reformers, 43–54, 57–73, 79–85, 87–93, 97–98, 147–49, 215, 222, 228; reversal of policy of, 212, 227, 230, 231, 233, 235, 238, 240, 254–56
Assiniboins, 99; on allotment, 177
Association of Indian Tribes, 217
Athearn, Robert G., 90, 131–32, 152–53, 260
Atkins, J. D. C., 58
Atnas, 127

269

Atsinas, on allotment, 177
Aztecs, 119

Bahmer, Robert H., 11, 260
Baker, E. M., 134, 141
Baird, W. David, 118, 155, 156, 215–21, 222, 223, 260
Bannocks, 127
Baptists, in Indian affairs, 48, 49, 96, 97
Beatty, Willard, 252
Bell, C. M., 109
Berkhofer, Robert F., 44, 79–86, 98, 260–61
Berthrong, Donald J., 89, 155–56, 261
Biddle, Ellen McG., 133
Bigman, Max, 185
Blackfeet, 99, 106, 127; and Collier, 177, 185; as stockraisers, 162; hostility of, 104, 157; photo, 236–37
Blackfeet Sioux, 202
Black Hawk, 5
Black Kettle, 138
Bland, Theodore A. *See* Thomas A. Bland
Bland, Thomas A., 6, 92
Blood Indians, 102
Blue Lake, 243
Blue River Baptist Association of Indiana, 49
Bluewater incident, 141
Board of Foreign Missions of the Reformed Church, 60
Board of Indian Commissioners, 44, 189, 223; abolished, 233; policies in 1880s, 57–78, 79, 90; records of, 28
Boudinot family letters, 113, 118
Bourke, John G., 133
Boyd, Mrs. Orsemus B., 133–34
Brainerd, 47, 49, 50
Bret Harte, John, 96
Brooks, Erastus, 68
Brown, Dee, 8
Brown, John F., 113
Bruce, Louis R., 226, 251, 258, 261; on BIA in 1970s, 242–50
Brulé Sioux, 184, 185, 205
Bruner, Joseph, 189, 217, 223
Buchanan, James Shannon, 112
Buck, Joe, 186
Buck, Solon J., 15
Buffalo, 103, 152–53, 251–52
Bureau of American Ethnology, 22, 27

Bureau of Indian Affairs, xviii, 43, 45, 68, 173, 175, 225, 226, 240, 256, 257; policies after Civil War, 57–61, 65, 67, 69–70, 96, 135, 142, 147, 157, 161, 163, 207; policies in 1920s, 229–32; policies in 1930s, 171, 186, 188, 192–93, 227, 232–33, 239, 252–53; policies in 1970s, 242–50, 251, 258–59; records of, 13–23, 28–30, 33–42, 88–89
Bureau of Reclamation, 22, 239
Bureau of the Budget, and Wheeler-Howard bill, 178, 185, 191
Burke, Charles, 229, 230, 232
Burke Act, of 1906, 88
Bursum bill, 229
Bury My Heart at Wounded Knee (Brown), 8
Buy Indian Act of 1910, 244

Caddos, 127
Cahuillas, 127
Calhoun, John C., 45
Carlisle Indian School, 67
Carter, William H., 133
Cash, Joseph H., 123
Cass, Lewis, 6, 29, 53
Catholics, in Indian affairs, 52, 90, 106, 184
Cayugas, 127
A Century of Dishonor (Jackson), 8
Chaffee, Adna R., 140, 147
Chapman, Berlin, 15
Chemehuevis, 127
Cherokee Cavaliers (Dale and Litton), 113
Cherokee Female Seminary, 114
Cherokees, 127, 128; alphabet, 51, 117; and Wheeler-Howard bill, 177, 190, 219; court cases, 7; on trail of tears, 6; records of, 17, 112, 113, 115, 118; schools, 47, 114
Cheyenne River Agency, 177, 184; map, 202
Cheyennes, 59, 63, 89, 127, 128, 159, 163, 208, 210; and guns, 105; and Wheeler-Howard bill, 189; in movies, 150; Washita incident, 138
Chickasaws, 127; and Wheeler-Howard bill, 190; records of 112, 113, 115

Index

Chilocco Indian Industrial School, plat, 63
Chippewas, 53, 127, 164
Chiricahua Apaches, 140; reservation maps, 135, 200–201
Chivington massacre, 158
Choctaw Academy, 97
Choctaws, 97, 127; and Wheeler-Howard bill, 190; persons, 51, 53, 118, 156; records of, 112, 113, 115
Chontals, 128
Chronicles of Oklahoma, 97
Civilian Conservation Corps, 238, 239
Civilization program, under McKenney, 45–56, 97
Civil Works Administration, 238
Clallams, 127–28
Clark, N. G., 66
Clark, W. P., 102
Cleveland, Grover, 58, 68, 69, 73
Clothing, sent to Indians, 102–4, 160
Cochise, 135
Cochitis, 128
Cocopas, 128
Coeur d'Alènes, 128; persons, 186
Coke bill, 65, 67, 70, 71, 72
Collier, John, xx, 17, 155, 212, 225, 226; adopted by Blackfeet, 185; articles on, 171–200, 215–21, 222–23, 227–41, 251–59; photos, 170, 236
Colnett, James, 103
Colvilles, and Wheeler-Howard bill, 177
Comanches, 63, 128, 155, 173, 208; and Wheeler-Howard bill, 189; hostility of, 157, 158, 159
Commissioners of Indian Affairs. *See* Bureau of Indian Affairs
Committee of Twenty-five, 68–69, 71, 72
Committee on Human Development, 253
Compere, Lee, 52
Connecticut Indian Association, 68
Continental Congress, 17, 20
Cosmos Club conference, 173, 177, 190
Costo, Rupert, 188
Council Fire, 92
Courts, Indian records of, 7, 26–27, 115, 117; proposed in Wheeler-Howard bill, 171, 179–80, 191, 193, 234

Crampton, C. Gregory, 100, 261; on Duke oral history project, 119–128
Crawford, Richard, 27
Creeks, 128; agent, 96; civilization of, 97; on Wheeler-Howard bill, 190; persons, 97, 117, 189, 217, 222; photo, 236–37; records of, 17, 112, 113, 115, 129; schools, 51–52
Crees, 128
Crook, George, 137, 140, 142, 147
Crow Creek Sioux, 184; agency photo, 203; persons, 185
Crows, 128; and guns, 105; persons, 185, 251–52; rations, 163
Cunas, 128
Curtis, Charles, 220
Custer, Elizabeth B., 133
Custer, George A., 133, 134, 138
Cutcheon, Byron, 67

Dakota Indians, 157, 158, 159; on reservations, 160–61, 165; rations for, 163, 208. *See also* Sioux
Dale, Edward Everett, 6, 15, 112–13
Danielson, P. W., 175
Daugherty, Harry, 232
Davies, Bruce, 223
Dawes, Henry L., 66, 67, 69, 70, 72, 149, 222
Dawes Act, 4, 43, 58, 65, 68, 73, 88, 90, 209; effects of, 149, 165, 200, 222, 223–24, 228–29; repeal of, 171, 173, 178, 179, 182, 193, 227, 231. *See also* Allotment
Dawes Commission, 21, 115, 117, 121
Debo, Angie, 15, 96, 99–100, 261–62; on Indian records in Oklahoma, 112–18, 129
Delaware Indians, 121, 128
Dempsey, Pauline, 102
Department of Justice, and Indian records, 26, 38
D'Ewart, Congressman, 256
Die Gartenlaube, of Munich, 108
Dieguenos, 128
Dobyn, Henry, 84
Dodge, Mabel, 172
Dougherty, John, 53
Douglas, Lewis, 185
Dragging Canoe, 220
Draper, Andrew S., 59
Driver, Harold E., 3

Duke, Doris, oral history project, 119–28
Dutch Reform Society of Foreign Missions, 96

Education, of Indians, 4, 123; after Civil War, 59, 61, 68, 158, 163–64, 166; as means of assimilation, 62, 63, 72–73, 79, 82, 83, 163–64; in 1930s, 171, 179, 233, 234, 252–53; in 1970s, 40, 247–48, 249. *See also* Schools
Ellis, Richard N., 90, 131, 146–51, 262
Employment Assistance Program, 245, 246
Eskimos, 128
Evarts, Jeremiah, 6
Ewers, Ezra P., 140
Ewers, John C., 99, 152, 153, 262; on Indian history, 8–9; on artifacts, 101–11

Fall, Albert B., 229, 230, 232
Farm Security Administration, 238
Federal Court of Indian Affairs. *See* Courts, Wheeler-Howard bill
Federal Emergency Relief Administration, 238
Finerty, John F., 134
Fire Thunder, 185
Fisk, Clinton B., 58, 59, 68, 71, 72
Five Civilized Tribes, 68, 116; and allotment, 149, 186–87; and Wheeler-Howard bill, 173, 175, 189–90; records of, 15, 112, 113–15, 117, 129. *See also* Cherokees; Chickasaws; Choctaws; Creeks; Seminoles
Flatheads, 99, 128; and Wheeler-Howard bill, 186; persons, 226
Fletcher, Alice C., 68–69, 70–71, 72
Florida Indian, 128
Ford, John, 133, 134, 142, 143, 149
Ford Foundation, xvii
Foreman, Carolyn Thomas, 15, 118
Foreman, Grant, 15, 113, 114, 115–16, 118
Forest Service, 239
Forsyth, George A., 133
"Fort Apache," 133
Fort Belknap Reservation, 177, 185
Fort Berthold Reservation, 207–11
Fort Hall agency, 186
Fort McDowell, 188

Fort Peck Reservation, 184
Fort Yuma Reservation, 188
Fox Indians, 128
Fritz, Henry E., 43, 44, 90, 96, 222, 223, 262; on Board of Indian Commissioners, 57–78

Gabriel, Ralph Henry, 6
Gadsden Purchase treaty, 181
Galinee, René de Brahant de, 102
Garfield, James A., 59
Garrison, William Lloyd, 134
Garrison Dam, 210
Gates, Merrill E., 72
Gates, Paul Wallace, 155–56
General Accounting Office, 37
General Land Office, 21, 70
Genizaros, 128
Geological Survey, U.S., 21, 22
Geronimo, 135, 140
Gilbert, Sir Humphrey, 102–03
Gilcrease, Thomas, 117
Goodwin, Ralph W., 223
Gordon, Milton, 81, 83
Gosiutes, 128
Gosnold, Bartholomew, 102–3
Grant, Ulysses S., 59, 61, 200
Graphic, of London, 108
Graves, Slemp, and Calhoun, 182
Grierson, Benjamin H., 147
Griffin, Victor, 217
Gros Ventres, 128; photo, 236–37
Guess, George. *See* Sequoyah

Hagan, William T., xx, 3, 91, 155, 207, 208, 212, 213, 215, 220, 262–63; on Dawes Act, 222; on reservation policy, 157–69, 209, 210, 223
Haidas, 128
Haile, Berard, 252
Halchidomes, 128
Harlan, James, 157, 158, 159, 207
Harpers, 108
Harrington, John P., 252
Harrison, Benjamin, 165
Haskill Institute, 194
Hastings, W. W., 220
Hastings Act, 15
Havasupais, 128
Hayes, Joseph W., 190
Hayes, Rutherford B., 59, 62, 200
Hayt, Ezra A., 60, 61, 65, 96

Index 273

Head Start programs, 37, 40
Heckaton, 220
Henderson, Annie Heloise Abel, 16
Hertzberg, Hazel, 91–92
Hidatsas, 128; on reservation, 207–11
Hill, Edward, 27, 28
Hillers, John, 22
History of the Santee Sioux (Meyer), 91
Hitchitis, 128
Holmes, Oliver W., 11, 39, 263; on Indian records, 13–32
Holy Rosary Mission, 184
Hoopes, Alban W., 16
Hoover, Herbert T., 123
Hopis, 128, 174
Hornaday, William T., 153
Howard, Edgar, 178, 192, 193, 235
Howard, Oliver Otis, 135, 140, 147
Hualapais, 128
Hudson's Bay Company, 103
Hunkpapa Sioux, 128, 205
Hunter, Robert F., 181
Hunter-Martin claims, 181–82
Huxley, Julian, 178

Ickes, Anna, 173
Ickes, Harold, 16; and Collier, 192–93, 232–33, 256
Illustrated London News, 108
Illustrated Weekly, 109
Indian Action Team, 246, 249
Indian Claims Commission, and Indian records, 26–27, 38
Indian Historian, xvii
Indian history, Indian study of, xvii–xx, 98, 238, 242, 253
Indian National Confederacy, 189, 217
Indian Removal (Foreman), 116
Indian Reorganization Act, 219, 220, 239; Collier's views of, 194, 216, 238–40, 256; provisions of, 193–94, 216, 233–35, 248, 251, 253. *See also* Wheeler-Howard bill
Indian Rights Association, 6, 91, 165; and Collier, 173, 190; and Dawes Act, 67, 68, 70
Indian Service. *See* Bureau of Indian Affairs
Indian Territory, records of, 15, 21, 117
Indian Tribal Claims Branch, 25
Indian Truth, 190–91

Institute for Government Research, 173, 230
Interior Department, Indian records of, 14, 17, 21, 22, 23, 28; policies after Civil War, 57–62, 69–70, 71, 73, 157–59, 164–65, 207; policies in 1920s, 229–30; policies in 1930s, 173, 178, 181–82, 192–93, 232–33, 256; policies in 1970s, 243, 246–47, 248
Iowa Indians, 128
Iroquois, 8, 117
Irving, Joe, 185
Ishadore, 186
Isleta pueblo, 128

Jackson, Andrew, 5, 6, 45, 96, 97
Jackson, Helen Hunt, 8, 92
Jackson, William H., 22
Jefferson, Thomas, 7, 254
Jeffords, Tom, 135
Jemez pueblo, 128
Jesuits, and Collier, 184
Jicarilla Apaches, 224
Job Corps, 37, 41
Johnson, Sir John, 117
Johnson, Richard M., 97
Johnson, Sir William, 117
Johnson-O'Malley Act, 233, 247
Jones, Robert M. McDonald, 97
Joseph, 5, 19, 64, 140
Josephy, Alvin M., Jr., 225–26, 258, 263
Jumper, John, 113

Kalispels, 128
Kanine, Jim, 186
Kansas Quarterly, 89, 91
Kelly, Lawrence C., xx, 225, 226, 258–59, 263–64; on Indian New Deal, 227–41, 252, 253–54
Kendall, H., 71
Kentucky Baptist Society, 48
Keres, 128
Kershner, Frederick D., 223
Kickapoos, 128; Remolino incident, 141
King, Charles, 134
Kingsbury, Cyrus, 47, 51
Kinney, Sara T., 68
Kiowa Apaches, 128

Kiowas, 63, 99, 128, 208; and Wheeler-Howard bill, 189; hostility of, 157, 158, 159
Kirkwood, Samuel, 60, 66
Kirkwood bill, 69–70
Knox, Henry, 254
Koyukons, 128
Kutenais, persons, 186, 226
Kwakiutls, 128

LaCourse, Richard, 258
LaFarge, Oliver, 173–74
Laguna pueblo, 128
Lake Traverse Reservation, 204
Lamar, L. Q. C., 71
Land-in-Severalty Act. *See* Dawes Act
La Pointe, Sam, 185
Lawyer, Archie B., 64
Leaves Her Behind, Molly, 256
Leighton, Alexander, 253
Leslies, 108
Lightner, Isaiah, 65, 66
Linquist, G. E. E., 189
Linton, Ralph, 173
Lipan Apaches, 115
Lipps, O. H., 175
"Little Big Man," 133, 134, 150
Little Bronzed Angel, 184
Litton, Gaston, 113
Long, John D., 59
Luisenos, 128
Lumbees, 128
Lyon, William H., 58

McCoy, James, 205
McDonald, James, 53–54, 83, 87–88, 97
McGillivray, Alexander, 117–18
MacGregor, Gordon, 253
McKenney, Thomas L., 43, 80, 82, 98; photo, 46; promotes assimilation, 45–56, 79, 96–97
Mackenzie, Ranald, 141
McLean, John, 53
McNaughton, Ray, 189
McNickle, D'Arcy, 226, 263–64; on Collier, 223, 251–57, 258; on Dawes Act, 223–24
Makahs, 128
Mandans, 128; and guns, 105; on reservation, 207–11
Mardock, Robert, 90–91, 148
Maricopas, 128

Marshall, John, 7
Martinez, Carpio, 177
Meacham, Alfred B., 92
Meeker massacre, 121
Menominees, 248
Mereness, Newton D., 16
Meriam, Lewis, 173, 230–31
Merk, Frederick, 43
Mescalero Apaches, 229
Methodist Board of Missions, 60
Meyer, Roy W., 91, 155, 207–11, 264
Miami Daily News-Record, 218
Miami Indians, 128
Micco, Hulbutta, 113
Miccosukees, 244
Midcontinent American Studies Journal, 91
Miles, Nelson A., 133, 140
Military policy, regarding Indians, 90, 131–43, 146–50, 152
Miniconjou Sioux, 202, 205
Missionary societies, and agents, 59–61, 66–67, 79, 96; and Indian education, 47–53, 68, 105–6, 184, 230; on allotment, 61–62, 65–67; on intermarriage, 83; oppose Wheeler-Howard bill, 184, 187, 189, 192
Mission Indians, and Wheeler-Howard bill, 176, 188; reservation map, 175
Mississippi Baptist Association, 49
Mocktum, Peter, 186
Modoc War, 5
Mohawks, persons, 226
Mohonk conferences, 59, 67, 68, 70, 71, 72
Mojave Indians, 128; and Wheeler-Howard bill, 188
Monahan, A. C., 188
Monroe, James, 48
Monteith, John B., 64
Moody, Marshall Dwight, 57
Morgan, Brent, 17
Morgan, Dale, 28
Morgan, Lewis Henry, 106
Morgan, Thomas J., 59
Morton, Rogers, 246
Museum of Modern Art, 237
Museum of the American Indian, 109
Muskogee Daily Phoenix, 217

Nambe pueblo, 128
Narragansett Indians, 128

Index

National Archives, Indian records in, xvii-xix, 11, 13–32, 33, 36–42, 88–89, 98, 120, 121, 147, 215
National Association on Indian Affairs, 173
National Congregational Council, 66
National Congress of American Indians, 245
National Council on Indian Opportunity, xviii, 245
National Park Service, 22
National Tribal Chairmen's Association, 244–45, 249
Navajos, 128, 175, 213, 225; and Collier, 186–87, 252–53, 257; as shepherds, 162; assimilation of, 92; photo, 236–37; property of, 174
Nevins, Allan, 115
New Deal, 149, 225, 240; articles on Collier, 170–200, 215–21, 227–41, 251–57
New York Public Library, holdings on Indians, 120
Nez Percés, 140; agency photo, 203; persons, 19, 64, 186
Night Hawk Keetoowah Society, 190
Nixon, Richard M., 242, 243, 244, 258
Northern Overland Survey, 22
Northern Pacific Railroad, 69
Northwest Indian Congress, 185–86
Nunamiuts, 128

Oberly, John H., 59
Office of Economic Opportunity, xviii
Office of Indian Affairs. *See* Bureau of Indian Affairs
Office of Indian Trade, 25, 28, 35, 45, 53
Office of Indian Water Rights, 246–47
Office of Territories, 22
Oglala Sioux, 128, 205; persons, 226
Oklahoma Historical Society, Indian records at, 15–16, 112, 113–17, 118
Oklahoma Indians, assimilation of, 191–92; effect of allotment on, 183; oppose Wheeler-Howard bill, 219, 220, 223, 235; records of, 15, 21, 112–18. *See also* specific tribes
Oklahoma Indian Welfare Act, 219–20
Omaha Indians, 109; allotment among, 62, 68, 69, 72
O'Malley, Thomas, 192

Oneida lace, 105–6
Onondaga reservation, 226
Oral history, 88, 115–16; article on Duke project, 119–28
Osages, 115, 128, 189
O'Sullivan, Timothy H., 22
Otippoby, James, 189
Otos, 128
Ottawa Indians, 53, 128
Owens, Robert L., 220

Paiutes, 128
Papagos, 128; and Wheeler-Howard bill, 188; land claims, 181–82, 193
Pan-Indian movements, 91, 214
Parker, Arthur C., 91
Parker, James, 133
Passamaquoddys, 52
Pawnees, 128
Peace Commission, 159–60
Peace policy, 59–61, 66–67, 90, 96
Penn, Arthur, 133, 134, 142, 143, 149, 150
People's Institute, 171–72, 227
Peoria Indians, 66, 128, 189
Phillips, Wendell, 134, 148
Philp, Kenneth R., 155, 212, 215, 216, 219, 220, 222, 223, 264; on Wheeler-Howard bill, 171–200
Photographers, of Indians, 108–10
Picuris pueblo, 128
Piegans, 134
Pimas, 128; on Wheeler-Howard bill, 188
Pine Ridge reservation, 161, 184, 185, 208, 210, 226
Pitchlynn, Peter P., 118, 156
Plains Indian Congress, 182–85
Plains tribes, and army, 131–32, 136, 158–59, 160; and Wheeler-Howard bill, 177, 182, 235; artifacts of, 104–5, 107; in art, 108; records of, 113, 116. *See also* specific tribes
Pocahontas, 121
Pojoaque pueblo, 128
Poncas, 109, 128
Pope, John, 131, 140
Potawatomis, 53, 128, 206
Powell, John Wesley, 22
Pratt, Richard, 67, 71, 82, 92
Presbyterian Board of Home Missions, 71

Presbyterian Indian Committee, 66
Price, George F., 133
Price, Hiram, 61, 67, 69
Priest, Loring B., 16, 43-44, 57, 87-95, 264
The Problem of Indian Administration (Meriam), 173, 232
Prucha, Francis Paul, xx, 43, 91, 97, 264; on Indian history, 1-10
Public Works Administration, 238, 239
Pueblo Indians, and Collier, 172, 174, 177, 228, 229, 233. *See also* specific pueblos
Pushmataha, 220
Puyallups, 69
Pyramid Lake reservation, 188

Quakers, and Indian education, 49; persons, 45, 47, 53, 65, 160, 232
Quapaws, 128, 156; oppose Wheeler-Howard bill, 189, 216-20
Quinaielts, persons, 186
Quinton, Amelia S., 68

Rahill, Peter, 90
Randall, George M., 140, 147
Rations, 161-63, 166, 208
Records of the Bureau of Indian Affairs, Preliminary Inventory No. 163, 28, 29
"Red Atlantis," Collier's idea of, 172, 194, 214, 215, 216, 218, 219, 220, 222
Red Cloud, 103
Reeves, Frank B., 28
Reformers, after Civil War, 57-73, 79, 90-92, 147-49; goals and methods of, 80-85, 92-93, 147, 149-50; in 1820s, 45-54, 79; in Collier era, 171, 173-94, 216-20, 227-40
Reformers and the American Indian, 148
Reid, James M., 60, 61
Remington, Frederic, 134, 142
Remolino incident, 141
Removal policy, 5, 54, 80; effect of, 89
Reservation Acceleration Program, 37, 245
Reservation policy, 155; Collier's reforms, 171-94, 215-20, 227, 233-35, 253; development of, 157-66; effects of, 83-84, 89, 207-11, 212-14; maps, 135, 176, 200-201, 202;
military view of, 152; missionary view of, 62, 65
Resettlement Administration, 238
Reuben, James, 64
Rhoads, Charles, 232
Ridge family letters, 113, 118
Riggs, Alfred L., 65, 66, 67, 69
Riggs, S. R., 66
Roberts, Rush, 66
Roberts, W. O., 176
Rodenbough, Theodore F., 133
Roe Cloud, Henry, 171
Rogers, Will, 115, 192, 220, 223
Roosevelt, Franklin D., 17, 171, 177, 183, 223, 233; and Wheeler-Howard bill, 193, 219, 222
Rosebud agency, 128, 176, 184, 185; sketch of, 205
Ross, John, 6, 114, 118
Ryan, Carmelita S., 11, 264; on BIA records, 33-42

Sacramento agency, 175, 186
Saenz, Moises, 173
Sahagun, 119
Saint Regis Reservation, 226
Salish Indians, 128; persons, 226
Sam, Thomas, 186
San Carlos Apaches, agents, 96; and Wheeler-Howard bill, 188
Sand Creek incident, 141, 148
Sandia pueblo, 128
Sandoz, Mari, 28
San Felipe pueblo, 128
San Ildefonso pueblo, and Wheeler-Howard bill, 187-88
San Juan pueblo, 128; and Wheeler-Howard bill, 177
Sans Arc Sioux, 202, 205
Santa Ana pueblo, 128
Santa Clara pueblo, 128; and Wheeler-Howard bill, 174, 188
Santa Rosa reservation, 188
Santee Sioux, 128, 184; allotment among, 65-66; on reservation, 208-11
Santo Domingo pueblo, 128, 187
Satz, Ronald, 96
Sauk and Fox Indians, 128; persons, 5; records of, 115; schools, 116
Saunkeah, Jasper, 189
Scales bill, 65, 70

Index

Scattergood, Henry, 173
Schellenberg, T. R., 34
Schools, illustrations, 63, 114, 116, 202, 204; in 1820s, 47–53, 97; in 1870s, 163–64; in 1920–30, 184, 230, 232, 239, 252–53. *See also* Education
Schreyvogel, Charles, 134
Schurz, Carl, 59–60, 61, 65
Scouts, 137
Search for an Indian Identity (Hertzberg), 91
Seax, 103
Self-determination policy, 92, 225–26, 242–44, 248–50
Sells, Cato, 229
Seminoles, Miccosukees, 244; records of, 112, 113, 115, 117, 118
Senapaw, 97–98, 222
Senecas, 128
Sequoyah, 117
Shale, Harry, 186
Shaul, David L., 129
Shawnees, 115, 128, 177
Sheridan, Philip H., 134, 140
Sherman, William T., 138, 140, 141
Shoshonis, 128, 139
Shults, A. B., 109
Sioux, 99, 109, 128, 155; agency illustrations, 202–5; and guns, 105; and Wheeler-Howard bill, 175, 177, 184, 191; cloth for, 103; language, 252–53; reservations, 65–66, 69, 208–11. *See also* Dakota Indians
Sioux Benefits, 185, 191
Sisseton Sioux, 66; sketch of agency buildings, 204
Sisters of the Nativity, 106
Sitting Bull, 226
Smiley, Albert, 67
Smith, John, 121
Smith, Michael T., 222
Smithsonian Institution, 22, 27
Sniffen, M. K., 190–91
Snodgrass, Jeanne O., 109
Society of American Indians, 91
"Soldier Blue," 133
South, Charles, 27
Southard, Henry, 48, 49
Spokans, 128
Spotted Eagle. *See* John Collier
Spotted Tail, 205
Standing Rock reservation, 161, 184

State Department, Indian records of, 24–25
Steere, Jonathan, 190
Stevens, Ernie, 258–59
Stevens, Isaac, 22
Stewart, Omer C., 129
Stockraising, 158, 162, 187, 207, 257
Strong, William, 67
Summerhayes, Martha, 133
Sumner, William Graham, 89
Surveys, western, records, 22
Swinomishes, 128

Taft, Robert, 108
Taos pueblo, and Collier, 172, 228, 257; council jailed, 257; land claims, 243
Taylor, Theodore W., 222
Taylor, Zachary, 118
Teller, Henry M., 61, 67
Termination policy, 149, 229, 240, 243, 246, 248
The Territorial Papers, 16
Tesuque pueblo, 128
Thomas, Elmer, 191–92, 193, 219, 235, 239
Thomas Gilcrease Institute, Indian records at, 112, 117–18
Thompson, Vern E., 217, 218, 219
Thurber, James, 214
Tibbles, T. H., 93
Tiguas, 128
Tillamooks, 128
Tiwa, 128
Tlingits, 128
To Be an Indian (Cash and Hoover), 123
Tonkawa agency, 115
Towa, 128
Trade goods, 101–6
"Trail of Tears," 6
Treasury Department, Indian records of, 25, 26
Treaties, 4, 24–25, 103, 159, 181; allotment provisions of, 62, 69, 159
Tribal Acceleration Program, 245
Truman, Harry S., 26
Tsimshians, 103
Turner, Frederick Jackson, 142
Tutchones, 128
Two Kettle Sioux, 202

Umatillas, and Wheeler-Howard bill, 182, 186

Uncle Sam's Stepchildren (Priest), 88, 90
Union agency, 114
United Traders Association, 187
University of Arizona, 119, 125
University of Chicago, 253
University of Florida, 119, 125
University of Illinois, 119, 125
University of New Mexico, 119, 125
University of Oklahoma, 119, 126; Indian records at, 112–13, 115, 118
University of South Dakota, 119, 126
University of Utah, 119, 122, 126
Utes, 128; and Wheeler-Howard bill, 177
Utley, Robert M., 131, 146, 150, 153, 265; on frontier army, 133–45, 147, 152

Viola, Herman J., 43, 87, 98, 265; on McKenney, 45–56, 80, 96–97
Vitorio, 254

Wallace, Henry, 193
Ward, Lester F., 89, 172
Wardell, Morris, 15
War Department, 90, 148, 152; and schools, 47, 49–50; Indian records of, 22–24, 26, 28, 35
Washakie, 139
Washington Daily News, 192
Washita incident, 138, 141
Watie family letters, 113, 118
Wayland, Francis, 59
Wayne, John, 133
Wehmann, Howard H., 20
Welsh, Herbert, 6, 68, 165
Werner, Theodore, 180–81
Wesley, Edgar B., 16
Wheeler, Burton K., 178, 191, 193, 232, 235, 238, 239
Wheeler-Howard bill, 171, 172, 215, 222; opposition from Indians, 182–90, 216–20, 223–24, 251–52; opposition in Congress, 180–82, 191–92, 219; provisions of, 178–80, 216, 233–35, 253; support from Indians, 190, 219. *See also* Indian Reorganization Act
White, Bruce, 152
White Bull, George, 184–85
White Cow Killer, Jacob, 185
Whittlesey, Eliphalet, 58, 65, 66, 68, 70, 71–72
Wichita Indians, 63, 128
Wilbur, Ray Lyman, 181, 182, 193
Wilkins, Thurman, 99–100, 265
Williams, Mark, 64
Wilson, John, 186
Wilson, Woodrow, 181
Wind River Reservation, 177
Winnebagos, 109, 128; persons, 170
Woehlke, Walter, 188
Women's National Indian Association, 67, 68
Worcester, Samuel, 49
Work, Hubert, 230
Works Progress Administration, 115–16, 238
Wounded Knee incident, 141
Wright, Muriel, 15, 97
Wyandots, 128

Yakimas, 128; persons, 186, 258
Yankton Sioux, 128
Yaquis, 128
Yavapais, 128
Yellow, George, 185
Young, Mary E., 155–56, 212–14, 265–66

Zia pueblo, 128
Zimmerman, William, 186; photo, 237
Zuñis, 92, 102, 128, 244